lonely planet

EPIC
HIKES
of AUSTRALIA and
NEW ZEALAND

Explore Australia and New Zealand's most thrilling treks and trails

CONTENTS

© kenichiiki / Getty Images; daw88888 / Shutterstock

© Posnov / Getty Images; pisaphotography / Shutterstock

INTRODUCTION

Australia and New Zealand were both originally explored on foot. The first Indigenous Australians, from up to 50,000 years ago, criss-crossed the continent, creating 'songlines' or dreaming tracks that told the stories of their people and the landscapes. In New Zealand, Māori people, such as the Waitaha and Ngati Wairangi, walked deep into the South Island's valleys in search of greenstone or *pounamu*, which was crafted into tools and weapons.

In both nations, walking routes today help us connect with and understand some of that history. On Tasmania, the wukalina walk, founded by palawa elder Clyde Mansell, is managed by an Aboriginal-owned business that provides visitors with guides who can introduce their culture, entwined as it is with a beautiful stretch of the east coast. Walkers discover some of the bush tucker of the area and practise crafts such as kelp basket-making, while supporting an Indigenous community. Over on the west coast of New Zealand's South Island, the Greenstone and Caples tracks lead into river valleys along routes used by Māori long before Europeans arrived.

Both walks are described in first-person accounts in this book, alongside 48 more hiking stories from Australia and New Zealand. Some of the routes are familiar melodies in each country's greatest hits: the Routeburn and Milford tracks in New Zealand or the Bibbulmun Track in Australia. But there are some very exciting new entries, including Queensland's Scenic Rim Trail and the Paparoa Track in New Zealand, which opened in 2019 and was created to commemorate the deaths of 29 miners in the Pike River Mine.

What they have in common is that they're all doorways to the natural world, where we can connect with nature. Recent research clearly shows how beneficial it is for our minds, bodies and spirits to be immersed in nature, to feel awe and peace among the trees, rocks and warbling birds. Our stress levels fall, our creativity rises and we become in tune with a deeper rhythm of life, governed by seasonal cycles. Slow down and take time to appreciate spring's golden blooms of wattle or winter's frosts. Few experiences match waking to a sunrise over Wilsons Promontory National Park or watching a wallaby go about its day on the Overland Track.

To compile this book, we asked some of Lonely Planet's seasoned hikers to share their adventures in Australia and New Zealand. And guests, such as Bob Brown, senator and leader of the Australian Greens, recount some of their personal hiking tales.

'Epic' is a relative term and while some hikes are certainly physical and mental challenges – the ultra-long Larapinta or Grampian Peaks trails, for example, will require a level of experience and preparedness – others are capable of being completed by the more relaxed rambler.

Time is a consideration for anyone planning a trip away from the nine-to-five, and the hikes here include a mix of time frames. There are plenty of day hikes, while other hikes are more epic undertakings. Most recognised routes in both nations are very well-established with signposting and accommodation that may need to be booked long in advance.

Australia and New Zealand are a walking wonderland in terms of the variety of terrain, climate and landscape that can be found, not to mention the fascinating cultures, histories and people you encounter along the way. We hope that the walks in this book will inspire you to reach for your boots and strike out somewhere new.

HOW TO USE THIS BOOK

The main stories in each chapter of the book feature first-hand accounts of fantastic hikes in those regions of Australia and New Zealand. Each includes an orientation toolkit to help plan the trip – when is the best time of year to hike, how to get there, any special equipment required. But beyond that, these stories should inspire other ideas. We have started that process in the 'more like this' section following each story, which offers other ideas along a similar theme, or in the same region. On the contents page, the hikes have been colour coded according to their difficulty, which takes into account not just how long, remote and arduous they are but their logistics and local conditions. The index collects different types of hike for a variety of interests. It's important to note that many of the routes in this book are challenging. Whether you're a seasoned hiker or a novice embarking on your very first trek, please ensure that you're adequately prepared and have taken appropriate safety precautions to help prevent dangers to yourself and others.

Clockwise from left: Aboriginal guides can provide unique insights of the places through which you're walking; a wintry Mt Feathertop in Victoria; looking out over a valley on New Zealand's Routeburn Track

Opening spreads from left: Cradle Mountain-Lake St Clair National Park through which the Overland Track passes; a wallaby in Tasmania; Wilsons Promontory National Park coast; cassowaries are a rare sight in Queensland's Daintree Rainforest

© FiledIMAGE / Shutterstock

NEW SOUTH WALES & VICTORIA

THE JAGUNGAL WILDERNESS

The peaks and plains of northern Kosciuszko National Park offer wild adventure for hardy bushwalkers, with sweeping views from boulder-clad mountains to rustic huts and abandoned mining relics.

Ask any Australian where the highest peaks in the country are and Kosciuszko National Park is a likely reply. It's here where Mt Kosciuszko presides over a barren landscape dotted with rocky outcrops and glacial lakes. But in the remote north of the park sits the Jagungal Wilderness, a land of alluring peaks, forested ridges, rolling frost plains and historic gold diggings – and a paradise for walkers seeking solitude in a largely untamed environment.

Our walk begins in the boom-to-bust gold town of Kiandra, just north of the Jagungal Wilderness. Prospectors flooded to Kiandra in 1860 to chase their dreams and strike it rich. Few succeeded. Most left with their tail between their legs, driven away by poor yields, bitter cold and deep winter snows. Fleeting discoveries kept the town alive, but by the early 1900s Kiandra's population was just a few hundred. Now, there's little left aside from a few buildings, ugly sluicing scars and other relics, and a cemetery.

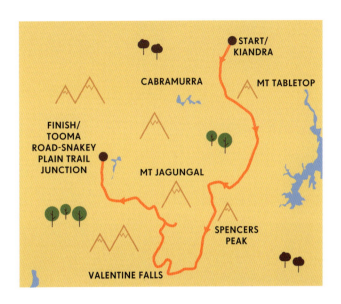

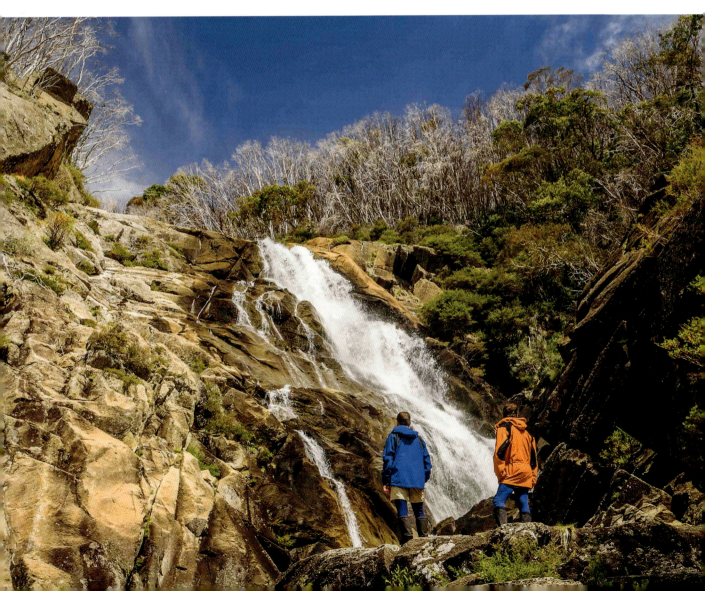

Heading south on the Australian Alps Walking Track (AAWT), we've barely started walking before I'm dripping in sweat, and I distract myself with thoughts of infinity pools and exotic beaches. Within a couple of hours my companions – Steve and Tony – and I have set up camp outside the Four Mile Hut. It's a tiny building full of mining artefacts and there is little room: perhaps just a couple of people could sleep here in a pinch. But like most huts in the mountains, sleeping inside is discouraged except in emergencies, and for our walk, accommodation will be purely tent-based.

The crisp morning air is laden with the scent of flowering snow gums and other alpine herbs, but the day warms nicely as we press on to Mt Tabletop, which rises 200m (656ft) above the plains. On top, the first panorama of the trip reveals itself – and many of the high peaks of the Snowy Mountains are assembled on the horizon to the south, including one of our checklist peaks, Mt Jagungal.

Happys Hut looks inviting as we set up camp, reaching it in the afternoon after a shortcut through the forest. The picture is not so pleasant the next day; heavy clouds brood, squalls shake the tent, and the straps of my rucksack flap angrily as we break camp. The storm catches us as we struggle south along Grey Mare Trail, but by the time we reach Mackays Hut bright sunshine bathes the high country in shimmering afternoon light.

Heavy frost coats everything by morning, and our socks airing outside the tent are as stiff as cardboard, but a piercing blue sky bodes well for the day ahead. On our way, we leave the AAWT

"Heavy frost coats everything by morning, and our socks airing outside the tent are as stiff as cardboard, but a piercing blue sky bodes well for the day ahead"

behind and take an off-track route past Spencers Peak and Cesjacks Hut, the eastern flank of nearby Mt Jagungal still graced with snow drifts from the past winter. We make camp in a shallow pass below Bulls Peak while being stalked by a Wedge-tailed eagle circling on the breeze above us like a plane in holding pattern. In the evening we make the short scramble onto Bulls Peak where a play of light and shadow parades before us as day ebbs towards night.

The aroma of Steve's freshly-brewed coffee draws us from our sleeping bags in the morning, and soon we amble across open plains on another cross-country route. From Mawsons Hut a faint trail guides us to incongruous Valentine Hut, painted glossy red and standing out like a sore thumb on the edge of the forest. Close by, a trail leads downstream beside the rushing Valentine Creek to a rock platform between two of the larger cascades of Valentine Falls. Another must-see on our checklist is duly ticked-off.

The next morning we pass through the former gold workings at Grey Mare, yet another spot in these inhospitable ranges where, from the late 1890s, gold prospectors eked out an existence. Despite

KIANDRA, BIRTHPLACE OF AUSTRALIAN SKIING

The hardy souls of Kiandra braved bitter winters, and soon discovered it was easier to get around on snowshoes and a form of skis they called 'skates'. First used in Kiandra in 1861, these rudimentary skis were renamed 'Kiandra Kick-Ins' and then 'Butterpats'. Formed in the same year, the trailblazing Kiandra Snow Shoe Club is one of the world's earliest recorded ski clubs.

Clockwise, from far left: Mackays Hut; pitch for the night near Bulls Peak; Snowy Mountains view to Mt Feathertop from Mt Fainter South. Previous page, from left: hikers near Cesjacks Hut; Kosciuszko National Park's Valentine Falls

being back on the AAWT, we seem to have the trail to ourselves. But we're not alone; swarms of the ubiquitous Australian bush fly and its bite-loving big brother, the March fly, keep us company.

At the head of the Tooma River, magpies swooping nearby remind us that it's nesting season and to keep a wide berth. Here we split; Tony heads straight for Derschkos Hut where we will rendezvous later in the day, while Steve and I take a bearing for Mt Jagungal's sky-piercing 2061m (6762ft) summit. Greeted by a birds-nest view of the Snowy Mountains, I take some photos but can't really do justice to the outstanding panorama. We pause to snack among the cool fractures of the summit boulders, the same outcrops that local Aboriginal peoples once sought out in summer to feast on the fat- and protein-rich Bogong moths that migrated there.

What might be our final day starts off as an easy jaunt under an increasingly heavy sky as we descend into Pretty Plain. We pass more signs of former gold diggings on the way to timber-slabbed Wheelers Hut, a sure winner of any charming-hut awards. It's only midday when we arrive but with a storm brewing we find it impossible to pass up a night here so we call it a day.

Lightning and thunder are unwelcome visitors overnight, but by morning the storm has abated. A few hours later, content though a little tired, our walk ends at Tooma Rd. The car coughs as it warms up, and as we head home the mountains recede behind us. Yet as I turn for a final glimpse, I'm almost unaware that I've started planning my next foray into the High Country. **GV**

ORIENTATION

Start // Kiandra
Finish // Tooma Rd-Snakey Plain Trail junction
Distance // 98km (61 miles)
Duration // 8 days
Getting there // Bring your own wheels or rental car; there is no public transport. Melbourne (540km/335 miles) and Sydney (490km/304 miles) are the nearest state capitals.
When to go // Some park roads are closed in winter, and the walk is also under snow, so November to May is the best time to hike here.
What to pack // Self-sufficiency is key: carry a tent; food; fuel-stove for cooking; cold-weather sleeping bag; and clothing and gear for a week-long trek.
More info // nationalparks.nsw.gov.au/visit-a-park/parks/ kosciuszko-national-park. Park access fees apply. Snowy Region Visitor Centre: 02 6450 5600.

Opposite, clockwise from top: evening rays light up Mt Cobbler; snowbound Pretty Valley Pondage at the start of the trail to Mt Fainter; Alpine everlasting daisies carpet Bogong High Plains

MORE LIKE THIS
AUSTRALIAN ALPS PEAK-BAGGING

MT COBBLER, VICTORIA

Likely named after the Cobbler in Scotland, which also has an imposing boulder-adorned summit, Mt Cobbler squats at the northern end of a long ridge in the Alpine National Park. The out-and-back route starts beside the King River and ascends the (at times) scrambly-steep Muesli Spur to reach the crest of the range. The route then becomes relatively easy. The walk itself is pleasant, but it's the appealing mountaintop that is the highlight of this walk. The spectacular vistas from the summit ridge are to die for, with views to far-away ranges from cliffs that horseshoe around the peak. Mt Cobbler can also be reached from Lake Cobbler, though it's a long drive and you may need a 4WD vehicle to navigate the steep access track.
Start/Finish // King Hut
Distance // 20km (12.4 miles)
Duration // 6-7hr

THE JAITHMATHANGS & MT FAINTER, VICTORIA

Fainter Spur, an off-shoot ridge of the Bogong High Plains near Falls Creek ski resort, forms a divide between endearing bushwalker-favourite Mt Feathertop and the deeply-incised valley of the Kiewa River to the west, and the more tame rolling hills of the Bogong High Plains to the east. This unofficial route starts on a good trail before passing over the Jaithmathangs range where extensive panoramas unfold for walkers keen to navigate off-the-beaten-track. Once back on the main trail, Mt Fainter South offers perhaps the finest view of the journey, before making a return along Fainter Fire Track. Consider extending this journey to two days, with camp made near Little Plain below Mt Fainter South.
Start/Finish // Pretty Valley Pondage
Distance // 24km (15 miles)
Duration // 7-9hr

GLACIAL LAKES CIRCUIT, NEW SOUTH WALES

As Australia's highest walking trail, the Main Range Track might well be the classic day-walk of the Snowy Mountains, indeed the Australian Alps. Forming a stunning loop-walk over a range of bulging peaks, ascending Mt Kosciuszko (2228m/7310ft) – Australia's tallest mountain – and passing five glacial lakes (the only direct evidence of glaciation on mainland Australia from the last ice age), this is an immensely popular route in the warmer months. The trail is almost entirely above the treeline so in fine weather prepare to be absorbed by constantly unfolding vistas. But if conditions are foggy, wet or otherwise inclement, find another destination; this walk is a fine-weather outing only.
Start/Finish // Charlotte Pass
Distance // 22km (13.7 miles)
Duration // 7-9hr

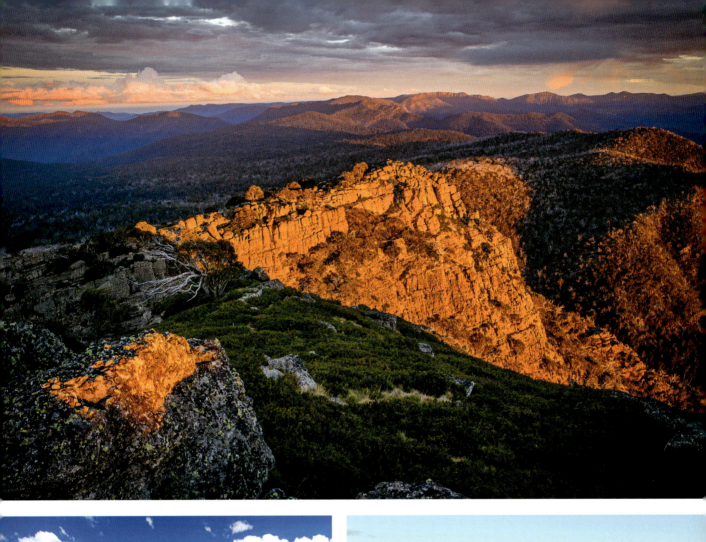

THE GREAT OCEAN WALK

Ditch the car and pull on your hiking boots to venture beyond the tarmac and deep into the Great Ocean Road's stunning natural surrounds, where rugged ocean meets serene rainforest.

The Great Ocean Road may be one of the world's most stunning coastal drives, but that doesn't mean you need a car to enjoy it. In fact, there's a whole lot you can't see from the road, and that's precisely where the Great Ocean Walk (GOW) comes into play – to immerse you deep among its superb coastal wilderness.

So here I am in the seaside hamlet of Apollo Bay on Victoria's southwest coast, ready to embark on one of Australia's most spectacular overland walks. The boots are on and the backpack's fastened as I take my first steps along this purpose-built trail that stretches 104km (65 miles) to the iconic Twelve Apostles.

Depending on your fitness level (and how rushed you are for time), the walk takes anywhere from four to 10 days, but I'm here to do it in five. And given all campsites need to be pre-booked, this is a detail you'll need to be sure on beforehand.

Departing Apollo Bay, I follow the yellow GOW directional markers as holiday homes give way to pastoral farmland. The trail briefly lands me on the sand before winding up through coastal heath via a hilltop offering my first glimpse of the superb ocean vistas ahead of me. It's grey and blowing a gale, but this being the Shipwreck Coast you can expect some stormy weather, so pack for all seasons!

From here the trail heads down to rugged Shelly Beach before leading into the superb Great Otway National Park, among the eucalypt-scented trail of manna, blue gum and giant mountain ash (some as high as 65m/213ft) before hitting verdant gullies of tree ferns and grass trees. After two hours I reach the GOW campsite at Elliot Ridge, but with daylight savings I'm pushing on for another 12km (7.5 miles) to Blanket Bay. Koalas are regularly sighted here so don't forget to look up. And don't forget to look down – snakes also are around.

I arrive at 6pm in time for a poke around Blanket Bay's aquarium-like rock pools before returning to settle into camp. Rainwater tanks are found across the campsites but you'll need to filter all drinking water. Be aware too that tanks can run dry, so for peace of mind, bring plenty of bottled water; otherwise tour operators can arrange water drops between campsites.

Day two: I'm up at sunrise for brekky and a cuppa before diving straight into what will be the longest day of the hike; a 35km (22-mile) tramp to Johanna Beach. It's a stunning mix of cliff-top walks, isolated beaches and coastal heath. I take my first break at the resplendent Cape Otway Lightstation (c. 1848), one of the highlights along the GOW, and a stop made even more memorable by spotting a koala snoozing up a nearby manna tree. It's a wonderful moment and brings a spring to my step as I continue ahead to Aire River, where I take lunch as I encounter a wallaby grazing in the scrub.

"My break at Cape Otway Lightstation is made even more memorable by spotting a koala snoozing up a nearby manna tree"

Castle Cove marks the official halfway mark and after another detour through the Otways I'm back on the sands along wild and rugged Johanna Beach; just me and a couple of hooded plovers to keep me company. Perched on a clifftop overlooking the beach, tonight's campsite is spectacular. I celebrate with a sneaky wine as I enjoy a magnificent sunset and the knowledge that tomorrow's 15km (9-mile) hike will be easier. And with blisters forming, I need it.

Day three is characterised by similar scenery, but with the addition of an echidna waddling along drilling for ants, a mob of eastern grey kangaroos and a blue-tongue lizard that scares the hell out of me as I mistake it for a tiger snake. There's another unexpected sight too: an old grizzly sea captain named Bert. He greets me in front of his upturned boat with offers of water, apples and marmalade. And while Bert's actually a mannequin, it's nice to have some company all the same. Arriving at Ryans Den campsite, I'm thrilled to get another wonderful sunset, but not so much by the discovery of leeches. Now where's that salt...

CAPE OTWAY LIGHTSTATION

Mainland Australia's oldest surviving lighthouse, Cape Otway (lightstation. com) is easily one of the GOW's highlights. Book a tour to climb to the top, learn about the Aboriginal Gadubanud people (the land's Traditional Owners), and hear tales of shipwrecks; from June to September, keep an eye out for migrating whales, too. You can also spend a night in its historical lightkeeper's cottage.

Left to right: marking the Great Ocean route; Cape Otway Lightstation; lush trails in Great Otway National Park. Previous page, from top: the Twelve Apostles; beach-hiking on the Great Ocean Walk

ORIENTATION

Day four: I awake well rested and eager for what looms as a challenging, but spectacular 25km (15.5-mile) hike. Gables Lookout is today's highlight with views out from some of Australia's highest cliffs. At low tide, take the stairs down for the 3.5km (2.2-mile) walk to Wreck Beach to pass the rusty anchors from a couple of old shipwrecks, just two of 180 ships to have met their demise along this treacherous coast. A steep climb leads up to Devils Kitchen GOW camp – featuring one of Australia's all-time best toilet views – before continuing inland through coastal scrub to reach Gellibrand River. Here I spend my final night camping in Princetown Recreation Reserve alongside grazing roos. And while the Twelve Apostles are only 6km (3.7 miles) from here, I've timed my arrival so as to catch the bus tomorrow morning.

On day five I'm packed and ready to go by 7am. Before long I get my first glimpse of the majestic Apostles as I make my way along the home stretch. Here hikers are treated to exclusive views from the designated GOW lookout, free from the selfie-stick wielding masses waiting ahead. From here it's down Gibsons Steps to see Gog and Magog rock formations before taking the underpass beneath the Great Ocean Road for the final kilometre. Reaching the finishing line at the Twelve Apostles, I can't think of any more fitting climax than the spectacular sight before me as seven limestone pillars jut miraculously out from the sea-mist cloaked Southern Ocean. It marks a wonderful endpoint and leaves me on a high as my bus zips me back to Apollo Bay. **TH**

Start // Apollo Bay
Finish // The Twelve Apostles
Distance // 104km (65 miles)
Duration // 4-10 days; six days average
Getting there // Apollo Bay is 196km (122 miles) southwest of Melbourne. V-Line (vline.com.au) run daily trains/buses via Geelong. Port Campbell-Apollo Bay buses are thrice-weekly.
When to go // March-April/September-November are best.
What to pack // All-weather gear; sturdy boots; hat; thick socks. Hiking tent and camp supplies; water filter.
Where to stay // Hike-in campsites come with shelter, picnic table, eco toilet, fresh rainwater tank.
Where to eat // Cape Otway has a daytime restaurant.
Tours // Hike2Camp (hike2camp.com.au), Great Ocean Walk (greatoceanwalk.info) and Walk 91 (walk91.com.au).
Things to know // Book campsites ahead at parks.vic.gov.au

Opposite, clockwise from top: juvenile emus, Tower Hill Reserve; making for the breaks at Bells Beach; Triplet Falls

MORE LIKE THIS
GREAT OCEAN ROAD EXTENSIONS

TOWER HILL RESERVE

It's a shame most finish their Great Ocean Road journey at the Twelve Apostles as the road ahead takes in many more coastal highlights. This includes the superb Tower Hill Wildlife Reserve, a unique extinct volcano formed over 32,000 years ago. Here you'll find several walking trails that lead you among beautiful forested scenery that offers memorable wildlife encounters. As well as abundant birdlife, you're pretty much guaranteed to spot koalas, kangaroos and emus, as well as echidnas and wallabies. Among several trails, the highlight is the 'Journey to the Last Volcano', a 2.2km (1.4-mile) return walk leading to views of the crater lake and the ocean looming in the distance. The Gunditjmara Traditional Owners run guided tours that offer fascinating insights into their culture, dating back some 30,000-plus years.

Start/Finish // Tower Hill, off Colac-Lavers Hill Rd
Distance // 2.2km (1.4 miles)
Duration // 1hr
More info // towerhill.org.au

SURF COAST WALK

Taking in the first leg of the Great Ocean Road is this spectacular 44km (27-mile) coastal trail that runs from Torquay to Fairhaven. Rarely leaving sight of the ocean, the walk passes endless beautiful beaches, cliff-top lookouts, iconic surf breaks, coastal towns and the Great Otway National Park. Gung-ho walkers can do it in a day, but most prefer to break it up over a few days or tackle it as individual walks so as to allow time for swims and leisurely lunches. Starting off from the 'Surf capital of Australia' in Torquay, you'll see lovely beaches and famous breaks – most notably Bells Beach, home to the pro event Bells Classic. Here the path winds through coastal scrub and grass trees, all the while taking in dramatic ocean vistas and ochre cliffs. After passing along Anglesea's cliff-top trail and attractive heath, you'll reach the grand finale – Aireys Inlet's Split Point Lighthouse. Here you can take a tour up for magnificent views before a short jaunt to Fairhaven beach, where there's a bus stop to whisk you back to Torquay or Geelong.

Start // Torquay
Finish // Aireys Inlet
Distance // 44km (27 miles)
Duration // 1-2 days
More info // surfcoastwalk.com.au

TRIPLET FALLS WALK

The Otways are blessed with hundreds of idyllic walks and waterfalls so it's hard to settle on just one, but for an enchanting snapshot into the magic of the Otways it's hard to pass up Triplet Falls. This easy one-hour loop boardwalk trail offers a wonderful opportunity for forest bathing as you stop and listen to the sounds of nature: the distant hush of cascading waterfalls among crisp notes of native birds and gentle rustle of leaves from the forest canopy. The evocative tree fern gullies among eucalypt trees take you down a steep track to different vantage points of the three-tiered falls, before leading up past abandoned rusty artefacts from an historic timber mill site.

Start/Finish // Great Otway National Park (off Colac-Lavers Hill Rd)
Distance // 1.8km (1.1 miles)
Duration // 1hr

MINYON FALLS
WALKING TRACK

Leave Byron Bay's beaches behind to tackle this half-day waterfall hike in an ancient rainforest that inspired a famous film.

I
f you were a child of the '90s, you might remember *FernGully: The Last Rainforest*, an animated fantasy film that sees the creatures of an Australian rainforest (including a discombobulated fruit bat voiced by Robin Williams) unite to protect their home from being destroyed by loggers. Now what if I told you that you could hike through its enchanting rainforest setting in real life?

Adapted from the book of the same name by Diana Young, *FernGully* was inspired by the subtropical rainforest that rises up behind the Byron Bay hinterland village of Federal in the NSW Northern Rivers, where Young lived while writing the book in the '80s. Thanks to protesters who campaigned to halt logging here in the '70s, this biodiversity-rich slice of nature was officially protected as Nightcap National Park in 1983.

Now forming part of the Unesco World Heritage-listed Gondwana Rainforests of Australia – an ancient wilderness area protected by 41 national parks and reserves stretching from the

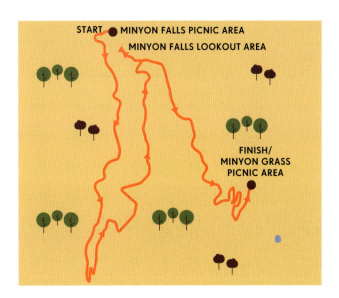

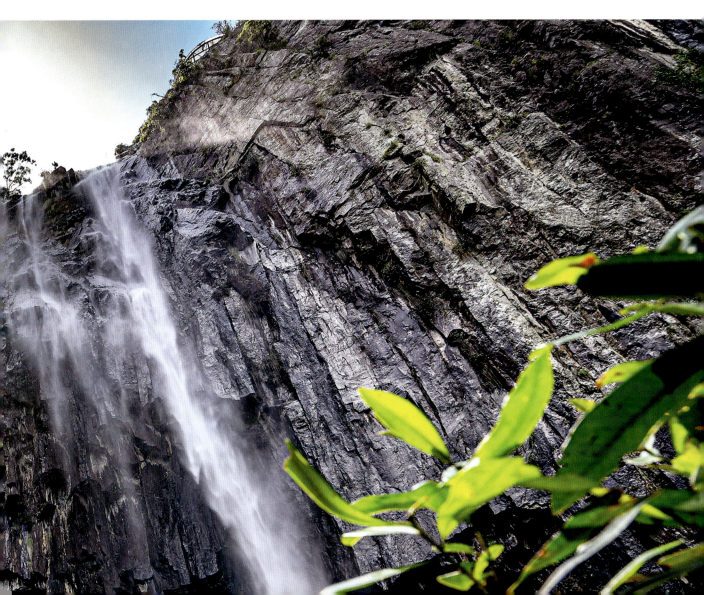

NSW Mid-North Coast into southeast Queensland – Nightcap is laced with a handful of superb walking trails. But by far the most famous is the Minyon Falls Walking Track.

As a Byron Bay native, I have traversed this spectacular loop walk more times than I can count. And while the trail has become busier over the years, its magic is never lost on me. After all, there can't be many places in the world where you can drive 45 minutes from a buzzy beach town and end up in a veritable Jurassic Park, where dozens of plant and animal species date back to the break-up of the Gondwana supercontinent, some 180 million years ago. And thanks to a major upgrade of the Minyon Falls precinct in 2021, this stunning public space is more user-friendly than ever.

The hike begins at the picnic area at the top of Minyon Falls, which drops 100m (328ft) off jagged rhyolite cliffs into a valley so lush you'll be itching to hike down into it. Admiring the expansive views across the rainforest from the Minyon Falls Lookout is obligatory before following the stepping stones across Repentance Creek that mark the trailhead.

Tracing the Nightcap escarpment, the track begins in wet sclerophyll forest (tall eucalypts with an understory of shrubs and ferns) before descending into a cooler, wetter, greener subtropical wonderland as the rainforest canopy begins to close in towards the bottom of the valley.

> *"There can't be many places where you can drive 45 minutes from a buzzy beach town and end up in a veritable Jurassic Park"*

Along the way, it's tempting to take the detour to Quandong Falls, which peels off to the right. But I'm a sucker for the next section of the main trail, which weaves along the rainforest floor towards the base of the falls. I always feel like a kid again as I trudge past huge Bangalow palms, yellow carabeen, black booyong and other rainforest trees that shoot up into the sky, the occasional thunk of seed pods dislodged by chattering cockatoos high up in the canopy providing the bassline to the rainforest soundtrack. Indeed, the strangler fig 'caves' along the trail formed by rotted-out tree carcasses were favourite hiding places of mine as a child. I keep my eyes peeled (and ears open) for the Albert's lyrebird – a pheasant-sized brown bird with long tail feathers thought to be descended from the world's first songbirds. Every now and then I get a glimpse of a pademelon, one of Australia's smallest (and cutest) macropods, bouncing through the undergrowth.

The path becomes rockier towards the falls, requiring a scramble over moss-covered boulders to reach the pool at the bottom, where it's wise to have your swimwear handy for a dip in the fresh, cool water. Sometimes I pack a picnic to enjoy here while gazing up at the unusual rock formations shaped by the elements over 20 million years since the Tweed Volcano erupted

BIRTH OF A MOVEMENT

In 1979, Terania Creek, some 10km (6.2 miles) west of Minyon Falls as the crow flies, was the scene of Australia's first major forest 'war'. The protests, which saw activists block bulldozers, were a watershed moment in Australia's environmental movement, cited as the first time a natural resource was physically defended by non-Aboriginal people (though Traditional Custodians were involved). The protests prompted then-NSW premier Neville Wran's historic 1982 'rainforest decision', which saw 100,000 hectares of forest removed from timber production.

Clockwise from top left: red-eyed tree frog at Minyon Falls; rushing waters in Nightcap National Park; keep eyes peeled for koala on Minyon Falls Rd; red-legged pademelon.
Previous page: Minyon Falls

for the last time, spewing lava across the landscape. With a backdrop like this, it's easy to understand why Nightcap holds deep cultural significance for Bundjalung people, the region's Traditional Custodians, who continue to use ceremonial and sacred sites within the national park today.

I tend to return to the top of the falls the same way I came down, because I prefer the gentler gradient, but if this is your first time here, continuing along the classic loop (which can be tackled in either direction) is a must. Hugging the bottom section of Repentance Creek for around a kilometre, this is your last taste of the rainforest before the trail ascends to the top of the escarpment via a series of steep switchbacks. It can be a particularly sweaty hike on a hot day (carry plenty of water), but it's worth it for the cracking front-on views of Minyon Falls in its glory from the Minyon Grass Picnic Area at the top.

The trail officially ends here, but you'll need to factor in an extra 20-minute (1km/0.62-mile) walk along Minyon Falls Rd if you've left your car at the top of the falls. It's a good opportunity to look for koalas, which can sometimes be spotted dozing in the eucalypts around the top of the escarpment, but watch out for traffic. Huge lace monitors also patrol the two picnic areas along with greedy kookaburras known for stealing many a sausage from the communal barbecues; be mindful that feeding wildlife is not permitted.

Just 2.5km (1.6 miles) further along Minyon Falls Rd, the Rummery Park Campground offers a chance to enjoy this lush wilderness for a little longer. But completing the Minyon Falls Walking Track always leaves me feeling suitably refreshed and ready to face the real world again, just a short drive away. **SR**

ORIENTATION

Start // Minyon Falls Picnic Area
Finish // Minyon Grass Picnic Area
Distance // 13km (8.1 miles)
Duration // 3-4hr
Getting there // The trailhead is an hour's drive northwest of Ballina Byron Gateway Airport, and a 1.5-hour drive southwest of Gold Coast Airport. There is no public transport.
When to go // Year-round, but be mindful that the falls can slow to a trickle during dry periods.
Where to eat // Just 20 minutes down the road in Federal, modern Japanese restaurant Doma makes an ideal lunch stop.
Tours // Learn more about this unique ecosystem on a Minyon Falls walk led by environmental scientist Wendy Bithell of Vision Walks Eco-Tours (visionwalks.com.au).
Things to know // Mobile phone reception can be patchy to non-existent.
More info // nationalparks.nsw.gov.au

Opposite, from top: sunlit cascades at Wentworth Falls, Blue Mountains National Park; suspension bridge at Dorrigo National Park

MORE LIKE THIS
WATERFALL WALKS
IN NEW SOUTH WALES

WENTWORTH PASS LOOP, BLUE MOUNTAINS NATIONAL PARK

Pair dazzling waterfalls with glorious Blue Mountains vistas on the popular but challenging Wentworth Pass Loop, less than 1.5-hours' drive west of central Sydney. Soak up the views across the Jamison Valley to Mt Solitary from the Wentworth Falls Picnic Area before plunging deep into the Valley of Waters; notice the eucalypt forests give way to vibrant green ferns and moss-covered rocks during your descent. Take a breather at the serene pool below Wentworth Falls before continuing on through the lush valley to Sylvia Falls and Empress Falls, then climb up to Conservation Hut, where you can grab a restorative coffee or a snack before taking the Shortcut Track back to the Wentworth Falls Picnic Area. If you're not big on climbing down ladders backwards, consider walking this loop in an anti-clockwise direction.
Start/Finish // Wentworth Falls Picnic Area
Distance // 5km (3.1 miles)
Duration // 4-5hr

TWEED BYRON HINTERLAND TRAILS

Scheduled to be completed in 2022, the pièce de résistance of the AU$7.35 million Tweed Byron Hinterland Trails Project in the NSW Northern Rivers is a four-day hiking trail that will link two of the region's most beautiful waterfalls: Mt Jerusalem National Park's mystical Unicorn Falls and Nightcap National Park's dramatic Minyon Falls, and plenty of other cascades and viewpoints in between these neighbouring reserves. Taking walkers deep into sections of ancient Gondwana rainforest previously inaccessible to bushwalkers, the challenging trail is pegged to become NSW's answer to Queensland's superb Scenic Rim Trail (see p188), which opened in 2020. There'll be picturesque bush camping along the way.
Start // Manns Rd Trailhead, Mt Jerusalem National Park
Finish // Minyon Falls Picnic Area, Nightcap National Park
Distance // 45km (28 miles) one-way
Duration // 4 days

CRYSTAL SHOWER FALLS WALK, DORRIGO NATIONAL PARK

Mist-shrouded Gondwana rainforest towers above you on this short but stunning walk in Dorrigo National Park on the NSW Mid-North Coast, an hour's drive west of Coffs Harbour, which takes you behind its namesake Crystal Shower Falls. Once you reach the fairy-tale-like falls, a suspension bridge carries you across the valley in front of the cascade for Insta-worthy views of the waterfall plunging into the pool below. If you're keen to extend the walk, continue to Tristania Falls and loop back to the Rainforest Centre on the 6.2km (3.8 miles) Wonga Walk. There's a picnic area and a cafe at the Rainforest Centre, and don't miss the attached Skywalk Lookout, a 70m (230ft) boardwalk boasting superb views across the verdant rainforest canopy towards the coast.
Start/Finish // Dorrigo Rainforest Centre
Distance // 4.4km (2.7 miles) return
Duration // 1.5hr

THE GREAT SOUTH WEST WALK

Lose yourself in Australia's natural world and find wildlife wonders aplenty on this multi-day hike through southwest Victoria's lush landscapes of forest, river, beach and bush.

After stretching my legs and lungs along the clifftops and beaches of Portland Bay, I turn into the lush greenery of Cobboboonee National Park. At first all I hear is the leafy shuffle of my feet on the path, but gradually the quiet of the bush envelops me with rustling and soft calls. And then I hear something scary – the sound of padding feet and a soft drumming behind me. Carefully turning around I lock eyes with a tall, elegant and beautifully clad local – an emu, making a weird noise in its throat. Head cocked to the side, checking me out, it seems quite unconcerned about sharing the track. So I move on slowly until I find an open space where I can stand aside, then watch as it saunters

slowly by, giving me a cursory glance as only a real local would. This was just the start of a walk that would sharpen my senses to the 'sounds of silence' and give me time to reflect on my place in a world that already seemed far away.

The Great South West Walk is a 250km (155-mile) loop in Victoria state's southwest corner. It unwinds through breathtaking landscapes of towering gum trees, a river of untouched beauty, magnificent ocean beaches and cliffs, and a magical world of flowering native bush. It also offers numerous shorter walks, so you can do as little or as much as you like. At a gentle pace, the whole hike takes between 11 and 14 days, and most of it is easy going.

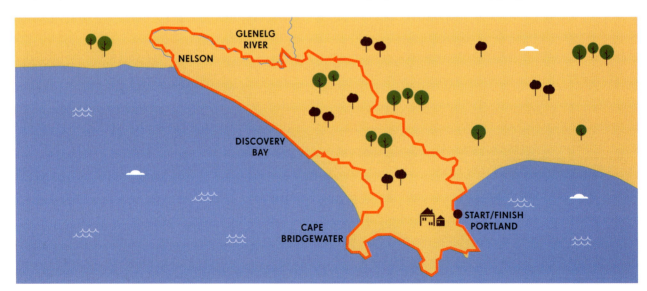

I wasn't sure when I set out if I was going to do the whole walk, but now that I'm here, I just want to keep going. I feel like I'm connecting with nature; walking, sleeping and waking with it all around me. And as I blend into the natural world around me, I become more aware of the animals, birds and insects everywhere; this walk is famous for its wildlife and I'm seeing dozens of emus and countless wallabies, kangaroos, echidnas and koalas, and none of them seem worried by my presence. And the shuffling and hooting of possums and owls are guaranteed night-time sound effects. I even start to feel a bit like an animal myself, moving quietly through the bush, sneaking up on fellow creatures to see how close I can get to them.

Soon I find myself alongside the serenity of the wide Glenelg River as it winds its way through gleaming limestone cliffs and enormous gorges. I'm having trouble keeping up with the birdwatching – wrens, robins, ducks, egrets, Wedge-tailed eagles, friendly bristlebirds, and a rare sighting of the endangered red-tailed black cockatoo, to name just a few. I'm not keeping count but I've heard that serious birdwatchers have noted 110 different bird species along this walk.

I watch groups in canoes gliding by in this beautiful riverscape and feel a stab of envy; another perfect way of being alone among nature. Some of the river campsites are only accessible by walking or water, which makes this river trek section even more exotic. After a night at the historic Pattersons Canoe Camp, established in the 1920s by the Patterson family of Warrock Station, I head into the small town of Nelson to stock up on supplies and overnight with a hot shower at the local campsite.

Next morning I'm up early and on my way along Discovery Bay beach, with crashing waves, flocks of seabirds, and a salty wind providing an exhilarating soundscape. This is a beachcomber's paradise, and I see lots of curios among the whale bones and other debris. There are remnants of human life too; walking through huge coastal dunes, some up to 70m (230ft) high, I spy an ancient Aboriginal midden site with scattered shells and pieces of flint from toolmaking, reminding me of the rich cultural history here.

ANCIENT LANDSCAPE

As you walk through the colossal sand dunes near Swan Lake, on Discovery Bay, you will pass flat beds of grey soil that have been exposed by the moving sand. These are actually the remains of ash from local volcanic eruptions that happened more than 5000 years ago. Middens of shells and flint chips, found near these deposits and along the clifftops, show that Gunditjmara Aboriginal people were living in this area over 11,000 years ago. If you happen to come across one of these middens, don't disturb it.

Clockwise from above: capes and cliffs of Discovery Bay; meet New Holland honeyeaters and wild emus; the petrified forest.
Previous page: winding Glenelg River

"I feel like I'm connecting with nature; walking, sleeping and waking with it all around me"

ORIENTATION

Halfway along Discovery Bay I have the choice of continuing on the coastal trail or heading inland; I choose the latter, and am soon surrounded by massive gum trees and the fabulous flora of Mt Richmond National Park, where one minute I'm staring up at two koalas in a eucalyptus tree, the next spotting a flock of New Holland honeyeaters feasting on the enormous flowering spikes of grass trees. As I'm absorbing the colours and shapes of some beautiful wildflowers, I notice a tiny, exquisite native orchid at my feet.

This wonderland of bush botany and wildlife gives way to rolling grasslands as I head towards the rugged cliffs of Cape Bridgewater. The views of the wild Southern Ocean are spectacular from these huge volcanic cliffs, and equally intriging are the pumping blowholes, a petrified forest and the noisy but cute seal colony that has both Australian and New Zealand residents.

My return to the everyday world starts via the small but lovely Bridgewater Bay village, before heading out along the clifftops to Cape Nelson and the welcome smells of coffee and food from the cafe at the base of an historic lighthouse. It's here that I learn how work started on the GSWW in 1981, and has been maintained by a group of local volunteers for the past four decades. The Friends of the Great South West Walk are mainly retired men who travel out to do track maintenance on a weekly basis. And at the time of writing this, one of its original founders, Bill Golding, is still pulling on his boots and gloves as part of this dedicated team.

Finally, I'm strolling along the last part of my journey – heading to Portland on a coastal track, watching for whales, surfers and diving gannets. I'm almost at the end of this wonderful walk, and feeling like a different person. There's no doubt that losing myself among the nature here has refreshed my body, mind and soul. **SN**

Start/Finish // Portland – you can walk in either direction.
Distance // 250km (155 miles), but with the option of lots of shorter walks too (10-22km/6-13 miles) .
Getting there // Portland is 357km (222 miles) southwest of Melbourne. You can fly or there's a daily train service to Warrnambool, with connecting bus to Portland.
When to go // September to March.
What to pack // Binoculars; sturdy walking boots; camping supplies; insect repellent; sunscreen.
Where to stay // There are 14 well-kept campsites along the trail that come with shelter, picnic table, eco toilet, fresh rainwater tank and a fire pit.
More info // Friends of the GSWW (greatsouthwestwalk. com) for general information, links and helpful phone numbers for planning.
Things to know // Most campsites are in state or national parks and require bookings and payment through the Parks Victoria website at parkstay.vic.gov.au/gsww

Opposite, from top: ghostly snowgums
in the Australian Alps; Sealers Cove

MORE LIKE THIS
MUST-DO VICTORIA HIKES

LITTLE DESERT DISCOVERY WALK

This four-day walk is through surprising landscapes in the semi-arid Mallee region of western Victoria. Despite the dryness, the Little Desert National Park is anything but barren, with vast areas of native wildflowers, flame heath and woodlands of yellow gum and slender cypress found in its heathlands, salt lakes, rolling dunes, dry woodlands and river red gum forests. The range of birdlife is amazing too; from the tiny blue wren, exotic gang-gang cockatoos and honeyeaters to the fascinating mound-building malleefowl. You literally wake and retire to birdsong. The full 84km (52-mile) trek is best suited to experienced walkers, but there are options for one- to four-day hikes, and two campsites along the way. Avoid the summer, which gets very hot.
Start/Finish // Horseshoe Bend camping ground, Kiata
Distance // 84km (52 miles)
Duration // 4 days

CROSSCUT SAW & MT SPECULATION

Best done over three days in November to April, this is one of the must-do hikes in the scenic Alpine National Park. Starting at Upper Howqua Camping Area, it crosses the Howqua River several times, before a challenging climb up Howitt Spur to Mt Howitt. The trail then traverses the jagged angles of the Crosscut Saw, which include the interestingly named Mt Buggery and Horrible Gap, then a steep hike up to Mt Speculation. The breathtaking panoramas of the Australian Alps and the remote and spectacular Razor Viking Wilderness are unforgettable. The return is back across the Crosscut Saw to Mt Howitt and then either down Thorn Range or via Howitt Spur back to the Upper Howqua Camping Area. Walkers usually overnight at the two campsites, the first at Macalister Springs, and the other at Mt Speculation.
Start/Finish // Upper Howqua Camping Area
Distance // Approx 38km (24 miles)
Duration // 3 days

SEALERS COVE

The Prom (see p38), at the southernmost tip of Australia, has spectacular scenery of all kinds; huge granite mountains, pristine rainforest, sweeping beaches and coastlines. There are some great walks from the Tidal River campground, and Sealers Cove is one of the best, often described as a 'walker's paradise'. That's partly because it's accessible only by boat or on foot, but also because it boasts clear turquoise waters, golden sand, a shady idyllic campsite and arresting wildlife. On the upward walk there are brilliant views and lush rainforest before heading downhill to the coast. It's about three hours each way, but birdwatchers and plant lovers will want to do it at a more leisurely pace to make time for all the photos. The track is good year-round, with boardwalks across winter streams, but the best walking weather is in spring and autumn.
Start // Tidal River
Finish // Sealers Cove
Distance // 12.5km (8 miles)
Duration // 6hr

SYDNEY'S SEVEN BRIDGES

Circle shimmering Sydney Harbour in a 27km (17-mile) loop, crossing iconic Sydney Harbour Bridge (and six others), taking in historic urban areas, beaches, bush and more.

I've been a bit of a bridge geek ever since building one out of popsicle sticks in grade school science class, so getting to see seven up close is more thrilling than I'd like to admit. This hike is best known as part of a yearly event called the Sydney Seven Bridges Walk, which raises money for cancer research. But my husband and I have decided to tackle it on an ordinary Tuesday in November.

We live near Sydney's CBD (Central Business District), so we decide to start the hike at its southeastern point, Pyrmont Bridge. Crossing Cockle Bay in the shiny entertainment district of Darling Harbour, the pedestrian-only Pyrmont, festively decked in coloured flags, looks more like a wide beach pier than a traditional urban bridge. Opened in 1902, it's one of the oldest working examples of an electric swing bridge, which means its middle chunk swings open to allow tall boats to pass. We don't get to see that in action today, but we do get a good eyeful of the pleasure yachts that moor here in the shadow of the CBD's modern skyscrapers. Crossing the bridge, we edge around the top of Pyrmont peninsula, passing wharves that once smelled of fish and reverberated with the sounds of shipbuilding. Today they're upmarket apartments and cafes, and many of the adjacent warehouses have been razed and replaced with waterfront green space.

Turning the bend to the western side of Pyrmont, we see it in all its glory: the Anzac Bridge. The Sydney Harbour Bridge may be the city's most famous, but true bridge geeks dig the Anzac more, with its cables like strings on a massive harp. The 805m (2640ft) bridge honours the Australian and New Zealand Army Corps (ANZAC), which fought in, among many others, WWI's Battle

of Gallipoli. Far above our heads, an Australian flag flutters against the clear blue sky on the bridge's eastern pylon, while a New Zealand flag ripples on the western pylon. Walking on the pedestrian lane beside eight lanes of Sydney morning traffic, we have views over the disused Glebe Island Bridge, which has sat rusting at the mouth of Rozelle Bay for more than two decades.

We exit the Anzac and we're in Rozelle. We wander the residential backstreets of this rapidly gentrifying neighbourhood, where traditional brick bungalows and wooden cottages sit cheek-by-jowl with Modernist boxes of glass and concrete. At the peninsula's western edge, we enter Callan Park. Here, a

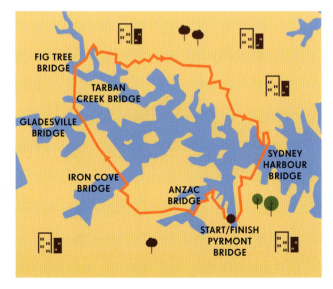

> *"The mighty steel arch stretches across the harbour between pylons of Australian granite"*

complex of Neoclassical sandstone buildings sits eerily quiet amid lush, slightly gone-to-seed parkland. Once the Callan Park Hospital for the Insane, the buildings are now home to an arts college. People say the area is haunted, and it's easy to believe. Somewhere in the distance, an ice-cream truck plays a tinny version of *Greensleeves* over and over. I shudder slightly and wipe sweat from my face. It's midday now, and getting hot.

Next up is the Iron Cove Bridge, a mid-century Art Deco beauty. A second Iron Cove Bridge, opened in 2011, runs parallel. We choose to cross the older bridge, huffing up the stairs and on to the pedestrian walkway. Exiting into the upscale residential neighbourhood of Drummoyne, we stop for flat whites at a cafe in a shopping complex overlooking the Parramatta River. The water is dotted with tiny islands, including Cockatoo Island, home to a 19th-century prison, and Spectacle Island, once used for manufacturing naval explosives.

The next bridge, the tall, graceful Gladesville, offers even more spectacular views (and quite a quad burn too). The afternoon is clear enough for us to see all the way down to the Sydney Harbour Bridge and the CBD some 6km (4 miles) away. The bridge itself is a 579m (1900ft) concrete arch, once the longest of its kind. Elegant white sailing boats glide through the deep blue waters below and ferries chug along, carrying passengers from one suburb to the next.

In quick succession we zip across the Tarban Creek Bridge and the Fig Tree Bridge, a span bridge and a girder bridge respectively.

PORT JACKSON

Sydney Harbour is part of a larger body of water known as Port Jackson (though the entire area is often referred to colloquially as Sydney Harbour). It's 19km (12 miles) long, extending from its western tributary, the Parramatta River, to the Sydney Heads, where it opens into the Tasman Sea. Geologically, it's a 'ria', a river valley flooded thousands of years ago. Much of Sydney's colonial history took place along its banks, which are now home to the most densely settled parts of the city.

Clockwise, from above: Luna Park and Sydney's North Shore; a kookaburra sits on a suburban gate post; enjoying the shade from palm trees.
Previous page: the Opera House peeks from below Sydney Harbour Bridge

From the footpath we goggle at the real estate of Sydney's North Shore – multimillion-dollar houses tucked into hillsides of gum trees and jacarandas, paths leading to docks where sailing boats and speedboats bob patiently. Just beneath the Fig Tree Bridge is Fig Tree House, a turreted yellow cottage built in the 1830s by Mary Reibey, who arrived in Australia as a convict in 1792 and made her fortune in shipping (you can see her picture on the AU$20 note).

The next two hours are bridge-less, as we traverse the neighbourhoods of the North Shore. There's a lot more real-estate gawking to be done here as we wind through well-heeled streets overlooking the harbour. The highlight of this section is a bushwalk beneath a canopy of gnarled gum trees along Tambourine Bay.

Finally, we drop down through North Sydney to Milsons Point and the star of the show comes into view: the Sydney Harbour Bridge. The mighty steel arch stretches across the harbour between pylons of Australian granite, a testament to the power of engineering. It opened in 1932 to great fanfare, with as many as a million Australians gathering to watch flotillas and sing specially composed bridge anthems. From up here it's a feast of iconic Sydney landmarks: the Opera House just to the east, the vintage carnival lights of Luna Park below, the ferries of Circular Quay across the water.

Coming full circle with a stroll among the 19th-century terrace houses of The Rocks, we sit down at a local pizzeria to revel in our achievement over pizza with pumpkin and sausage. First, a toast: to bridges, to engineering, to the glorious city of Sydney. **EM**

ORIENTATION

Start/Finish // Pyrmont Bridge (or anywhere along the loop)

Distance // 27km (17 miles)

Getting there // Sydney International Airport is about 7km (4 miles) south of the city centre, connected by bus and rail.

When to go // Sydney is generally pleasant year-round, but its mild winters (June-August) are especially nice for hiking.

Where to stay // If you plan on starting the walk at the Sydney Harbour Bridge or Pyrmont Bridge, staying in or near the city centre would be most convenient.

What to take // Wear long sleeves and a floppy hat. And as any Sydneysider will tell you, it pays to carry sunscreen.

More info // Cancer Council NSW hosts a Seven Bridges Walk to raise money for cancer research each spring. Their website (7bridgeswalk.com.au) has a detailed map of the trail. If you're in town for the actual event, sign up!

Opposite, from top: rowing on the Yarra River, Melbourne; hanging at Bronte Beach, Sydney

MORE LIKE THIS
AUSTRALIAN CITY HIKES

BONDI TO COOGEE WALK, SYDNEY, NEW SOUTH WALES

Explore two of Sydney's most famous beaches on this beloved 6km (4-mile) paved urban trail. Start in Bondi, the pin-up model of Sydney beaches, with a bracing swim in the blue-green surf and an exploration of the tidal pools on the northeastern rocks. From here you'll wind south along a clifftop path edging Sydney's posh eastern suburbs. Heading out of Bondi, don't miss the Aboriginal rock carving of a shark or whale on your left. About 15 minutes later you'll hit the beach town of Tamarama, home to the tanned and toned surf set. A bit further on, at Bronte, check out the 'bogey hole' (rock pool) on the beach's south end. Ramble another mile or so along the rocky, scrub-covered cliffs to Clovelly Beach, working up a bit of a sweat on the steep stairs, then on to busy Coogee. Celebrate with a dip in one of the beach's aqua rock pools and a beer at one of the cafes set back from the sand.
Start // Bondi Beach
Finish // Coogee Beach
Distance // 6km (4 miles)

CAPITAL CITY TRAIL, MELBOURNE, VICTORIA

This 29km (18-mile) loop circles central Melbourne, running along the Yarra River and Merri Creek much of the way. It's an urban trail, which means walking under highways and over bridges, following train tracks and passing walls covered in graffiti. It's all part of the charm. You'll pass directly by or near many of Melbourne's top sights, including the Royal Botanic Gardens, the Melbourne Zoo and the Abbotsford Convent complex, an imposing former convent turned mixed-use arts and entertainment centre with an adjacent children's farm.
Start/Finish // Princes Bridge, near Flinders St Station (this is a popular and convenient starting point, but you can start wherever you'd like)
Distance // 29km (18 miles)

DARWIN CITY TRAIL, NORTHERN TERRITORY

Located on the shores of the tropical Timor Sea, Darwin has a frontier feel that's only enhanced by knowledge that dinosaur-proportioned saltwater crocodiles inhabit the creeks and sometimes sunbathe on the city's beaches. Built on a headland, it's ideal for foot-based exploration. After hand-feeding wild fish at Doctors Gully, wander east through Bicentennial Park to tunnels built into Darwin's cliffs during WWII. At the Waterfront, plunge into a croc-free saltwater lagoon or surf some breaks in the wave pool. Continue around the headland and bear east to Charles Darwin National Park, adding a bushwalk to this urban adventure, before cutting back across towards Fannie Bay to the Museum and Art Gallery, where fascinating exhibits include a terrifying immersive experience about Cyclone Tracy, which flattened the city over Christmas 1974. End your mooch at Mindil Market, where Darwin's melange of cultures and cuisines fuse together in a spectacular fashion.
Start // Doctors Gully
Finish // Mindil Beach
Distance // 20km (12.4 miles) or more

WILSONS PROM SOUTHERN CIRCUIT & LIGHTHOUSE

This stunning four-day wilderness adventure leads through Australia's southernmost mainland point, taking in pristine beaches and bushland rich in wildlife and biodiversity.

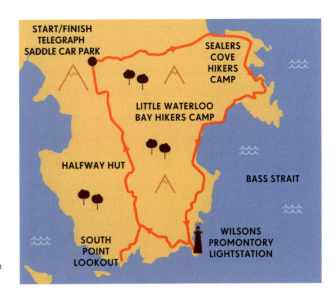

Wilsons Promontory map showing: START/FINISH TELEGRAPH SADDLE CAR PARK, SEALERS COVE HIKERS CAMP, LITTLE WATERLOO BAY HIKERS CAMP, HALFWAY HUT, BASS STRAIT, SOUTH POINT LOOKOUT, WILSONS PROMONTORY LIGHTSTATION

When it comes to dramatic first impressions, few national parks can compete with the moment Wilsons Promontory first comes into view: a swathe of primordial paradise where turquoise waters and looming islands meet the Prom's shaggy hinterland. And it's at this moment I know I've made the right decision to come to trek South Gippsland's magnificent wilderness.

I'm here to tackle Wilsons Promontory's Southern Circuit, a hike that passes the ancient and spectacular landscapes of the Boon Wurrung, Bunurong and Gunaikurnai people. It's a trail that loops through the national park over two nights and three days – but somewhat perversely I've decided to tack on a few extra days to the journey. For two reasons: one, I'm wanting to stand at the southernmost tip of mainland Australia; and two I've always wanted to spend a night in a lighthouse. And that's the beauty of this Southern Circuit – you can customise your trip to anything from half-day strolls to week-long hikes.

The trailhead leaves from Telegraph Saddle where I lug my bag onto my shoulders to set out beneath a blazing blue sky. It's a somewhat leisurely 10.3km (6.4-mile) first leg that cuts east through the Prom to Sealers Cove, a trail that begins among a valley dotted with boulders, wildflowers and the skeletal branches of bushfire-ravished trees. The forest thickens into a shady trail among elegant tree ferns before reaching a grassy clearing at Windy Saddle, where I lay down my pack to dry while admiring a Wedge-tailed eagle circling high above.

> *"I arrive at stunning Sealers Cove, and though camp lies just ahead, it'd be madness not to swim somewhere as beautiful as this"*

Back on trail the path softens to pass through a fern gully before journeying across a boardwalk over the boggy forest floor to arrive at stunning Sealers Cove, with perfect golden sands and calm teal waters. And though camp lies just ahead, it'd be madness not to swim somewhere as beautiful as this. But from here one challenge remains: a tidal crossing where Sealers Creek meets the sea. Frustratingly I can see my campground literally across the water, so it's a cruel turn of events to stumble at this final hurdle. But it's not a surprise, I've timed my run to avoid high tide, but the only problem is it's not quite low tide either. And while it's hard to know how deep it is, fortunately I'm still wearing my board shorts, so I'm able to tentatively wade across to discover it's thigh deep – so luckily I don't have to swim. I arrive and set up camp in the open woodland to enjoy my curry with a few wines and to fall asleep to the sounds of nature.

Awaking to an overcast sky, I set out for today's 13.6km (8.5-mile) hike to Little Waterloo as the trail returns to the Prom's forested interior. I head up a ridge to overlook Sealers Cove before continuing through a valley of prehistoric-looking grass trees until the path opens to coastal heath for more coastal views. After two hours I'm back on the chalk-white sands of Refuge Cove and admiring the mesmerising turquoise waters. Again I stop for a swim and lunch before embarking on the steady climb up to Kersop Peak to take in screensaver-worthy views over fetching blue waters. Here I spot the lighthouse in the far distance – my destination for tomorrow night now within sight. The trail continues for another 2km (1.2 miles) through the hinterland till again I'm on blissful white-quartz sands of North Waterloo Bay. And when I reach my campsite, I come to the realisation that literally every sight gets better than the last, as I marvel at what's an even nicer beach as I arrive at Little Waterloo Bay's pristine sands, glass-clear waters and lichen-splattered boulders.

TO THE LIGHTHOUSE

Only reachable by foot (and an 18km/ 11-mile one-way hike at that) Wilsons Prom's iconic lighthouse sits on a remote peninsula overlooking Bass Strait. Laying claim to be Australia's most southerly mainland light, here trekkers can spend a night in the historical lightkeepers' cottages. Built in 1859 by convict labour, the lighthouse is steeped in fascinating maritime history, and you can climb to its top on a tour to enjoy dramatic 360-degree views.

Clockwise, from above: scenic shores along Tidal River; Southern Circuit views; taking a break at Windy Saddle. Previous page: a bird's-eye view of the Wilsons Prom coastline

Windy Saddle Elevation 300m

← Sealers Cove Camp 6.6 km | 2 hrs

→ Telegraph Saddle Car Park 2.9 km | 1 hr

The third day is when hikers on the Southern Circuit return to Tidal River, but I'm heading on to the lighthouse, an 11km (6.8-mile) hike through eucalypt-scented forested trails to the Prom's southeast tip. Passing more life-affirming coastal panoramas, the lighthouse appears within reach as I take a steep path past rock formations to finally arrive. Dating to 1859, this historic brown-brick beauty is every bit as remote and dramatic as I hoped. I jump at the chance for a tour with the friendly caretaker, and I'm regaled with stories of its seafaring past while climbing to the top to gaze out over the romantic and tempestuous Bass Strait. Back on the ground, I come across a lumbering resident wombat before I head off to settle in for 'luxuries' like a hot shower, a kitchen and a real bed, even if it is a bunk bed.

My final morning is rainy and gloomy, but if inclement weather suits anywhere, it's an isolated, windswept lighthouse. However, I'm less enthused when it's actually time to leave as I take off in the drizzle for the 8km (5-mile) hike to the South Point. It's a path of ups and downs through dense tracts of bush brightened with a smattering of wattle and late wildflower blooms. At Roaring Meg Campground I detour down to witness mainland Australia's most southerly spot. The rain's eased, but it's hard to make out much on this bleak and blustery day – I can see outlying islands before being on my way for the final 15km (9-mile) stretch. The rain's really picked up now, so I skip Oberon Bay (which supposedly has a beautiful beach) to push on for another two hours through forest, coastal heath and over an escarpment to arrive back by 3pm. My phone pings to mark my return to civilisation and officially completing what I would describe as a genuine bucket-list trail for all hikers out there. **TH**

ORIENTATION

Start/Finish // Telegraph Saddle car park
Distance // 69km (43 miles)
Duration // 4 days
Getting there // Wilsons Promontory is 226km (140 miles) southeast of Melbourne and driving is the only option to get here. During busy periods a shuttle runs between Tidal River and Telegraph Saddle car park.
When to go // Year-round.
What to wear // Rain gear; sturdy boots; hat; thick socks.
What to pack // Hiking tent and camp supplies; water filter; swimwear; insect repellent, sunscreen; body wipes; towel; first aid kit; power bank.
Where to stay // The park has hiking-dedicated campsites that come with shelter, picnic table, eco toilet and rainwater tank. You can also stay at the lighthouse, which has dorm rooms, kitchen and bathroom.
Where to eat // BYO all food and water.
Things to know // Arrange campsites through Parks Victoria (parks.vic.gov.au) and book well ahead if you're coming in peak season (December-February).

Opposite, from top: spy Skull Rock
on the Three Bays Walk; Wilsons
Prom from the summit of Mt Oberon

MORE LIKE THIS
WILSONS PROM WALKS

NORTHERN CIRCUIT HIKE

For hikers seeking a challenging trek, Wilsons Prom's 60km (37-mile) overland Northern Circuit is ideal. Following an unmarked trail, this grade-5 circuit is for experienced hikers who are both self-sufficient and have good navigational skills. Starting out from Five Mile Rd car park, the first 18km (11-mile) leg cuts through the Prom's forested interior to pass Barry Creek camp before pushing along to Five Mile Beach to pitch your tent. The following day is a 29km (18-mile) hike leading you north along the coast before passing through mountainous terrain to camp at Tin Mine Cove, overlooking the pristine Corner Inlet Marine National Park. The final day then takes you down south along the coastal trail before returning inland to Lower Barry Creek campground, and then on to Five Mile Rd car park for what is a 22km (13.6-mile) sprint to the finish.
Start/Finish // Five Mile Rd car park
Distance // 60km (37 miles)
Duration // 3-4 days
More info // parks.vic.gov.au

THREE BAYS WALK

If you're not up for a multi-day overland adventure, rest assured the Prom has plenty of scenic day-walks too. And none is better than this 12.4km (7.7-mile) return hike that delivers with a trifecta of unique, stunning beaches. Starting from Tidal River, the trail winds around to Pillar Point for breathtaking views over Norman Beach and the enigmatic Skull Rock before continuing to the first of three bays at stunning Squeaky Beach. Along with its azure waters and unique boulders, here its bone-white sands do indeed squeak like a dog's toy as you make your way across the quartz-grained beach. Next along is Picnic Bay, which is perfect for just that, so bring along a packed lunch and enjoy a swim here before continuing to the final stop at Whisky Bay. This here is a regular nominee for the Prom's best beach and with its pure white sands and photogenic boulders, it's easy to see why. Take it all in before retracing your steps back to Tidal River.
Start/Finish // Tidal River
Distance // 12.4km (7.7 miles) return
Duration // 4hr
More info // parks.vic.gov.au

MT OBERON SUMMIT

In a national park blessed with countless scenic trails, it's hard to pick just one, but for many the hike up to Mt Oberon is the Prom's best. It may not be the most strenuous hike but it's uphill, so there's a base fitness level required to reach the top. Setting out from the Telegraph Saddle car park, the walk zigzags its way up the steep forest track among a diversity of eucalyptus and tree ferns, where you can often spot wallabies. Stairs lead to the top where you'll scramble across the summit to take in astonishing panoramic views of Wilsons Prom stretching over Tidal River and beyond to its islands.
Start/Finish // Telegraph Saddle car park
Distance // 6.8km (4.2 miles)
Duration // 2hr return
More info // parks.vic.gov.au

THE JERUSALEM BAY TRACK

This Sydney day-trip checks all the boxes — secluded wild swimming, a decent uphill challenge and a friendly pub waiting at the end. All accessed by train.

At Jerusalem Bay I dipped my toes in the transparent water, careful to avoid the oysters. Other than a fishing boat in a quiet cove a couple of kilometres away, I had the place completely to myself. I was at the head of the long and lovely inlet, looking down 5km (3.2 miles) of waterway with thick wilderness climbing steeply up both shores. It was hard to believe that I'd left my home in busy, inner-city Sydney just a few hours before.

I had taken the train north from Central Station, careful to sit in the back carriage, as the platform at my destination, Cowan, was only three carriages long. The hour-long trip took me from the clamour of the city centre, through its leafy northern suburbs and straight into the dense and gorgeous bushland that surrounds Sydney. I got out at the little station, which is just about the only thing in Cowan, and took a pedestrian bridge across the noisy Pacific Motorway into the peace of the bush.

This is Gai-mariagal Country, and neat graffiti on a railing near the start of the track reminds walkers 'Always was, always will be,

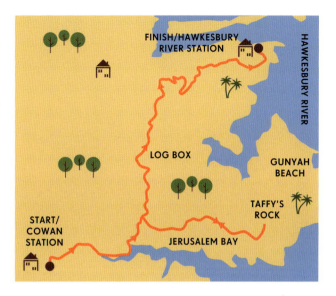

"It was hard to believe that I'd left my home in busy, inner-city Sydney just a few hours before"

Aboriginal land'. Nearby, a short detour leads to a group of four rock engravings etched into a platform, including a human, an eel and a bird. The largest is 5m (16.4ft) long — some interpretations say it's a sea creature with human arms, though it may be a creation spirit.

From here, the track took me another 2km (1.2 miles) down, following a tributary of Cowan Creek, which starts as a little trickle in a rocky cradle and widens out to a broad, sandy expanse flowing into the tidal waters of Jerusalem Bay. The bush was beautiful, small lizards sunning themselves on the trail darted away ahead of me and I was brushed, and occasionally pricked, by the spikes of grass trees, which always seem so shiny and healthy though they may be 400 years old.

Floating in the bay, I could see the jutting lip of the Jerusalem Bay cliff jump on the far side of the creek. For some, this heart-stopping, 9m (29.5ft) leap into the clear water is the main reason to come here. If you time the tides right, it's an easy wade across

the shallows of the creek to the rock that overhangs the deeper water of the bay. This, combined with good fishing, can make the spot busy on weekends, especially in summer. In 1895, George and Agnes Rhodes set up a boat-rental business here to attract visitors from Sydney, and built the walking track down from the station. They also planted the slightly incongruous palm tree which stands above the bay.

I was tempted to rest a while on the grass that's pretty much all that's left of their home site, but the truth was I hadn't earned it. The hardest part of the walk was just about to start. I bit the bullet and began the thigh-burning climb up onto Govett's Ridge from the bay. Here the walk rises over 200 vertical metres (656ft) in 1km (0.6 miles). It was a scramble, but vastly improved by the endorphins of a good workout and increasingly beautiful views as I heaved myself up onto the ridge.

One of my favourite things about Sydney bushland is the sandstone that is everywhere, breaking through the skin of the soil like the bones of the land. It rears up in steep escarpments, curls into waves and erodes into delicate lacework, sometimes swirling like ice cream with ripples of gold, white and pink. The trail wound over great grey lumps of the stuff, and I scrambled over boulders and through channels that squeezed the track between walls of stone only half a metre apart.

Eventually the terrain levelled out before dropping to cross Campbell's Creek where cabbage-tree palms grew thick. Their huge leaves, concertinaed like Chinese fans, screened the sunlight into patterns of light and shadow.

I climbed up a set of iron rungs set into the rock and reached the green metal log box containing a sheet for walkers to record their trek. I noticed that only two people had entered their details that day. I sympathised with the comments like 'hard walk, but worth it' and 'lots of steep ups and downs' and one wit who asked 'where's the lift?'

But the worst was over. The final 6km (3.7-mile) stretch headed downhill on an easy fire management trail, roughly following a telephone line. While not as beautiful as the first half of the walk, this section offers peeping views of the waterways and inlets of the boat-speckled Hawkesbury River. I could see the distant arched bridge that carries the train line north from Long Island, not far from my destination. This bridge is the emblem of the Hawkesbury Brewing Co, which makes my favourite Yowie ginger beer, named after the legend of a local bush monster. But it was the thought of the beer, more than the monster, that spurred my pace in the final stretch.

The trail wound down to Brooklyn Dam, with its pretty sprinkling of yellow water lilies, and I took the short cut through the basic campground that branches left just before the water. The last section of the trail was an extremely steep descent on a concrete road, which delivered me into the sleepy town of Brooklyn, just in time to drop into the historic Angler's Rest for a quick beverage before jumping on the train back to Sydney. **MP**

TAFFY'S ROCK

A fantastic side trip for seasoned hikers, Taffy's Rock is a 10km (6.2-mile) return detour off the Jerusalem Bay Track, offering stunning views stretching to the Broken Bay entrance. The tough, sometimes overgrown track starts just after the steep climb out of Jerusalem Bay. It's an unsigned trail hidden directly behind a sign pointing to Jerusalem Bay and Brooklyn Dam. Check AllTrails for details and download a map before you start out.

Left, from top: fan-like fronds of cabbage-tree palm; the Hawkesbury River's Brooklyn Bridge. Previous page: boat-speckled inlets along the banks of the Hawkesbury

ORIENTATION

Start // Cowan Train Station
Finish // Hawkesbury River Train Station
Distance // 12km (7.5 miles)
Duration // 4hr
Getting there // Take the hourly train linking Sydney and Newcastle – Cowan is one hour from Sydney's Central train station.
What to pack // Bring your swimwear for a dip in the bay, plus plenty of water for the steep sections of the hike.
Where to eat // Angler's Rest Hotel will pour you a welcome drink at the end of the walk.
More info // Search for 'Great North Walk – Ku-ring-gai Chase National Park' on the National Parks and Wildlife Service website (nationalparks.nsw.gov.au), or Jerusalem Bay Track or Taffy's Rock on AllTrails (alltrails.com).

Opposite, from top: espy Barrenjoey Lighthouse on the West Head Loop; Putty Beach rockpools, Bouddi National Park

MORE LIKE THIS
COASTAL TRAILS IN NEW SOUTH WALES

WEST HEAD LOOP

With twinkling water views to Barrenjoey Lighthouse, this loop walk from a car-free community is a stunner. The walk starts at Great Mackerel Beach (population 36), which is only accessible on foot or by boat (including a ferry from Palm Beach). The community's grassy paths are sprinkled with houses ranging from fishermen's shacks to designer getaways. From here, the trail hugs the steep shore of Pittwater, an arm of Broken Bay on Sydney's northern fringe. It passes isolated Resolute Beach, also inaccessible by car, and historic gun emplacements installed during WWII. The track hits the road at beautiful West Head Lookout (which is an alternative trailhead, where you can park a car). Follow the road south to the trailhead for the Basin Trail, where you head back down to Mackerel Beach via a superb Guringai rock-art site, considered one of Sydney's best.

Start/Finish // Great Mackerel Beach
Distance // 8.5km (5.3 miles)
Duration // 5hr
More info // nationalparks.nsw.gov.au

THE GREAT NORTH WALK

The Great North Walk picks its way between two of Australia's biggest cities traversing suburban streets, wetland boardwalks, isolated wilderness and golden-sand beaches. You can tackle the walk in many different stages, from its starting point at Circular Quay, just east of the Sydney Harbour Bridge, to its end at Queens Wharf in Newcastle. One of the loveliest sections is the Benowie Track, starting in Sydney's northern suburb of Thornleigh and winding north towards the Jerusalem Bay Track. Heading north of Brooklyn, you can take a ferry (book ahead) or water taxi to the pretty village of Patonga and then hike over scenic Mt Wondabyne to the Cedar Brush Track, Watagan Track and the ocean-side Yuelarbah Track to Newcastle. The walk is well signposted and there are camping options along the way. If camping's not your cup of tea, you can book 'inn to inn' accommodation for most walk stages.

Start // Sydney
Finish // Newcastle
Distance // 260km (161.6 miles)
Duration // 16 days
More info // thegreatnorthwalk.com

BOUDDI COASTAL WALK

This walk links a string of beaches surrounded by Bouddi National Park wilderness, in a well-to-do corner of the Central Coast, 1.5-hours' drive north of Sydney. The wildflower-sprinkled moors in the northern section give way to a bush trail, with wonderful coastal views, that traverses steep gullies until it hits an idyllic arc of golden sand at Maitland Bay, named after an 1898 shipwreck that claimed 24 lives. The headland south of the bay is a fantastic whale-watching spot. In season (May to November), over 30,000 whales travel between Antarctica and the Pacific along the 'Humpback Highway' just off the coast.

Start // MacMasters Beach
Finish // Putty Beach
Distance // 8.5km (5.3 miles)
Duration // 4hr (one-way)
More info // nationalparks.nsw.gov.au; wildaboutwhales.com.au

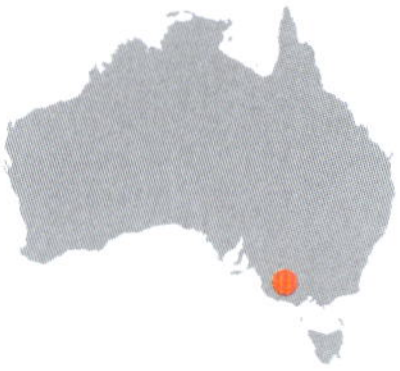

THE GRAMPIANS PEAKS TRAIL

Embark on this 160km (99-mile) expedition through the heart of the Grampians as you journey across their entire length to scale spectacular peaks, ancient bushscapes and extraordinary views.

Some 20 years in the making – and with many unforseen setbacks along the way – finally Victoria's most highly anticipated overland walk, the Grampians Peaks Trail (GPT), is officially open for business. Launched in late 2021, this 160km (99-mile) trail leads hikers deep into the remote wilderness of the Grampians (Gariwerd) National Park. Constructed in consultation with the Djab Wurrung and the Jardwadjali Traditional Owners, this 13-day/12-night adventure starts from Mt Zero in the north, and traverses the park's majestic plateaus and mountain summits before finishing up in Dunkeld in the southern Grampians.

Though it's more suitable for the fit and seasoned, self-sufficient walkers (the kind who are prepared to lug around two-weeks' worth of supplies), there are alternatives for everyday walkers. And that's where Grampians Peaks Walking Company steps in to make the walk accessible for all by offering guides, gear hire and hiker support – from transfers to food/water drops.

If the prospect of 13 days sounds a little daunting, the trail's designed to be broken into individual sections – from overnight walks to multi-day hikes. Unfortunately my visit happened prior to the official opening – so it's the latter I'm here to do, a 37km (23-mile) GPT 'taster' known as Stage One. This was the first section rolled out to hikers in 2015, a three-day, two-night loop through the central Grampians.

I sneak in one last taste of civilisation with an egg-and-bacon brekky roll before it's pack on the back to depart Halls Gap for today's 8.6km (5.3-mile) hike to Bugiga Campsite. I pass grazing kangaroos and emus – a common sight around here – as I officially enter the Grampians (Gariwerd) National Park to follow

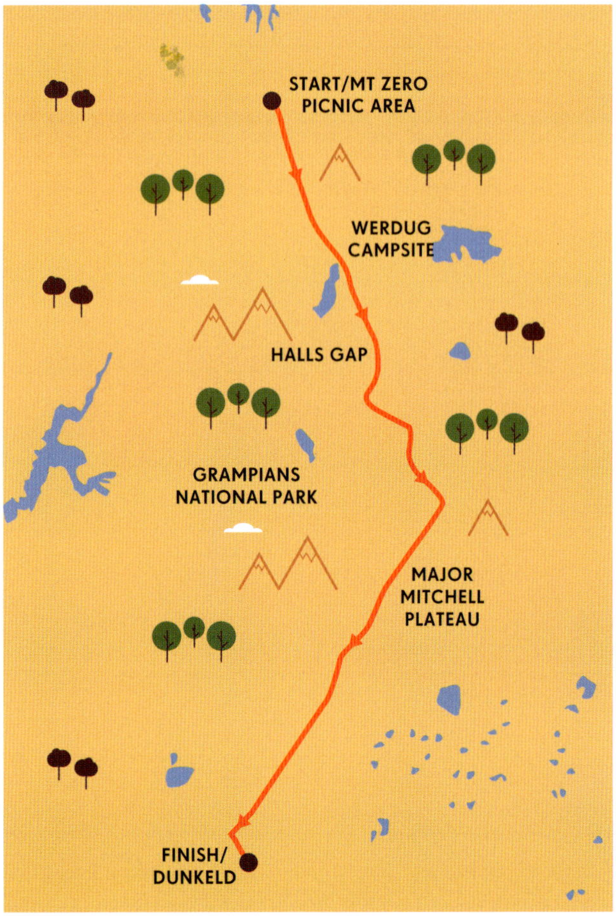
START/MT ZERO PICNIC AREA
WERDUG CAMPSITE
HALLS GAP
GRAMPIANS NATIONAL PARK
MAJOR MITCHELL PLATEAU
FINISH/ DUNKELD

the signed track to the Pinnacles and the Wonderland Range. The first stop is at the evocatively named Venus Baths, where its alluring sculpted rock pools beckon as a swimming hole come summer. Not far on awaits Splitters Falls, a short detour leading among the Grampians' famed spring wildflower blooms. Back on track, I follow the painted yellow arrows up a rocky outcrop to arrive at another scenic detour down to the 'Grand Canyon', an impressive rocky gorge that's worth the steep climb down. Back on the 'path' again, next I'm passing through the sandstone gorge 'Silent Street' to arrive at the Pinnacles. This here is the Grampians' most famous lookout, and it doesn't disappoint. The views are astonishing – reaching out over vast and ancient landscapes where textured dense bushland meets the Grampians' distinctive sandstone peaks and Lake Bellfield in the distance. It's a popular destination, so I'm one of many here enjoying the view, and after 20 minutes I'm on my way again.

The trail takes me up over a ridge looking over pristine valleys before I take the track leading to tonight's campsite at Bugiga – one of the 11 hike-in campgrounds built specifically for the GPT. While some have raised their eyebrows at the $47 camping fee, once you see its timber tent pods, boardwalks, well-maintained non-flush toilets and shelter you'll see why they're slightly pricier than the norm. It's wonderfully secluded too, and my tent overlooks Mt Rosea and Mt William at the southern end of the Wonderland Range. (Top tip: for the tent pods bring along extra rope to tie it to the attached cable). I prepare my dinner in the hangar-like shelter, enjoying a dehydrated Thai curry with a few wines as I sit back and enjoy the stillness of these wonderful bush surrounds.

On day two I awake to the raucous squawk of cockatoos, and enjoy a leisurely morning reading my book among the sounds of nature. I'm in no great rush to leave this beautiful spot, but eventually I set off taking the forested trail along messmate

INDIGENOUS CULTURE

A land of great spiritual significance to the Djab Wurrung and the Jardwadjali people, Gariwerd is one of Victoria's premier destinations for Aboriginal culture. In Halls Gap, don't miss the excellent Brambuk Cultural Centre, where you'll get a fascinating overview of the region from an Indigenous perspective. Gariwerd's also home to the state's largest collection of ancient rock art and features some beautiful sites that can be visited solo or with the accompaniment of Aboriginal guides.

Clockwise from above: sharing the views at the main Pinnacles lookout; Chatauqua Peak near Halls Gap; kangaroo mob in Grampians (Gariwerd) National Park. Previous page: vertiginous ledge views from the Pinnacles lookout

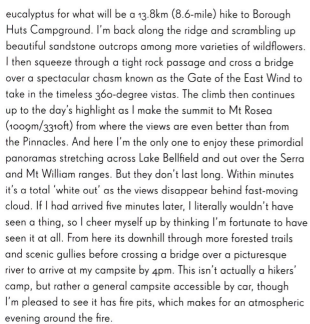

"I awake to the raucous squawk of cockatoos, and enjoy a leisurely morning reading my book among the sounds of nature"

ORIENTATION

eucalyptus for what will be a 13.8km (8.6-mile) hike to Borough Huts Campground. I'm back along the ridge and scrambling up beautiful sandstone outcrops among more varieties of wildflowers. I then squeeze through a tight rock passage and cross a bridge over a spectacular chasm known as the Gate of the East Wind to take in the timeless 360-degree vistas. The climb then continues up to the day's highlight as I make the summit to Mt Rosea (1009m/3310ft) from where the views are even better than from the Pinnacles. And here I'm the only one to enjoy these primordial panoramas stretching across Lake Bellfield and out over the Serra and Mt William ranges. But they don't last long. Within minutes it's a total 'white out' as the views disappear behind fast-moving cloud. If I had arrived five minutes later, I literally wouldn't have seen a thing, so I cheer myself up by thinking I'm fortunate to have seen it at all. From here its downhill through more forested trails and scenic gullies before crossing a bridge over a picturesque river to arrive at my campsite by 4pm. This isn't actually a hikers' camp, but rather a general campsite accessible by car, though I'm pleased to see it has fire pits, which makes for an atmospheric evening around the fire.

The next day's alarm clock is the manic laugh of kookaburras and it's a cracking morning with clear blue skies for the last leg back to Halls Gap (12.8km/8 miles). It takes me along an undulating sandy track through lovely forest, but the soft surface makes the climbs tough going. Spotting an echidna, wallaby and emu energises me along the way as I continue on the path that skirts Lake Bellfield, and before I know it I'm on the main road back into Halls Gap. Though just a small taste of the GPT, it's enough of a glimpse to have me raring to come back for more. **TH**

Start // Mt Zero

Finish // Dunkeld

Distance // 160km (99 miles)

Duration // 13 days/12 nights

Getting there // Halls Gap is 253km (157 miles) northwest of Melbourne. V-Line (vline.com.au) run public transport to/ from Halls Gap and Dunkeld. For Mt Zero you'll need to book transport through Grampians Peaks Walking Company.

When to go // September-November for wildflowers

What to pack // All-weather gear; sturdy boots; hat; thick socks; sunglasses. Hiking tent and camp supplies; food for two weeks; water filter; insect repellent; sunscreen.

Where to stay // There are 11 hike-in campsites with shelter, eco toilet and water tanks. Book night four accommodation at Halls Gap in advance, especially in peak season.

Where to eat // You'll need to be self sufficient and carry a gas cooker. On day four you can stock up in Halls Gap.

Tours // Grampians Peaks Walking Company (grampianspeaks.com.au) offers tours, transport and food.

Things to know // Book campsites ahead at parks.vic.gov.au

Opposite, from top: Mt Arapiles-Tooan State Park; Hanging Rock

MORE LIKE THIS
VICTORIAN SUMMITS AND CIRCUITS

LAVA CANAL WALK, BUDJ BIM NP

Along with the Grampians, Budj Bim National Park is one of Victoria's best destinations for walkers wanting to immerse themselves in Aboriginal culture in a beautiful natural setting. An hour's drive from Dunkeld in southwest Victoria, this Unesco World Heritage-listed site is famous as the residing place of the Gunditjmara people for millennia, and where they established one of the world's oldest aquaculture systems among ancient lava flows. To learn more about this fascinating area, don't miss one of the Indigenous-led walking tours (budjbim.com.au), but if you're looking for a self-guided hike through these volcanic landscapes take the Lava Canal Walk. Circumnavigating the dormant volcano, this relaxed loop trail takes you past memorable views over the crater lake, before leading you along the old lava flow to visit caves set amid other natural features.
Start/Finish // Budj Bim Picnic Area
Distance // 6.5km (4 miles)
Duration // 3hr
More info // parks.vic.gov.au/places-to-see/parks/budj-bim-national-park

MT ARAPILES GULLY LOOP WALK

A shortish drive (67km/42 miles) northwest from Mt Zero in the northern Grampians leads to the Mt Arapiles-Tooan State Park, where you'll find the spectacular quartz and sandstone rocky outcrop of Mt Arapiles. Rising 365m (1197ft) dramatically from the Wimmera Plains, Arapiles is not only Australia's premier rock-climbing destination, but it features some beautiful walks. Starting at Centenary Park campground, follow the signed Central Gully Track that leads you up to the summit trail for stunning views that stretch out over the Wimmera Plains from both Bluff Picnic Area and Summit Picnic Lookout. Returning via Pharos Gully and the Central Gully walking tracks will have you circumnavigating this striking monolith as you admire classic Aussie bush landscapes and flora, including spring wildflower displays. For those seeking a longer walk, there is the longer 15km (9-mile) Circuit walk that loops around park's perimeter.
Start/Finish // Centenary Park camping and picnic area
Distance // 4km (2.5 miles)
Duration // 1-2hr
More info // parks.vic.gov.au/places-to-see/parks/mount-arapiles-tooan-state-park

HANGING ROCK

While the summit walk up to Hanging Rock is only 1.8km (1.1 miles) return, what this hike lacks in distance it makes up for with astonishing beauty and views. Immortalised in the famous novel and film *Picnic at Hanging Rock*, this is one of Victoria's most enigmatic natural sights, steeped in both mystery and a powerful spiritual energy. Dating back some six million years, Hanging Rock was once an active volcano, and today you can scale it via a hiking trail that leads up through its scenic bushland. Along the way stop to take in the unusual rock formations before reaching the summit for far-reaching vistas out over the Macedon Ranges. Before you venture up, drop into the Discovery Centre to get an understanding of Hanging Rock's volcanic background and cultural significance to its Traditional Owners – the Dja Dja Wurrung, Woi Wurrung and Taungurung people. Be sure to pack a picnic to enjoy at its base on grassy lawns among grazing kangaroos, where you can also do the base walk around this beautiful rock (1.8km/1.1 miles, 30 minutes return).
Start/Finish // Hanging Rock Discovery Centre
Distance // 1.8km (1.1-mile) return
Duration // 50min return
More info // mrsc.vic.gov.au/See-Do/Our-Region/Natural-Attractions/Hanging-Rock

THE BUDAWANGS

Discover remnants of ancient Gondwanaland in deep pockets of hidden rainforest as you weave through the maze of eroded sandstone bluffs in the Budawang wilderness.

Heavy dew drips off the edge of my tarp as I lie listening to the kookaburras' pre-dawn assault on Wog Wog Campground. I get a brew going in the half-light, hoping to get away before the nearby Outdoor Ed group wakes. My two companions are making similar rustlings in their own bivvies.

On the far western side of Morton National Park, above the Shoalhaven coast south of Sydney, Wog Wog provides access to the Budawangs, a protected wilderness area of dry, rocky plateaus and crumbling sandstone peaks, of hidden valleys and narrow canyons, all containing unique and diverse microclimates. Accessed only by foot and with minimal signage, the countless opportunities

for off-track exploration make the Buddos a favourite destination for experienced bushwalkers looking for multi-day epics.

The track starts easily enough, heading east, down and across Wog Wog Creek, then climbing slowly through dry, eucalypt forest bearing the scars of previous fires. Turning south into conglomerate country, a large outcrop known as Tinderry Lookout offers average views over scrub and farmland. More outcrops, then a downclimb squeezed between two tall formations before the route eventually gains the Corang Plateau, turning east again.

After the somewhat oppressive forest it was a relief to traverse the open rock platforms and low scrub of the exposed plateau and we

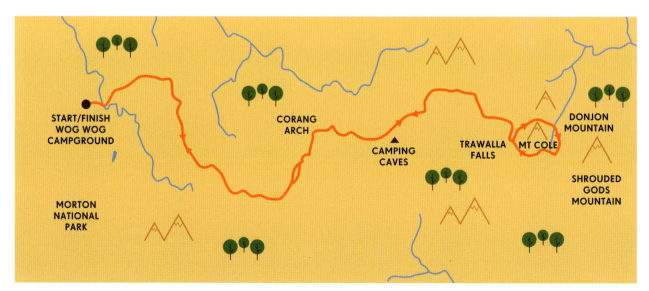

START/FINISH
WOG WOG
CAMPGROUND

MORTON
NATIONAL
PARK

CORANG
ARCH

CAMPING
CAVES

TRAWALLA
FALLS

MT COLE

DONJON
MOUNTAIN

SHROUDED
GODS
MOUNTAIN

took every opportunity detouring to unmarked viewpoints, one after Korra Hill revealing a panorama of distant Pigeon House Mountain.

Keeping left at a track junction, a short, steep, scrubby climb led to the top of Corang Peak where we downed packs, devouring cheese and crackers below the scrub, out of the wind. Re-joining the lower track, we crossed rocky ground to Corang Arch, a natural stone bridge begging a photo op. The route continued north, losing height while divulging expansive views of a valley ringed by sandstone walls, before disappearing steeply down conglomerate to the valley floor.

Turning east again, the track crossed Canowie Brook, the first water since Wog Wog Creek, before zigzagging to a gap in the bluffs and a spacious campground by Burrumbeet Brook. Most groups however prefer the nearby 'camping caves' – atmospheric overhung rock shelters – a short detour under the imposing southern cliffs. Though tempting, we decided to push on, hoping for a shorter, packless day tomorrow.

Overgrown, the soggy path climbed alongside Burrumbeet Brook before rising to a flat plateau providing easier walking. Our original plan meant reaching the camping caves under Mt Cole but one companion, unused to overnight walking, was clearly fatigued so we searched for campsites after rounding Bibbenluke Mountain. A lovely site was found by the upper Corang River, a short wander down a side-track. We dumped our gear and made camp, a small blaze

taking the sting out of the winter evening. A quick meal and we were fast asleep under cold, clear skies.

A crisp, pink morning saw us in high spirits as we bounded unburdened across a scrubby saddle and up to the camping caves under Mt Cole's western cliffs. As close as they were to our campsite, in comparison the overhangs felt cold, dark, viewless and were already occupied so our decision the previous afternoon felt justified.

Following a narrow trail clockwise around Mt Cole, we skirted more camping caves to the tight, fern-filled gap below Donjon Mountain, revelling in the vegetation change – pockets of rainforest in deep, narrow chasms and eucalypts on the sunnier, drier slopes. Climbing one such conglomerate slope for a snack break, we were rewarded with impressive views of Shrouded Gods Mountain.

Rounding Mt Cole we headed south, passing the bizarre, cupcake-like Seven Gods Pinnacles before descending into the cool, green, rainforest-filled canyon of Monolith Valley, where the tinkling of running water was a glorious sound. Soon we were lunching on an incredible sandstone arch suspended beneath the verdant canopy, surrounded by birdsong.

After lunch, the route turned mongrel, splitting by a wooden bridge, the right branch launching up a near-vertical gully. We scrambled along ledges in dense forest, following a small stream, before the route turned south, climbing a steep ramp to a junction just below

BUSHFIRES

Fire has a complex relationship with southeast Australia's dry sclerophyll forests – too little fire and undergrowth fuel loads increase, too much and species don't regenerate. Many eucalypts establish regrowth quickly after average-intensity fires. Mountain ash and snowgums take longer, and wet gully rainforests usually remain unburnt. The hottest-on-record fires of 2019/2020 devastated southern forests, scarring the landscape for decades to come.

Clockwise, from top left: Corang Arch; hiking out of Burrumbeet Brook; navigating the fern-filled gully below Mt Donjon; Mt Owen view from the Bibbenluke Mountain plateau. Previous page: a bird's eye view of Pigeon House Mountain

ORIENTATION

Start/Finish // Wog Wog Campground, Morton NP
Distance // 41km (25 miles)
Duration // 3 days
Getting there // From Nerriga, 230km (143 miles) southwest of Sydney, Wog Wog Campground is 20km (12.5 miles) towards Mongarlowe on Charleys Forest Rd.
What to pack // Be fully self-sufficient. A good map, GPS and navigational experience are essential. Bring a fuel stove; sturdy shoes; gaiters; hat; sunscreen; two-litre water bladder; and a sleeping bag/groundsheet/ bivvy bag or tent/tarp.
Things to know // Walkable all year, though summers can be hot and water hard to find – fill up whenever you can. Check rfs.nsw.gov.au for updates on bushfires.
More info // alltrails.com; bushwalk.com

Mt Owen's summit plateau. Turning left, a sheer outcrop overlooked the ragged lump of Mt Nibelung. The other branch entailed a short, steep scrub bash onto the plateau where cairns guided us northwest towards the saddle with Mt Cole. Ignoring another string of cairns going south, we dropped into the saddle, eventually hung out on an airy sloping slab which we tiptoed across to a scrub band providing a safer descent into the tree-lined creek. The route was well defined through the narrow gorge and in no time we were back on the western edge of Mt Cole, completing our circumnavigation by passing the small Trawalla Falls.

We recrossed the saddle back to our homey campsite with the tiredness and satisfaction of an adventure-filled day. Cheese and wine, a vermillion sunset, cosy fireglow and full bellies brought on a deep, coma-like sleep.

Another heavy dew found us drying gear in the warming sunshine as we packed to leave. Clouds gathered as we retraced our outward steps, a quick detour to Yurnga Lookout for one last view of Pigeon House and Mt Owen and then we were climbing back onto Corang Plateau, easier going up than down. We bypassed the summit, the rain letting loose somewhere near Korra Hill. The forest track to Wog Wog seemed to have lengthened dramatically and it was with weary legs we finally stumbled into the car park. And drove straight to the Nerriga pub! **SW**

Opposite, from top: Mt Giles from Ormiston Creek; the view from Mt Speculation on the Viking Circuit

MORE LIKE THIS
RUGGED TRAMPS

MT GILES/LTARKALIBAKA, NORTHERN TERRITORY

Your navigational skills will be sorely tested on this hot, untracked route across a waterless valley to the Territory's third-highest peak: 1389m/4557ft Mt Giles in the remote Chewings Range. From Ormiston car park, follow the Pound Track east as it climbs through a barren, heat-blasted no man's land to a small pass. Descend into Ormiston Pound, turning east to cross open, undulating country, following the dry bed of Ormiston Creek. Giles is the obvious high point after the Pound corner and water is usually found up the gorge just west of the peak, with campsites by the gorge entrance. A rough, eroded track climbs steeply to the summit where there are several bivvy spots. Return to the Pound and head through scenic Ormiston Gorge to a swimming hole near the car park. The best conditions for the ascent are from May to September.

Start/Finish // Ormiston Gorge car park
Distance // 31km (19 miles)
Duration // 3 days
More info // nt.gov.au/parks; bushwalk.com

TABLETOP TRACK, NORTHERN TERRITORY

Pack your swimwear, mosquito dome and little else for this easy circuit around the dry savannah escarpment above Litchfield's lush tropical waterfalls and swimming holes. Accessed via 'link tracks' from several tourist spots, the circuit is walkable in either direction, and is best done from May to September (permits are required outside this time). Start each day early, aiming to reach camp before the afternoon heat. Florence Falls' link is the shortest, climbing quickly from Shady Creek to the rocky plateau. Turn left, following the obvious route to a campsite by a small creek. Unless you're missing tourists and ice cream, ignore the Wangi Falls turnoff. Walker Creek camp, down another side-track, has some lovely cascades to cool off in. Onward returns you to Florence where you won't want to leave its stunning plunge pool. So stay another day and explore Buley rockhole!

Start/Finish // Various points in Litchfield National Park
Distance // 41-50km (25-31 miles)
Duration // 3-4 days
More info // nt.gov.au/parks; bushwalk.com

VIKING CIRCUIT, VICTORIA

With its rugged terrain, navigational challenges and scant water sources, many hardcore walkers rate this gruelling circuit as one of Victoria's best. Prime time to hike it is between October and May (Howitt Rd is closed in winter). From the end of Howitt Rd, you start on the flattish track to Macalister Springs before tackling the vacillating Crosscut Saw, a thin, jagged ridge leading past The Terrible Hollow, over Mt Buggery and through Horrible Gap. Mt Speculation's summit has amazing views into the Wonnangatta Valley; find water down a side-spur. Traverse the un-signposted Wilderness Zone to the Razor via Mt Despair, camping in Viking Saddle; again, hunt water off the sides. Climb energetically onto the Viking, crossing to South Viking to locate the correct descent ridge to the Wonnangatta River. Ascend the Zeka Track, leaving it ASAP for shortcuts leading to your outward route near Macalister Springs.

Start/Finish // Howitt Rd end, Alpine National Park
Distance // 41km (25 miles)
Duration // 4 days
More info // alltrails.com

MT GOWER

Gaze across an otherworldly Australian island after scrambling up its highest peak, which is cloaked in critically endangered cloud forest.

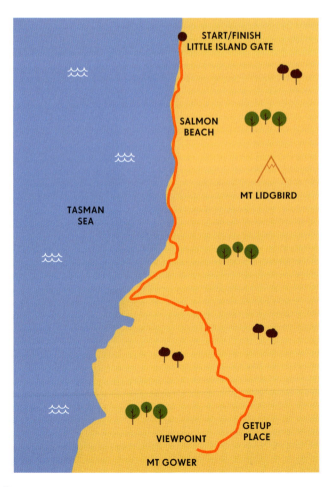

The view across Lord Howe Island's idyllic turquoise lagoon towards the volcanic hulk of Mt Gower is a classic postcard image of this remote New South Wales outpost, some 700km (435 miles) northeast of Sydney. While many visitors to the Unesco-listed jewel of the Pacific are content to enjoy the spectacle from sea level, others can't resist finding out what the views are like from the 875m-high (2871ft) peak – or at least attempting to. And I'm one of them. The 8-hour-return slog is widely considered to be Australia's best day hike, after all.

'I've done a lot of counselling on this ledge,' chuckles Dean Hiscox, owner and head guide of Lord Howe Environmental Tours, when we reach the Getup Place, around three quarters of the way up, from where fixed ropes become essential for hauling ourselves up the steepest part of the trail. There's no safety harnesses though – lose your grip, and, well, let's not think about that.

It's at this point that Hiscox typically makes a call on whether struggling hikers should stop to ensure the group will be off the mountain before sunset. With a natural granite seat and superb views past neighbouring Mt Lidgbird (777m/2549ft) towards the northern tip of the island, around 11km (6.8 miles) away, there are worse places to spend a few hours. But the last section of this challenging hike is the part you really don't want to miss.

As we near the summit, the subtropical rainforest morphs into an enchanted wonderland straight out of a fairy tale. Dripping in fuzzy mosses and frilly lichens in every shade of green, the critically endangered gnarled mossy cloud forest is unique to Lord Howe. When I pause to take a photo, a Lord Howe woodhen – an endemic flightless bird brought back from the brink of extinction in the 1980s – wanders out of the forest to investigate. The curious

nature of these bantam-sized birds made them easy meals for the island's first documented settlers, who arrived in 1894, yet even today woodhens show little fear of humans. An endemic pied currawong also seems to want a piece of the action, perching on a nearby tree branch after following us halfway up the mountain.

Having worked as a Lord Howe Island Board ranger for 16 years before launching his ecotourism business (one of two offering guided Mt Gower climbs), Hiscox knows a thing or two about this one-of-a-kind environment, pointing out endemic plants such as the scarlet pom pom-esque mountain rose – which like many local flora and fauna species doesn't occur anywhere else on earth – as we climb.

Sticking to the rough track meandering across the summit plateau is essential to avoid landing in one of the thousands of providence petrel nests that pockmark the forest floor. This season's fledglings have already flown the nest, but they return to the island in around March to mate; Hiscox tells me it's quite a sight to see the clumsy seabirds crash-land through the cloud forest canopy to nest.

The trail spits us out in a small clearing offering blockbuster views across the lush island, which makes a gentle arc around its iconic lagoon, protected by the world's most southerly barrier reef. While the grey skies don't make for blockbuster photos, Hiscox says we're actually quite lucky, as it's difficult to see anything through the shroud of mist that usually envelops the summit, helping this otherworldly ecosystem to thrive.

After devouring what's left of my sandwich, the strenuous climb calling for several snack breaks, I follow Hiscox back across the plateau to begin our descent. Looking down at this point is not the best idea if you suffer from vertigo. However, as the first part of the return hike is mostly spent kissing the granite as you shimmy down the ropes, this is easily avoided. While I bounce back down

AU REVOIR TO RATS!

An island-wide rodent eradication program enacted in 2019 has seen Lord Howe's rare and threatened flora and fauna rebound with flying colours. One of the biggest winners is the providence petrel, whose breeding success has jumped from 2-3% to over 70%. With the vulnerable seabirds known to nest only on Lord Howe Island (and on Philip Island, near Norfolk Island, in smaller numbers), it's an incredible win for conservation.

Clockwise from top left: Mt Gower and Mt Lidgbird; Lord Howe Island's endemic pied currawong; the island's reef-fringed coastline.
Previous page: view to Mt Gower across the lagoon

the trail with relative ease despite my dodgy knee, Hiscox makes it look like child's play. Indeed, he also offers an express climb option that gets you down by noon. With only one person allowed on each rope at any one time, it takes much longer to hike in a group of up to 15.

Towards the bottom, we retrieve the hardhats we'd left clipped to a rope bolted to a sheer cliff. With rockfalls known to occur along this stretch, I'm grateful to be wearing one as I shuffle along a narrow ledge, admiring elevated views across the island for the last time before we dip back into the lowland palm forest, then join the 1.4km (0.9-mile) Little Island Track, which follows a service road along the shoreline to the trailhead at the end of Lagoon Rd.

My legs feel like jelly as I climb into the tray of Hiscox's ute – a perfectly safe way to travel on an island where the maximum speed limit is 25km (15.5 miles) per hour, and seatbelts are optional. Gazing up at the formidable mountain as the ute cruises down Lagoon Rd towards my guesthouse at the opposite end of the island, it's hard to believe I was looking down from the top just a few hours ago.

Naturally, I reserved enough energy for a sundowner at the aptly named Sunset Bar & Grill, one of two public bars on the laidback island (home to just 380 residents) with Mt Gower views. Fortunately the venue has a complimentary shuttle, as walking back to my guesthouse is out of the question. **SR**

ORIENTATION

Start/Finish // Little Island Gate
Distance // 9.4km (5.8 miles)
Duration // 8-10hr
Getting there // Lord Howe is a two-hour flight from Sydney.
When to go // September-May. Many of the island's hotels and tour operators shut down during the winter months.
What to wear // Long, light trousers will protect against rock scrapes. Pack a rain jacket and a warm layer for the summit.
Where to stay // Luxe Capella Lodge (capellalodge.com.au) is closest to the trailhead, but hiking operators offer transfers.
Where to eat // Fresh local kingfish is usually on the menu at the Coral Cafe, next to the island's excellent museum.
Tours // Hiking Mt Gower without a licensed guide is not allowed; Lord Howe Environmental Tours (lordhoweislandtours.com) provide guiding and transport.
More info // lordhoweisland.info

Opposite, clockwise from top:
Wineglass Bay from Mt Amos;
Coxen's fig-parrot, Mt Barney;
Boyd's forest dragon, Mt Sorrow

MORE LIKE THIS
AUSTRALIAN MOUNTAIN CLIMBS

MT AMOS, TASMANIA

During the summer months, hundreds of people funnel through a pass on Tasmania's spectacular Freycinet Peninsula each day to gaze out over Wineglass Bay from a lookout platform. But the best views of this idyllic curve of white sand fringed by a ribbon of turquoise water are to be had from the peak of Mt Amos (445m/146oft), which looms above. The track to the summit of this granite mountain, part of the range known as the Hazards, is steep and strenuous, but in good weather the pay-off is worth it. Avoid climbing in wet weather, when the granite boulders you'll need to clamber over can be treacherously slippery.

Start/Finish // Wineglass Bay car park, Freycinet National Park
Distance // 3.6km (2.2 miles) return
Duration // 3hr
More info // parks.tas.gov.au

MT SORROW RIDGE TRAIL, QUEENSLAND

Despite the gloomy English name this peak was given by Captain Cook after the *Endeavour* struck a nearby reef, the view from atop Mt Sorrow (680m/2231ft) is sure to bring a smile to your sweaty face. Beginning 150m (492ft) from the Kulki day-use area at Cape Tribulation, in the heart of Queensland's Unesco-listed Daintree Rainforest north of Cairns, this steep and difficult trail is ideal for fit and experienced hikers, with log scrambling required in some places. Beginning in a lowland rainforest valley, the trail ascends into upland rainforest; look for Boyd's forest dragons perching on trees lining the track. The wind-sheared forest canopy opens out towards the summit, where you can gaze out over the Daintree coastline and the Great Barrier Reef beyond. Leave the summit by 2pm to allow enough time to hike down before sundown.

Start/Finish // Kulki day-use area
Distance // 7km (4.3 miles) return
Duration // 6hr
More info // parks.des.qld.gov.au

MT BARNEY, QUEENSLAND

Quite literally the pinnacle of bushwalking in southeast Queensland's Scenic Rim region, Mt Barney (1354m/4442ft) is a very challenging climb that should only be attempted by hikers with extensive bushwalking, scrambling and navigation experience – and ideally with a guide, as summit routes are not well marked. Located in Mt Barney National Park, which forms part of the Unesco-listed Gondwana Rainforests of Australia, this climb ascends through one of the world's most ancient ecosystems, home to rare and threatened flora and fauna species, including the colourful Coxen's fig-parrot and the adorable brush-tailed rock-wallaby. There are two routes to the top: the vertigo-inducing South East Ridge route and the slightly longer but less steep East Ridge route. Both routes descend via the East Ridge.

Start/Finish // Upper Logan Rd, Mt Barney National Park
Distance // 17.5km (10.9 miles) return
Duration // 1 day
More info // parks.des.qld.gov.au

FEATHERTOP TO BOGONG TRAVERSE

Grab some altitude on this stunning multi-day hike across the roof of Australia,
crossing the state of Victoria's fabled Bogong High Plains, home of the wild brumbies.

I n the crisp, still dawn, golden sunbeams creep slowly across the High Plains, falling spindrift-like into my open tent. I take another sip of coffee. Nearby, a copse of gnarled snow gums turns molten orange, while somewhere above, a lonely currawong warbles a welcome to the new morning. On Feathertop's South Face, remnants of winter snow are burning bright crimson. The temperature is just above freezing.

Content in my sleeping bag, I review my plan to link Victoria's three highest peaks in a leisurely five-day high-country amble. Yesterday afternoon, I'd left the car at 1700m (5577ft) on the Great Alpine Rd and walked north along the Razorback, a spectacular high ridge leading to Mt Feathertop, at 1922m (6306ft), Victoria's second-highest peak. The views were incredible, but nothing surpassed dusk from the summit – a searing, snow gum-framed sun sinking into scarlet oblivion beyond the 'horns' of distant Mt Buffalo.

Ahead was the Bogong High Plains, a high, desolate plateau sprinkled with historic huts and herds of brumbies (wild bush horses). Soon I'm packed and walking, but not before another quick summit dash to gaze on the aloof, table-topped Mt Bogong – aka Big Man, Victoria's highest peak at 1986m (6516ft) and my final destination. I head for Diamantina Spur, a steep, relentless two-hour knee-breaking descent down to the Kiewa River, through scarred snow gums and blackened mountain ash. Bushfires are a regular occurrence in alpine Victoria, as entire ridges of grey skeleton trees testify.

Surviving Diamantina, I refill my water bottle from the clear Kiewa before stopping for lunch at historic Blair Hut, idyllically located in a grassy, stream-side clearing. Echoes of long-gone

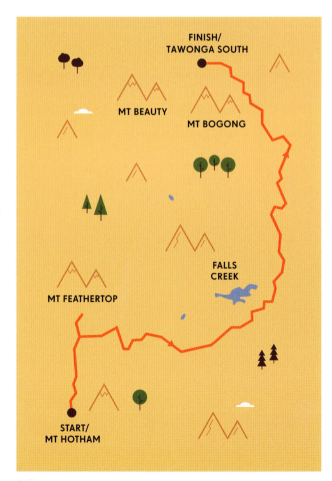

mountain cattlemen and their horses resonate from the now-dilapidated structure, until I look up from my cheese and crackers to find I'm surrounded by horse-trekking tourists. I quickly seek solitude in the steep climb to Weston Hut.

Flanking the High Plains, just inside the treeline, the original Weston Hut was constructed by cattlemen in the 1930s, and nearby, horse yards are still visible. It escaped the awful 2003 fires, but was reduced to cinders in 2006. Volunteers erected the present structure in 2011. The grassy surrounds make a pleasant campsite, and the hut offers refuge from the notorious High Plains weather.

The snow gums give way to tussock, brumby dung and alpine grasses as I ascend a snow-pole line on to the plateau. There's a stark, desolate beauty about this barren high country that stretches for miles in all directions. I push on to a track junction, pole 333. A set of numbered snow poles spike in from the south like abandoned telegraph poles — from Mt Hotham, they cross the Cobungra Gap and count the way to Bogong. Another set disappear northwest over my left shoulder, on to the Fainters, but I focus on the string beckoning forwards. In the melancholy late-afternoon sun, all is still, empty, not another soul to be seen.

A few kilometres further I pause to observe a herd of brumbies eyeing me warily. The stallion stands his ground, snorting. I keep moving, eventually setting up camp beside a group of snow gums above Cope Saddle as the temperature plummets with the sun.

"The last day's trip is short but it's the most magical. The sky is deep blue, the earth blindingly white and the air frigid"

Early the next day, I'm crunching through thin puddle-hiding-ice and the odd snowdrift. The pimply summit of Mt Cope (1837m/6027ft) sits tantalisingly close to my right, but I've got a more pressing goal — the long-drop toilet at Cope Hut.

Mission accomplished, I rush through this ski area on the eastern edge of the plateau. Missing the moody High Plains solitude, I push on cross-country and bag Mt Nelse North, Victoria's number three at 1884m (6181ft), and only marginally higher than the fire-trail beside it. Massive Bogong is looming ahead as I stroll downhill to Roper Hut.

The original Roper hut, dating from 1939, burnt in the 2003 fires, but arose phoenix-like in 2008 as an emergency shelter. I give myself the rest of the afternoon off, lounging in the sunshine and collecting water from a nearby cascade.

The following fog-shrouded morning is spent laboriously descending and ascending steep spurs covered in wet regrowth and fallen trees as I depart the High Plains, cross Big River and finally climb on to Bogong. From my welcome lunch spot on top

HIGH HORSES

In Australia, 'brumby' refers to any wild bush horse, and though herds are scattered across wilderness areas, they are commonly linked with the High Country, thanks to Australia's favourite bard, AB 'Banjo' Paterson, who immortalised them in his poem *The Man From Snowy River*. Their presence in alpine areas is contentious and while scientists call for culls, many others call for their protection.

Clockwise from far left: Cape Hut; a Bogong High Plains creek; here be wild brumbies; the Kosciuszko Main Range is visible on the walk.
Previous page: Mt Feathertop

ORIENTATION

Start // Diamantina Hut, Mt Hotham
Finish // Mountain Creek, Tawonga South
Distance // 77km (48 miles)
Duration // 5-6 days
Getting there // It's a 4-hour-drive from Melbourne; find transport at both ends via mtbeauty.com or ptv.vic.gov.au
When to go // September to May.
What to take // A good tent; sleeping bag; fuel stove; warm clothes; thermals and wet weather gear. Food for five days. Huts (except Cleve Cole) are for emergency use only.
Things to know // Shorter three-day circuits are possible: Mountain Creek, Eskdale Spur, Cleve Cole, Roper Hut, Timms Fire Trail, Bogong Creek Saddle, Quartz Ridge, Staircase, Mountain Creek; or Razorback, Feathertop, Diamantina, Weston Hut, Cobungra Gap, Dibbin Hut, Swindlers Spur.

of T-Spur, it's only a short walk through lush snow meadows to the Cleve Cole Memorial Hut, although I take a detour via the picturesque Howman Falls.

Nestled in a beautiful, sheltered bowl on the mountain's southeastern flank, the hut commemorates a local skier caught in a blizzard. Made from stone, with bunks, indoor plumbing and solar panels, it's one that's popular with walkers, and I exchange pleasantries, though still opt to sleep in my cosy bomber tent – orientated, as always, to catch the sunrise.

Early morning sunlight sparkles off the surrounding snow and draws long shadows from the ubiquitous snow gums as I crunch above the tree line one last time. While this last day's walk is short, it's the most magical of the whole trip. The sky is deep blue, the earth blindingly white and the air frigid as I follow the pole line on to Bogong's wide summit plateau.

The whole of the High Plains lies stretched out along my left, ending in the distinctive cap of Feathertop, while over to my right, a distant long white wall heralds the Kosciuszko Main Range, which is across the border in New South Wales. Clouds fill the valleys. I am absolutely alone, at altitude, and immensely happy. I take the mandatory selfie at Bogong's summit cairn, then drop down the atmospheric – and at times decidedly airy – Staircase, until the trees swallow me up and my thoughts stray to how I'm going to recover my car. **SW**

Opposite: snow-covered flowers in the heights of Alpine National Park on the epic Australian Alps Hike

MORE LIKE THIS
MULTI-DAY MARVELS

AUSTRALIAN ALPS HIKE, VICTORIA, NEW SOUTH WALES & AUSTRALIAN CAPITAL TERRITORY

Stretching out over a massive 655km (407 miles) from Victoria and NSW to the ACT, a walk in the park this is not! Instead, it's a full-blown five- to eight-week cross-country expedition through wilderness areas of Australia's iconic high country terrain. Traversing five national parks, it's not a hike for your average Joe – you'll need to be very well prepared, carry all the necessary equipment, and have a good fitness level to go with advanced navigational skills. In the high country, the route takes you through famed ski resorts – Hotham, Falls Creek, Baw Baw, Thredbo and Perisher – and scales the nation's highest peaks, including Mt Kosciusko (2228m/7309ft). Needless to say this is a hike best taken in summer (December to February) to avoid freezing conditions. But if that all sounds too much, you can break the route down into more manageable legs to give you a good taste for what is truly one of Australia's most epic hikes.

Start // Walhalla, Victoria
Finish // Tharwa, ACT
Distance / 655km (407 miles) one-way
Duration // 5-8 weeks
**More info // theaustralianalpsnational
parks.org/experience/aawt**

SUNSHINE COAST HINTERLAND GREAT WALK, QUEENSLAND

The Sunshine Coast's white sandy beaches and blissful year-round sunshine may bring in the crowds, but just a short distance inland a whole different kind of natural beauty awaits. And what better way to explore the beautiful hinterland of the Blackall Range and its subtropical rainforest, waterfalls, rock pools and stunning gorges than on foot along this four-day trek. One of Queensland's 'Great Walks' – a series of celebrated hikes initiated as a collaboration between the National Trust and Queensland Parks and Wildlife – this hinterland trek takes you through three national parks (Kondalilla, Mapleton Falls and Mapleton), in an area where the Jinibara people have resided for millennia. Like most of the Great Walks, this one is divided into different sections; all can be tackled as short jaunts or day-trips if you don't have all the gear for a multi-day camping adventure.

Start //Baroon Pocket
Finish // Delicia Rd entrance
Distance // 58.8km (36.5 miles) one-way
Duration // 4 days
**More info // parks.des.qld.gov.au/
parks/great-walks-sunshine-coast**

MT ARTHUR & TABLELAND, SOUTH ISLAND, NEW ZEALAND

Kahurangi National Park's excellent network of backcountry huts provide many multi-day tramping opportunities, and the Mt Arthur and Tableland area is spectacular. One challenging route climbs above Mt Arthur Hut (1310m/4298ft) to the summit of Mt Arthur (1795m/5889ft) then follows a high, exposed traverse to Salisbury Lodge (1130m/3707ft). With good weather, the views are superb; in bad it's abysmal and the alternate low-level route should be used. Continue on to the Tableland, a high limestone plateau covered in tussock, alpine flowers, snow and sinkholes. Pass Balloon Hut on the way to Lake Peel, a photogenic alpine tarn, before climbing the ridgetop for a sensational view of the Cobb Valley. Return to the car by the low-level route or drop down into the Cobb for further adventures.

**Start/Finish // Flora car park, Motueka
(or Cobb Reservoir, Takaka)**
Distance // 35km (22 miles)
Duration // 2-4 days
More info // doc.govt.nz

TASMANIA

THE WUKALINA WALK

Follow ancient footsteps along the extraordinary Bay of Fires, learning of Tasmanian Aboriginal culture as you walk some of Australia's most beautiful beaches.

In the far northeast of Tasmania, on the island's flattest corner, there's a hill that passes for a mountain. Rising just 215m (705ft) above sea level, Europeans called it Mt William, though to the palawa (Tasmanian Aboriginals) it's always been wukalina. To the Indigenous people, it has been something more than a mountain for hundreds, if not thousands, of years. From this summit, fire was used to signal the Furneaux Islands visible to the north, and today the mountain lends its name to the wukalina Walk, the first tourism venture owned and operated by the palawa community.

Launched in 2018, this four-day guided walk is an exploration of country and culture, climbing wukalina/Mt William and hiking the bright and beautiful Bay of Fires coastline. Dotted with middens and sites of ancient Aboriginal shelters, it's a coast that feels custom-made by nature for walking – the town of St Helens at the Bay of Fires' southern end was even known to palawa as kunnara kunna, a name that translates as 'easy walking place'.

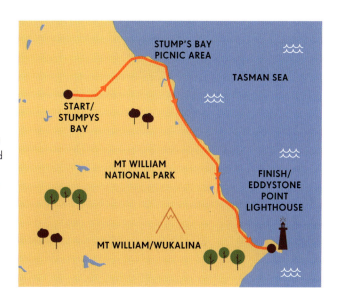

Suitably, the wukalina Walk begins on wukalina/Mt William, hiking across the flat lands of Mt William National Park and onto the mountain. It's a gentle climb through coastal scrub, with grass trees bursting from the earth, and the upper slopes flaked with rock outcrops. From the low summit, there's a mud-map view of the coast, with Swan, Rum, Preservation and Cape Barren islands afloat offshore, and the Strzelecki Peaks on Flinders Island rising above them all. Two dimples in wukalina/Mt William's summit rock may have been the firepits used to send out signals.

On the descent, we turn at a cleverly hidden junction, veering onto a trail cut specifically for the wukalina Walk that's like a secret portal from the mountain to the sea. The bush looks like nondescript coastal scrub, but it also turns out to be a rich larder. Guides point out edible plants such as pigface, currant bush, lettuce weed and the she-oak cones that palawa would chew to assuage thirst. A guide's hand forages beneath the foliage of a grass tree and pulls out a lump of sap.

'This is what was used to make glue,' he says. 'Mix it with something fibrous like roo poo and it makes a really strong glue.'

This night, and the next, we will stay in krakani lumi, the wukalina Walk's purpose-built camp. The beautifully designed 'place of rest' features a communal hub with a large dome cut into a main building and sleeping pods dotted around it. The cube-shaped pods winch open to reveal domed interiors – along with the domed hub, they're designed to replicate ancient palawa shelters from

"The place where I will sleep tonight has been sheltering people for thousands of years. It's a fitting spot to rest on a hike that's been all about country, culture and learning"

Tasmania's west coast. A classically spectacular Bay of Fires beach is five minutes' walk away, and a dinner of muttonbird and wallaby is cooking on the firepit as we arrive.

Though we are ultimately walking to larapuna/Eddystone Point, the next day is a gentle one of exploratory walks in the vicinity of the camp. Wind whips the coast, and pelicans blow across the sky as we wander the shoreline. On the beach, the sea has deposited a bounty of marine wonders: shark eggs; bluebottle jellyfish; the leathery strands of the bull kelp that palawa use to make baskets. Offshore, assaulted by waves, is George Rocks, where 19th-century sealers would send palawa women to hunt seals. Most striking of all, however, is a dune that's not really a dune at all. Glistening in its sands is a large pile of shells that betrays the dune as a midden – a place where shells were discarded by ancient palawa after countless thousands of meals.

The third day is the biggest day on the wukalina Walk, with a 17km (10.6 mile) hike from krakani lumi to larapuna/Eddystone Point. There are no trails between the two, so it's the beaches that

THE DEATH MYTH

It was long contended that the Tasmanian Aboriginal lineage ended with the death of Bruny Island woman Truganini in 1876, but the kidnap of palawa women to the Bass Strait islands by British and American sealers unintentionally helped the line survive. More than 4% of the Tasmanian population now identify as Aboriginal (higher than the Australian average), and 20-plus places have official English and palawa kani dual names.

Clockwise from top left: Eddystone Point lighthouse, perched atop a palawa midden; white sand and red rocks at the Bay of Fires; keep eyes peeled for a wukalina wallaby. Previous page: Bay of Fires coastline

will be our guiding line. The sand is white and fine grained, so that it's a little like walking on a sheet of paper. When clusters of rock appear – which they regularly do – they're coated in the orange lichen that all but defines this Bay of Fires coastline.

Schooled now in the nuances of this coast's bush and its tucker, I begin to see coastal shrubs that are like cases of fruit. Ahead, the 35m-high (115ft) lighthouse on larapuna/Eddystone Point becomes a constant presence, rising like a finish post for the walk. They're the kind of beaches you wish could stretch forever, but soon enough we're at Picnic Corner, where the sand yields to the frayed, rocky edges of larapuna/Eddystone Point. We cross the point and approach the lighthouse from the south.

The lighthouse and the point have been handed back to the palawa, and when I drop my pack in the lighthouse keeper's cottage that now forms the accommodation for wukalina Walk guests, there's one more short walk to be made around the point.

Larapuna/Eddystone Point is one of the most significant historical sites along this coast, for it is effectively a large palawa midden with a lighthouse staked atop it. On one side of the point, the shells and stone tools of the midden are visible like a skin, while on the other side there are depressions in the land where palawa shelters once stood. This place where I will sleep tonight has been sheltering people for thousands of years. It's a fitting spot to rest at the end of a hike that's been all about country, culture and learning. **AB**

ORIENTATION

Start // Stumpys Bay
Finish // larapuna/Eddystone Point
Distance // 33km (20.5 miles)
Duration // 4 days
Getting there // The wukalina Walk departs from Launceston, with a shuttle to the hike's start on the northeast coast.
When to go // The walk runs from October to April, with trips departing every week or fortnight.
What to pack // All bedding and food is provided, meaning you really only have to carry clothing. Backpacks and rain jackets can be supplied by wukalina Walk.
Where to stay // The first two nights are spent at krakani lumi camp, with the final night in the lighthouse keeper's cottage at Eddystone Point.
More info // wukalinawalk.com.au

*Opposite, from top: rock art
at Burrungkuy (Nourlangie);
hiking into Carnarvon Gorge*

MORE LIKE THIS
ANCIENT SITES HIKES

BARRK SANDSTONE WALK, NORTHERN TERRITORY

Burrungkuy (Nourlangie) is an outlier of the Arnhem Land escarpment adrift among the floodplains of Kakadu National Park. Two major rock-art galleries feature along its base, and they can be connected on one of the longest of the national park's day walks. The hike begins along the paved trail to the main Anbangbang Gallery, where paintings include creation beings such as Namarrkon (Lightning Man). The walk climbs and crosses Burrungkuy, at times through a virtual lost city of sandstone, before descending to Nanguluwur, a less-visited gallery where the paintings include 'contact art' of European sailing ships. From here, the track skirts Burrungkuy, crossing a rocky ridge and returning to the car park. Days can be brutally hot, even in winter, so carry plenty of water.
Start/Finish // Burrungkuy (Nourlangie) car park
Distance // 12km (7.5 miles)
Duration // 5-7hr
More info // parksaustralia.gov.au/ kakadu/do/walks/barrk-sandstone-walk

CARNARVON GORGE, QUEENSLAND

This deep incision, 400km (248.5 miles) inland from Bundaberg, is a work of art from both nature and ancient Indigenous painters. A track threads through the gorge to Big Bend, with several short trails detouring away into side gorges. Prime among them is the simply titled Art Gallery, where a 60m-long (197ft) line of cliffs is covered in more than 2000 Aboriginal paintings and ochre stencils – hands, animal tracks, boomerangs. The track is less maintained beyond the Art Gallery, but it's worth continuing to view Cathedral Cave, the second of Carnarvon's art sites. At this large overhang, the art includes a depiction of a rifle from early European contact. It's a short distance from here to the pool at Big Bend, where the walk turns back through the spectacular sandstone gorge.
Start/Finish // Carnarvon Gorge visitor area
Distance // 19.4km (12 miles)
Duration // 6-8hr
More info // parks.des.qld.gov.au/ parks/carnarvon-gorge

RED HANDS CAVE, NEW SOUTH WALES

Near the foot of the Blue Mountains, at Sydney's western edge, is this low overhang covered in stencilled ochre handprints. The walk sets out from near the Glenbrook entrance to Blue Mountains National Park and makes a lollipop loop, branching through Red Hands Gully to the cave and returning along Camp Fire Creek. It's thought that the track follows the route used by Aboriginal people for thousands of years to access the cave. Keep an eye out along Camp Fire Creek for grooves left in the rock from Aboriginal axe grinding – they're seen not long after the link track first reaches the creek. Back at the trailhead, there are a couple of nearby short walks leading to cooling swimming holes at Blue Hole (500m/1640ft walk) and Jellybean Pool (1km/0.62-mile walk).
Start/Finish // Glenbrook Causeway
Distance // 8km (5 miles)
Duration // 2-3hr
More info // nationalparks.nsw.gov.au/ visit-a-park/parks/blue-mountains-national-park

THE SOUTH COAST TRACK

A week-long traverse of Tasmania's wild south coast, stepping from beach to beach and over one of the most notorious mountain crossings in the state.

To unsettle a Tasmanian bushwalker, you need only mutter two words: Ironbound Range. Rising off the island's south coast, this mountain range has innocuous statistics, stretching less than 10km (6.2 miles) from end to end and topping out at little more than 1000m (3280ft) above sea level. And yet it presents perhaps the most notorious day of walking in Tasmania.

I'm camped at its foot, on the banks of Louisa River. It's the second night of my week-long walk along Tasmania's most committing and remote coastal trail, and nervous energy fills the camp as walkers contemplate the coming day across the Ironbounds. It's an energy tempered only by the relief of those who've just come across the range from the other direction.

The South Coast Track is a rare walk that begins (or ends) at an airstrip, flying in by light aircraft from Hobart to remote Melaleuca in the state's far southwest corner, deep inside the Tasmanian Wilderness World Heritage Area. As the name suggests, the South Coast Track beelines straight to the south coast at Cox Bight, and while there will be a couple of protracted inland stretches over the coming week, the walk stitches together nine wild beaches – and this one infamous mountain range.

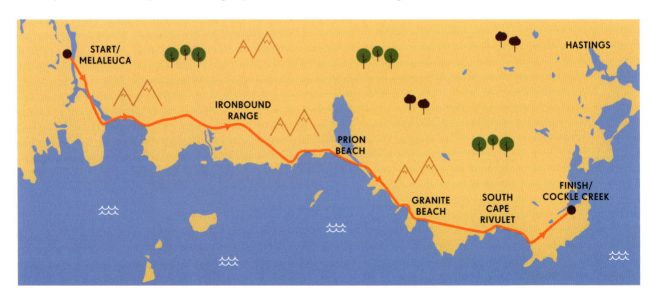

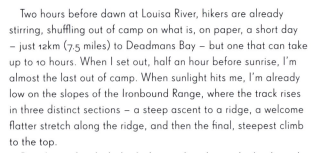

Two hours before dawn at Louisa River, hikers are already stirring, shuffling out of camp on what is, on paper, a short day – just 12km (7.5 miles) to Deadmans Bay – but one that can take up to 10 hours. When I set out, half an hour before sunrise, I'm almost the last out of camp. When sunlight hits me, I'm already low on the slopes of the Ironbound Range, where the track rises in three distinct sections – a steep ascent to a ridge, a welcome flatter stretch along the ridge, and then the final, steepest climb to the top.

But it's not the climb that's the toughest bit on the Ironbounds; it's the descent. I crest the range late in the morning, after hours of climbing through its alpine slopes. Around me, hikers take a few steps, pause for breath, and then take a few more steps. It's like watching people ascend at altitude, except that the Southern Ocean isn't far below us.

The descent begins gently enough, but as it enters the damp rainforest that smothers the range's eastern slopes, a punishing few hours are about to begin. The track is steep, muddy and slippery. Trees reach across the track, creating a gymnastic obstacle course – I climb under trees, through trees and over trees – and their roots alternate as slippery steps and secure handholds. By the time I stumble into camp late in the afternoon, Deadmans Bay feels like a description as much as a place. Ahead

"Trees reach across the track, creating a gymnastic obstacle course – I climb under trees, through trees and over trees"

of me now, however, the south coast rolls out like a welcome mat. In three days of walking to here, I've traversed just one beach – Cox Bight. Now eight more call at me like sirens.

In the morning I round little Turua Beach and step out onto Prion Beach, the longest strand along the track. For more than an hour, I sink into its sand as it narrows into a spit separating the Southern Ocean from New River Lagoon. As I finally turn in behind the dunes to the shores of the lagoon, there are two imposing sights: the looming bulk of Precipitous Bluff, one of Tasmania's most commanding mountains; and the amount of water I must cross to get to the other side of the lagoon. Fortunately, rowboats have been tied up to the shores for walkers to make the crossing. Momentarily, it's my arms doing the walking.

A storm chases me into camp behind Osmiridium Beach this night, stirring the Southern Ocean into a fury, but all is calm and clear the next morning as the beach-hop continues. The fierce beauty of this entire coast means there are now no surprises about the scene at Surprise Bay, despite its perfect combination

DENY KING

If Melaleuca seems a strange location for an airstrip – welcome to the middle of nowhere – you have Deny King to thank for it. The 'King of the Wilderness', he lived in Melaleuca for 55 years from 1936, mining for tin and becoming a noted naturalist and environmentalist. King's home still stands near the airstrip, which he carved out singlehandedly over three summers in the 1950s, transforming access to this place that feels as remote as anywhere in Australia.

Clockwise, from top left: waratah in flower, Ironbound Range; hiking the South Coast Track; Deadmans Bay; view to Cox Bight from the Ironbound Range. Previous page: South Cape Bay

of smooth sands, craggy boulders and the dark, tannin-stained Surprise Rivulet draining across the beach.

While many South Coast Track walkers build in a rest day somewhere like Deadmans Bay, I've planned a short walking day to Granite Beach – a quick headland crossing beyond Surprise Bay – where I spend the afternoon sat atop the cliffs at the campsite's edge watching the mesmerising motion of the Southern Ocean.

Granite Beach marks the point at which the second of the South Coast Track's range crossings begin. The South Cape Range is around half the height of the Ironbounds but has its own notoriety. This crossing to South Cape Rivulet can be a sloppy mess of mud, but in the middle of a dry summer, it's dried to a crust. The pits of black mud are just a rumour beneath my feet.

It makes for a quick crossing to South Cape Rivulet and my final night on the track, before the march inland to Cockle Creek, where the track ends and roads begin. Six days of attrition are weighing heavily on my body, but as the rivulet flows past camp and through the beach, it balloons into a deep pool that's cool and restorative.

As I sit on its bank, water, time and memories of nearly a week of some of Tasmania's finest wild beauty wash over me. A shower is a day away, Tasmania's southernmost point is in sight – next stop, Antarctica – and the end is nigh. But for the moment, I want to be nowhere but here. **AB**

ORIENTATION

Start // Melaleuca
Finish // Cockle Creek
Distance // 86km (53 miles)
Duration // 6-8 days
Getting there // Par Avion (paravion.com.au) flies to Melaleuca from Hobart. Tasmanian Wilderness Experiences (twe.travel) run a Hobart-Cockle Creek shuttle bus.
When to go // Access and weather are best December-March.
Where to stay // Camp at one of the route's 10 sites.
Tours // Tasmanian Expeditions (tasmanianexpeditions.com. au) and Trek Tasmania (trektasmania.com.au) operate South Coast Track walks covering flights to Melaleuca, Hobart-Cockle Creek return transport, camping gear and all food.
More info // parks.tas.gov.au/explore-our-parks/southwest-national-park/south-coast-track

Opposite, from top: head-spinning cliffs on the Tasman Peninsula; Castle Rock, Flinders Island

MORE LIKE THIS
TASMANIAN COASTAL HIKES

CRESCENT BAY, TASMAN PENINSULA

Ask any Tasmanian walker (or child) to name their favourite sand dunes on the island and the likely answer will be Crescent Bay. The trail to this lovely dune-lined beach begins beside Remarkable Cave in Port Arthur and passes the salty exhalations of Maingon Blowhole before crossing below Mt Brown to the bay. Tall, smooth sand dunes rise off the beach – they're a favourite spot for sandboarding – and there's an excellent view across the water to Tasman Island and Cape Pillar, the site of Australia's highest sea cliffs and the focal point of the popular Three Capes Track. If you want a lofty perspective on things, it's a short haul to the summit of 174m-high (571ft) Mt Brown – the track junction is in the low saddle just before you reach the beach.

Start/Finish // Remarkable Cave car park
Distance // 7.5km (4.6 miles)
Duration // 3-4hr
More info // parks.tas.gov.au/ explore-our-parks/tasman-national-park/crescent-bay

CASTLE ROCK, FLINDERS ISLAND

Flinders Island is an exceptional hiking destination – three of Tasmania's 60 Great Short Walks are on the island, including this coastal ramble to Castle Rock. The walk sets out from near Wybalenna – the haunting site of a former Aboriginal mission – and picks its way north along the Marshall Bay coast. It's less a track than a natural guiding line of sand and headlands, with the destination – the massive granite boulder known as Castle Rock, which towers directly out of the sands – visible from the outset. Smothered in orange lichen, Castle Rock dwarfs everything around it. It's a humbling spot to stop and ponder the world. The return route is simply back along the beach, or you can keep striding out north along the beach as far as you want to go.

Start/Finish // Allports Beach
Distance // 6.6km (4 miles)
Duration // 2-3hr
More info // parks.tas.gov.au/things-to-do/60-great-short-walks/castle-rock

CAPE QUEEN ELIZABETH, BRUNY ISLAND

If you've only ever seen one Instagram image of Bruny Island, it's likely to be Mars Bluff, where an arched rock rises out of the beach like a rainbow set in stone. This sea arch is found midway along the walk to Cape Queen Elizabeth, immediately north of Bruny's narrow isthmus. After rounding a large lagoon, the trail presents two options. If it's low tide, head to the beach and pick along the coast, squeezing through breaks in the cliffs to emerge by the rock arch. If the tide is higher, follow the trail up and over the bluff, returning to the coast through sand dunes – it's a short stroll back along the coast to the rock arch from here. The trail then continues along Miles Beach, ascending past muttonbird rookeries to fine views from Cape Queen Elizabeth.

Start/Finish // Beside Bruny Island airstrip
Distance // 12km (7.5 miles)
Duration // 3-4hr
More info // brunyisland.org.au

THE OVERLAND TRACK

Arguably Australia's top multi-day walk, the Overland Track is a 65km (40.4 mile), five-day odyssey through Tasmania's World Heritage-listed alpine highlands.

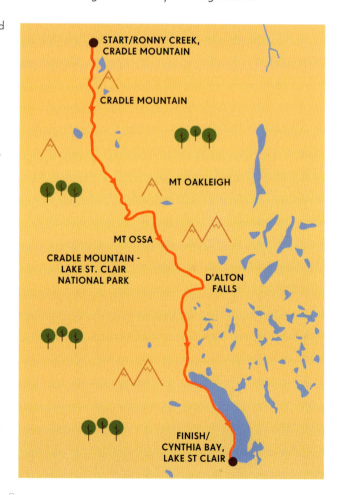

Back in the mists of time, my oldest friend and I graduated from high school in Hobart, Tasmania. With a long summer ahead, my friend said, 'Let's hike the Overland Track!' In those days, conditions on this long haul through Cradle Mountain-Lake St Clair National Park were rudimentary at best: knee-deep bogs; barely a boardwalk; meagre huts; unspeakable toilets. It was hard work, but we did it. We summited Cradle Mountain, then Mt Ossa, Tasmania's highest peak (1617m/5305ft). We were marooned in Windermere Hut by a biblical thunderstorm (we ate noodles and played chess). We poo-pooed the easy final-day Lake St Clair ferry ride and tramped around the lakeshore instead, stumbling into Cynthia Bay six mud-caked days after we'd begun. My friend's mum picked us up, we ate hamburgers – and it was epic!

And so, when I retraced the Overland Track 20-something years later with my wife and two good friends, would it still stack up? Or would 'epic' have matured into something more moderate and manageable, just as I had?

Indeed, some things had changed. The new visitor centre at Cradle Mountain for starters. This high-end architectural masterpiece is designed to cope with the park's 284,000 annual visitors – including 9000 Overland Track walkers. 9000! Where were they two decades ago? Perplexed, we jumped on a shuttlebus (another crowd-management initiative) to the Ronny Creek trailhead and tramped into the wilds.

Barely metres into our 11km (6.8-mile) first day, a wombat and her fluffy baby bumbled across the track. The sun broke through the clouds. Perplexity turned to joy. Spirits soared. Most of this swagger evaporated when, beyond deep-blue Crater Lake (not

actually a crater, but a glacial hollow), we were confronted by the sheer rock face of Marions Lookout (1250m/4101ft). It's a cruel blow to the confidence that the Overland's steepest climb hits you on day one. I didn't recall feeling such profound uneasiness the first time around, but once we'd scrambled onto the plateau (declining further terror on the Cradle Mountain ascent) it was an easy amble towards spectacular Waterfall Valley Hut.

Things that have changed the Overland Track #2: the huts. The sexy new 34-bed hut at Waterfall Valley is a stunner, with a huge gas heater, bunkrooms with doors, highly sociable areas and jaunty window designs. All the main huts and campsites along the Overland are first-come/first-served: the possibility of sleeping in this one might hasten your stride.

In the morning, we woke to see what had been concealed by clouds the evening before: the magnificent crest of Barn Bluff, jagging 1559m (5115ft) into the sky in clear sunshine. We hiked towards it, mesmerised. The well-made trail, interspersed with long sections of duckboard, tracked past gorgeous alpine tarns, windswept heath, and a couple of tiger snakes warming themselves in the morning sun.

> *"This is wild, ethereal country, where time is immaterial, humans are small, and for a few meditative days you can forget about everything except footsteps and mountains"*

Things that have changed the Overland Track #3: the mud. So well maintained is the track these days, that its infamous loose-your-boot bogs, ever-widened and deepened by walkers, have largely disappeared. We covered the 8km (5 miles) to Lake Windermere Hut on day two with clean gaiters (and no thunder this time).

Things that have changed the Overland Track #4: camping platforms. At Windermere, we were most pleased to discover that we could pitch our tents between pandanis and snow gums on nifty raised timber camping platforms, hovering safely above any moisture or snake-based inconveniences – and with awesome lake views. Who needs a hut? It was New Year's Eve: we lightened our packs by dispensing with some whisky and toasting life's excellence.

In the morning, the 17km (10.6-mile) stomp to Pelion Hut seemed a difficult proposition. Sore blisters, sore knees, sore heads – but the Overland soothed us with breezy buttongrass plains, arbors of deciduous beech (one of the species which helped prove the theory of continental drift), dense stands of ancient rainforest and sunshine. When we got to Pelion, everyone who'd cheerily left Windermere hangover-free at dawn was reclining in the best bunks and on the best platforms, sipping tea and looking smug. Note to self...

HIKING MT OSSA

Standing on a remote mountaintop and howling at eternity is hard to beat. Tasmania's highest peak, Mt Ossa, grants this opportunity. It's a difficult 5km (3.1-mile), four-hour return ascent from Pelion Gap on the Overland Track (day four). Alpine meadows turn to steep rocky shelves and fractured boulder fields as you ascend, with snowdrifts lingering into summer (check the weather beforehand: that snow could have blown-in yesterday). And the views? To eternity and beyond.

Clockwise, from top left: Tasmanian echidna; view from Mt Ossa; on the trail at Cradle Mountain; standing stones mark the start of the trail. Previous page: duckboard section on the Overland Track

And so, hut-to-hut, the days unravelled: 9km (5.6-mile) Pelion to Kia Ora; 10km (6.2-mile) Kia Ora to Windy Ridge; 9km (5.6-mile) Windy Ridge to Narcissus. At times we hiked single-file and quietly; at other times we hiked alongside one another, talking. We passed waterfalls, creeks, cushion plants, historic huts, steep climbs, steeper descents, summits (the view from atop snowy Mt Ossa was a knock out), and eventually, some serious mud.

When we arrived at Narcissus Jetty on Lake St Clair (at 200m/656ft, Australia's deepest), our pre-booked ferry was waiting – no hardcore 15km (9.3-mile) lakeshore trudge required this time around. Having enjoyed clear skies for five days, a vast roiling stormfront brewed up behind us, pursuing us across the lake. Fat bullets of rain pelted the Cynthia Bay jetty as we scrambled ashore laughing, bee-lining for the bar.

Every young person should test themselves in the wilderness at least once, right? I know, I know, I'm sentimental and I've probably watched *Into The Wild* more times than is necessary. But the Overland Track was, is, and always will be, the benchmark for Australian alpine multi-day hikes – a true challenge. In this self-propelled realm, the existential discomfort of carrying everything you need to survive on your back is very real – and looming above it all, the mountains! Cradle, Barn Bluff, Ossa, Oakleigh, Geryon, the Acropolis, Pelion East and West – this is wild, ethereal country, where time is immaterial, humans are small, and for a few meditative days you can forget about everything except footsteps and mountains. And it's astonishingly beautiful. **CR**

ORIENTATION

Start // Ronny Creek, Cradle Mountain
Finish // Cynthia Bay, Lake St Clair
Distance // 65km (40.4 miles) one-way
Duration // 6 days
Getting there // The northern trailhead at Cradle Mountain is a 2hr drive (102km/63.3 miles) from Launceston, or 1hr 15min(82km/50.9 miles) from Devonport (where the *Spirit of Tasmania* ferry from Melbourne docks). Alternatively, park at the southern trailhead (Cynthia Bay), then shuttlebus (twe.travel) back to the starting line at Cradle Mountain.
When to go // Summer (December-February) offers the most stable (though far from guaranteed) weather.
What to wear // Layers: be ready for all weathers.
Tours // Guided-hike operators offer cooked meals, lightweight packs and (sometimes) beds: see Tasmanian Expeditions (tasmanianexpeditions.com.au) and Tasmanian Walking Company (taswalkingco.com.au).
More info // Walker numbers are limited October to May: book ahead at parks.tas.gov.au/explore-our-parks/cradle-mountain/overland-track.

Opposite, from top: Tarn Shelf Track,
Mt Field National Park; Franklin
River swing bridge, Frenchmans Cap

MORE LIKE THIS
TASMANIAN PEAKS

TARN SHELF TRACK

In the shadows of misty Mt Field West (1434m/4705ft), the Tarn Shelf circuit track elevates you into Tasmania's World Heritage-listed alpine heights, looping past stands of snow gums, spiky pandanis and ice-cold tarns. Just 1.5 hours (88km/54.7 miles) from Hobart within Mt Field National Park – also home to one of Tasmania's only ski clubs – it's an accessible but demanding day-walk. You can tackle the five- or six-hour loop year-round: in spring, melting snow trickles beneath the boardwalks; in autumn, deciduous beech trees turn golden. From Lake Dobson, take the Urquhart Track to the ski fields and the start of the trail. The hike circles past shimmering Twisted Tarn, Twilight Tarn and Lake Webster – a glorious alpine day out. National Park fees apply.
Start/Finish // Lake Dobson car park
Distance // 12km (7.5 miles)
Duration // 5-6hr
More info // parks.tas.gov.au/explore-our-parks/mount-field-national-park/tarn-shelf

FRENCHMANS CAP

Within Franklin-Gordon Wild Rivers National Park, the bald, hat-like peak of Frenchmans Cap is shorter than towering Mt Ossa on the Overland Track: at 1446m (4744ft), it's a modest #30 on the list of 'Tasmania's Highest Mountains'. But Frenchmans Cap remains one of the island's most challenging summits, and a 'must-do' for experienced peak-baggers. This three- to five-day adventure crosses the legendary Franklin River, then skirts the notorious 'Sodden Loddons' buttongrass plain (into mud, much?). Your final ascent tracks past Lake Vera, exposed Barrons Pass and the high stone terraces above Lake Tahune. Unpredictable weather is a given: there are two huts to bunker down in (book ahead). National Park fees apply.
Start/Finish // Frenchmans Cap car park, Lyell Hwy
Distance // 54km return (33.6 miles)
Duration // 3-5 days
More info // parks.tas.gov.au/explore-our-parks/franklin-gordon-wild-rivers-national-park/frenchmans-cap

HARTZ PEAK HIKE

Looking for a bite-sized snapshot of alpine Tasmania? Hartz Peak beckons, an accessible 1254m (4114ft) summit within Tasmania's World Heritage-listed Southwest Wilderness, delivering astounding 360-degree views across the windswept wilds. To get started, head 1.5 hours south of Hobart through timber-town Geeveston to the Arve Rd, then onwards to the Hartz Rd trailhead, within Hartz Mountains National Park. Begin your ascent across alpine moorland, passing mirror-flat Lake Esperance and Ladies Tarn. From the top, clear-day views range across much of the Southwest, from Federation Peak to Precipitous Bluff to gem-like Hartz Lake, a classic 'cirque' lake gouged-out by a million years of ice. It's a rugged walk, but most people can reach the peak and return within five hours. Bring all-season gear: snowstorms blow through on a whim, even in summer, and there are no rangers to bail you out. National Park fees apply.
Start/Finish // Hartz Rd
Distance // 7.4km return (4.6 miles)
Duration // 5hr
More info // parks.tas.gov.au/explore-our-parks/hartz-mountains-national-park/hartz-peak

FEDERATION PEAK

Incredible scenery, terrible weather and huge exposure will challenge even the most experienced on this epic wilderness trek to South West Tasmania's Holy Grail.

As I inch out on the ledge, Lake Geeves, some 600m (1968ft) below, appears between my legs. I concentrate on the rock, counting myself lucky that the notoriously hideous South West weather hasn't eventuated.

A narrow finger of rock thrusts skywards into the Roaring Forties from the already jagged Eastern Arthur Range in the South West Tasmanian wilderness. Federation Peak's (1224m/4016ft) remoteness and difficulty has long been a beacon for hardcore bushwalkers. Several access routes exist though the most satisfying is the full Eastern Arthurs traverse, and despite track upgrades it still requires many gruelling days and a dollop of luck to reach this point.

I'd left Scotts Peak Dam five days earlier, heading south under a leaden sky on the Port Davey Track, across buttongrass plains and boot-sucking bog. Wildflowers, melaleuca and tea-tree lined the route as it wound towards distant hills. Junction Creek, with its tannin-stained water and sheltered tent sites proved an ideal camp after my late start.

Above the creek I'd turned left onto Mckays Track and headed east across the boggy Arthur Plains where the track regularly dipped into dense scrub and muddy forest at numerous creek crossings. Later, ascending a dry ridge south from Cracroft Plains, I caught my first view of the Eastern Arthurs, with the tooth-like Federation on the mist-tinged horizon. Eventually I reached Pass Creek nestled at the bottom of Luckmans Lead, where the preamble concluded and the traverse would now begin in earnest.

The clear ridge climbed steeply onto the craggy range, revealing tantalising views of the neighbouring Western Arthurs. Higher up, the bog returned and prickly scoparia and pandani

tested my gaiters, until I finally reached the ribbed cliffs of The Boiler Plates.

The going became easier, a stretch of boardwalk protecting the fragile montane ecosystem before the route weaved around rocky outcrops above a frigid-looking Lake Leo sunken under the bulk of East Portal. Under the massive quartzite Dial, the sun-kissed tent platforms of Stuart Saddle had proven too enticing and I'd lazed the afternoon away with countless cups of tea, Federation framed by a hole in the dense scrub.

That night it rained, continuing through the next morning. I'd waited it out then headed onto Goon Moor via more steep

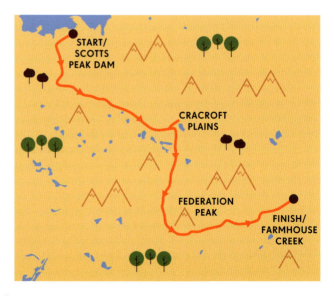

shenanigans and razor-thin traverses. After almost getting blown off the saddle, I retreated to Goon's sheltered tent-platforms where a nearby rock outcrop provided sensational sunset views towards Bathurst Harbour.

Next morning the weather was kinder and I quickly crossed Goon Moor to The Gables then threaded the maze of the Four Peaks to gain access to the near-mythical Thwaites Plateau and its excellent views of Federation. Rounding Devils Thumb, a rock window displayed the sobering sheerness of Feddo's northern face.

Dumping my pack at a track junction, I'd decided to seize the fine weather window. Turning left onto the Southern Traverse, the track had descended steeply, requiring some scrambling before I reached the large cairn signifying the start of the Direct Ascent route. Many groups come unstuck here, as a head for heights is needed for the meandering scramble up the rock face. The climbing is neither difficult nor technical though the exposure is formidable. Small cairns show the way, but if you're uncomfortable, turn back, especially if you've had to pack haul on the way in.

The route climbs steeply, rounds a corner, then ascends a crack that leads to the ledge. I ignore Lake Geeves, confident in the knowledge that at the end of this airy ledge there's a magical cleft providing a natural staircase up to safer, flatter ground. Yep, I've been here before. Crossing the small hanging plateau I make the final ascent to the surprisingly flat summit, being careful to mark my exit point. Summit logbook signed, I take in the incredible 360-degree view showcasing the jewels of the South West: remote bays, needle-sharp peaks, forgotten tarns and untrampled ridges,

> *"Despite track upgrades it still requires many gruelling days and a dollop of luck to reach this point"*

TASMANIAN MOUNTAIN PLANTS

Tasmania's remote alpine regions are home to unique endemic flora like pandani, or 'Dr. Seuss plants', with sharp serrated leaves, slender trunks and a leaning, fronded canopy. Also notable are bushwalker's nemesis scoparia, a prickly, stunted mountain dweller that tears into gaiters and skin alike; and cushion plants, fragile, slow growing clumps near bogs that bind together to form a dense mat. Fagus (or tanglefoot) is a small, beautiful, straggly deciduous beech whose leaves turn brilliant red in autumn.

Clockwise, from above: Hanging Lake; up high on Thwaites Plateau; sunrise-watching at Goon Moor; fagus (tanglefoot) in its autumnal glory. Previous page: the near-vertical Chockstone Gully climb

while keeping a weather-eye to the prevailing west. It's not a place to linger and I'm mindful of needing to retrace my steps.

Regaining my pack at the track junction, I follow the right branch down to beautiful Hanging Lake and set up camp on the cosy wooden platforms, later climbing nearby rocks for an unforgettable sunset.

The next day I recommence the precipitous Southern Traverse, now more challenging with my pack. There's plenty of breezy steepness until the near-vertical ascent of Chockstone Gully opens onto a beautiful high grassy shelf. The scariest part of the traverse is over. Bechervaise Plateau, a handy campsite if arriving from Farmhouse Creek, is visible far below as the narrow route winds steeply down rock slabs. Boardwalk crosses the plateau until the tree line and the start of infamous Moss Ridge. Steep, muddy, overgrown and badly eroded, there's not much to enjoy on the descent, other than the fact I'm not climbing it. By the time I reach the sanity of Cherry Creek and take a welcome break, it's mid-afternoon.

I push on, keen to make the most of the long southern summer days as the track emerges onto buttongrass crossing the Cracroft Valley, following the river east. Just on dusk I reach the South Cracroft, well tired but knowing I've knocked off most of the walk. I cook a quick meal and sleep like the dead. The following day is an easy few hours in lush riparian forest before reaching the road-end at Farmhouse Creek and hopefully my pickup. **SW**

ORIENTATION

Start // Scotts Peak Dam
Finish // Farmhouse Creek
Distance // 61km (38 miles)
Duration // 7-9 days (weather depending)
Getting there // Arrange drop-off/pickup with Tasmanian Wilderness Experiences (twe.travel).
What to pack // Be totally self-sufficient and come prepared for the worst possible weather. You'll need: a good tent; warm sleeping bag; fuel stove; warm clothes; thermals; sturdy boots; gaiters. Maps and wet weather gear are mandatory. Bring extra food and fuel for bad weather days.
Things to know // Check with Parks Tasmania for track updates. A Parks Pass is mandatory. Check the long range weather forecast.
More info // parks.tas.gov.au; bushwalk.com

*Opposite, from top: Boulder Lake
in the Dragons Teeth, New Zealand;
South West Tasmania's Lake Oberon,
Western Arthurs*

MORE LIKE THIS
HIGH WILDERNESS TRAVERSES

WESTERN ARTHURS, SOUTHWEST NP, TASMANIA

This classic South West traverse makes the perfect warm-up for the more committing Eastern Arthurs with which it can be combined into one magnificent skyline epic. From Scotts Peak Dam turn right after Junction Creek onto the Port Davey Track, heading for Alpha Moraine. Ascend into a world of mist-shrouded peaks, icy tarns, narrow footpads and vertiginous gullies where your vertical movement eclipses any forward motion. The scenery (if visible) is sensational and the weather usually horrendous as you tick off campsites at Cygnet Lake, Lake Oberon, High Moor and Haven Lake. Exit the range by Kappa Moraine, rejoining Mckays Track at Seven Mile Creek for the return to Scotts Peak Dam, or continue towards the Eastern Arthurs via Centaurus Ridge and the wild Crags of Andromeda.
Start/Finish // Scotts Peak Dam
Distance // 52km (32 miles)
Duration // 6-7 days
More info // bushwalk.com

THE DRAGONS TEETH (HIGH ROUTE), KAHURANGI NP, NEW ZEALAND

Rarely travelled, this legendary wilderness route above the treeline of Kahurangi's Douglas Range will stretch your backcountry skills. The first two days are long slogs up forested ridges from the Aorere Valley to Boulder Lake. Continue on to Adelaide Tarn, from where the route, marked with sporadic cairns and old tree markers, staggers drunkenly onto the range – off-track navigational skills are essential as losing the route is common. Camp by small tarns high on the side of Anatoki Peak. Follow the cairns along the range on a long day leading to exquisite Lonely Lake Hut. With the back of the 'Teeth' broken, it's pleasant walking down to Fenella Hut in the Cobb Valley with the car park only a few hours away.
Start // Aorere River
Finish // Cobb Reservoir
Distance // 60km (37 miles)
Duration // 6-9 days
More info // john.chapman.name/nz-dragon.html

PRECIPITOUS BLUFF, SOUTHERN RANGES, TASMANIA

You'll need good navigational skills and fitness for long days of fabulous ridge walking across Tasmania's wild Southern Ranges on this peak-baggers delight. Start at Mystery Creek near Ida Bay and ascend Moonlight Ridge to Pigsty Ponds. Follow the ridge to Ooze Lake, bagging flat-topped La Perouse on the way. Pindars Peak offers brilliant 360-degree views of the southern coast and distant mountains but then the unmaintained route descends into head-high scrub en route to scary-looking Precipitous Bluff. An exposed scramble leads to Plateau Camp before a long, trying descent through dense forest eventually reaches the shores of New River Lagoon far below. Wade the lagoon to reach the South Coast Track where several days of easy walking on a well-marked trail will seem like luxury.
Start // South Lune Rd, Ida Bay
Finish // Cockle Creek
Distance // 75km (47 miles)
Duration // 7-10 days
More info // bushwalk.com

TAYTITIKITHEEKER/ DRYS BLUFF

This walk takes in the plains south and west of Launceston, which are dominated by taytitikitheeker (Drys Bluff), a cliff-topped mountain that has fascinated people for thousands of years.

The boisterous little Liffey (tellerpanger) River flows around the northern flank of taytit (let's call it that for short), draining part of Tasmania's high Central Plateau and tumbling over the beautiful Liffey Falls along the way. Getting up taytit is one of the single biggest day-walks in Australia. Deans Track rises 1000m/3281ft from the river to the top (Melbourne's Eureka Tower is just short of 300m/984ft and Paris' Eiffel Tower is 324m/1063ft); it's definitely a climb for seasoned walkers only.

Nevertheless, everyone who makes it to the Liffey Valley is rewarded with the scenery: the river flowing between the small farms and forested foothills at the base of the mountain.

Taytit is an hour, on sealed roads, from Launceston and less than three hours from Hobart. The mountain is the northeast highpoint of the Tasmanian Wilderness World Heritage Area, one of the finest temperate wildernesses left on earth. Except for two remote highway crossings, you can walk from the top of taytit to the island's far extremity, South West Cape, without encountering a town, farm or building. In a straight line, that would be 230km (143 miles) through some of Australia's most rugged terrain, though, as far as I know, no one has ever tried it. Ditto for the 80km (49.8-mile) walk west to Cradle Mountain.

Taytit's top is plateau and the actual summit (1340m/4396ft) is a half hour's rough walk south. However, I recommend that once on top you clamber east to the highest point of the dolerite cliffs (it's called Proposal Peak, but that's another story), which is the best perch overlooking the Liffey Valley, its views extending to Bass Strait and Ben Lomond. There are rare King Billy pines in the cleft east of this lookout.

In 1973 I was a young doctor in Launceston when I drove out to see the Liffey Falls and, on the way back, spotted a white cottage on the south side of the river, directly below taytit's topping cliffs. A month later I was the owner of the cottage plus the forest and riverside paddocks which went with it. From there, my life has never looked back, though I have missed a cherished goal: to climb taytit as many times as my age. Here I am at 77 and have been to the top only 70 times and the years are gathering faster than my ascents.

Perhaps most memorable was the walk up in the night, aided only by a full moon, and a return to the cottage just as the dawn

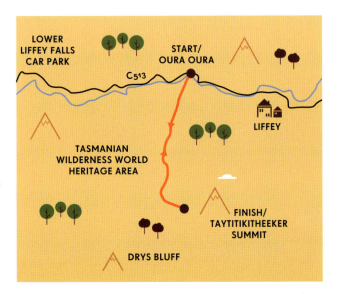

chorus of birds was in full throttle. On another night, a brilliant Aurora Australis made it look like there were searchlights up there on the clifftops.

For an easy-going, sight-seeing rambler it's four hours up and three back and, given an hour or two sitting up there looking across northern Tasmania to Bass Strait, that's a full day's expedition. Mind you, back in the 1980s my friend and fellow Franklin River campaigner Geoff Law, who was superbly fit and had spidery legs, accomplished the return trip in an hour and 45 minutes. I still can't believe it, but his entry is in the mountaintop logbook to prove it.

Taytit is much more than physical exercise rewarded with a view. It is like a floristic layer cake, from the remnant riverside sassafras trees, through grand old eucalypts to the stunted alpine rainforest and waratahs in the final climbing gully. On the summit plateau during the summer, there is a delightful scoparia show – pink, white, yellow and orange clusters of flowers on spiky stems.

Watch for the Wedge-tailed eagles catching the thermals near the cliffs and the peregrine falcons that nest in a sandstone overhang halfway up.

Long before my time, a Tasmanian tiger was snared on the mountainside and there are still Tasmanian devils, spotted-tailed quolls, Bennett's wallabies, bettongs and echidnas among the wildlife that a quiet walker may see along the trail.

> *"Most memorable was the walk up in the night, aided only by a full moon, and a return to the cottage just as the dawn chorus of birds was in full throttle"*

On my first ascent, early in 1974, I found ropes near the top to help where the boulders are otherwise no easy scramble. These had been placed by the cottage's previous owner, John Dean, who, with Stephanie and their three young children, made a number of trips up taytit in the early 1970s. Hence the name 'Deans Track'.

The intrepid Polish count Paweł Strzelecki climbed taytit from the east after his famous ascent and naming of Australia's highest mountain, Kosciuszko, in 1840. A decade earlier, palawa Aboriginal people led a colonial party down off the mountains east of taytit and back up again to the west: they went around the heavily forested Liffey Valley. Their ancestors had occupied the sandstone overhangs halfway up taytit during the last ice age, when the forests were largely replaced by grasslands. The palawa were perplexed by the British urge to climb the mountains rather than sensibly walk around them.

If going to the top is not your cup of tea either, I recommend the 500m (1640ft) walk from the little bridge over the Liffey, past

BOB BROWN

Environmentalist, doctor and former politician, Bob Brown was the guest writer of this trail. He led the Australian Greens from the party's foundation in 1992 until April 2012. In 1978, Bob was appointed director of the Tasmania Wilderness Society. He is perhaps best known for leading the campaign against the damming of Tasmania's Franklin River, which culminated in a 1983 High Court decision that permitted federal governments to block damaging projects. It also inspired Australians to protect their wilderness.

Clockwise, from above: admiring the taytitikitheeker/Drys Bluff views; the trail to Liffey Falls; 'taytit' from below. Previous page, from top: Liffey Falls; scoparia in flower

the cottage, to the fern-clad creek on Deans Track. That's the easiest part of the track, before it becomes relentlessly steeper. Or else, from the car park, just enjoy the path along the river to the footbridge and up to the cottage. There are storyboards courtesy of Bush Heritage Australia (partner Paul Thomas and I donated the property, Oura Oura, to BHA in 2011), new public toilets behind the hay-shed and good picnic spots under the old walnut tree or by the river.

The name taytitikitheeker comes from the local Panninher band of the palawa and is a sentence that includes the term for 'high in the clouds'. Nearby Quamby Bluff (an easier walk, also rewarded with panoramic views) was called lartitikitheeker. The names told a story of two related mountains. Such great features were highly significant for thousands of years for the Panninher. (The imposed name, Drys Bluff, comes from the landed gentry's Mr Dry who could see the mountain but never went near it.)

Taytit often wears a mantle of snow. In winter the waterfall in the climbing gully has icicles metres long and the tarns on top are sometimes solid ice. Summiteers can be assured that all year round there is water halfway up as well as on top.

These days it's the pleasure of hearing the adventures of younger walkers that keeps my relationship with this great mountain alive. That, and the occasional dip in the river below. There's no better finish to a walk up taytit than to share a swim in the tellerpanger with the resident platypuses. **BB**

ORIENTATION

Start // Oura Oura
Finish // taytitikitheeker/Drys Bluff summit
Distance // 8km (4.9 miles) return (1000m/3280.4ft ascent)
Getting there // Oura Oura is 1hr drive from Launceston and a 2.5hr drive from Hobart. Take the C513 from the nearby town of Bracknell through the village of Liffey. There is a white cottage at the walk's starting point.
When to go // March-April and September-November are ideal for the hike.
What to pack // Sturdy boots; thick socks; wet weather gear; insect repellent; sunscreen; first-aid kit.
What to eat // Bring your own water, lunch and snacks as there are no amenities at the trail. There are places to eat and pick up provisions in Bracknell (13km/8 miles from Oura Oura).
More info // greatwesterntiers.net.au/walk/full-day-walks/ drys-bluff

Opposite from top: Lake Angelus,
Nelson Lakes National Park; the Two
Thumbs Range from Lake Tekapo

MORE LIKE THIS
WALKS WITH MOUNTAIN VIEWS

LAKE ANGELUS TRACK, SOUTH ISLAND, NEW ZEALAND

Despite its relatively short length, this hike boasts all that's good about Nelson Lakes National Park. In fine weather, the walk along Robert Ridge is spectacular – seldom do hikes afford such an extended period across open tops. The Robert Ridge views will blow your socks off, and they will again as you descend into extraordinary Lake Angelus basin. You'll also enjoy the stopover at the Angelus Hut, a particularly fine specimen, built in 2010. At 1650m (5413ft) above sea level, perched on the edge of the lake among golden tussock, it has insulated walls, a capacious common area and a large sunny deck. Many walkers choose to spend two nights at Angelus Hut, which means you have a whole day to explore the beguiling environment of the 'glowing white lake', as the Māori call it.

Start // Mt Robert car park
Finish // Coldwater Hut
Distance // 21.5km (13.4 miles)

TWO THUMBS RANGE, SOUTH ISLAND, NEW ZEALAND

Within the extraordinary expanse of Te Kahui Kaupeka Conservation Park, near Lake Tekapo in the middle of the South Island, the wide glaciated valleys and ice-numbed peaks of the Two Thumbs Range offer off-piste adventures aplenty for ski mountaineers during winter. For those happier hiking than sliding, however, guided snowshoeing escapades offer an excellent day-walk alternative. Rex Simpson Hut, a 1300m (4265ft) eyrie on the edge of the range, makes a magical base for such missions. From here, slip on snowshoes and stomp along sinuous Snake Ridge to beautiful Beuzenberg Peak (2070m/6791ft) absorbing the surrounding Southern Alps, a twinkling tiara of peaks topped by not-too-distant Aoraki/Mt Cook. Outside of winter (June-August), green-season hiking here is sensational too.

Start/Finish // Coal River Bridge car park, off Lilybank Rd (near Lake Tekapo)
Distance // 11km (7 miles) one-way to Beuzenberg Peak, via Rex Simpson Hut
More info // alpinerecreation.com

YURREBILLA TRAIL, SOUTH AUSTRALIA

Completed in 2003, the Yurrebilla Trail provides Adelaide with an asset possessed by few other major cities: a multi-day walking track on its doorstep. As you wander through Waite Conservation Reserve on day two – after overnighting at Brownhill Creek Caravan Park – you'll be just 10km (6 miles) from the city, yet you're more likely to see kangaroos than people. The trail traces the line of the Mt Lofty Ranges, linking seven national and conservation parks, including a final day's winding tramp through what is arguably Adelaide's greatest natural asset, Morialta Conservation Park. You can walk the Yurrebilla Trail's entirety or use the suburban bus network to sample it in sections.

Start // Belair railway station
Finish // Ambers Gully
Distance // 54km (33.5 miles)

THE THREE FALLS CIRCUIT

Fall in love with Tasmania's oldest nature reserve on a manageable hike the whole family can enjoy, with some of the state's best waterfalls photo opps along the way.

t's a chilly, overcast spring morning when I pick up a hire car in Hobart, bound for Tasmania's favourite waterfall. With a multi-day hike on the Tasman Peninsula booked to begin the following day, I had only planned to stroll the first 1.4km (0.87 miles) of the Three Falls Circuit, a sealed wheelchair accessible trail that leads from the Mt Field National Park visitor centre to the base of Russell Falls. But when I get this far, I'm glad I decided to wear proper hiking boots, and packed some emergency snacks.

As I marvel at the splendid waterfall cascading gently over several siltstone benches framed by emerald tree ferns, it's easy to understand why Russell Falls – which is around 50m (164ft) tall – was chosen to grace Tasmania's first scenic stamp series in 1899. It's a perfect example of the raw natural beauty of this island state. Fortunately, Tasmania's colonisers recognised this early on, designating an area surrounding the falls as the state's first nature reserve in 1885. In 1916, Mt Field was named Tasmania's first national park, along with Freycinet National Park on the east coast.

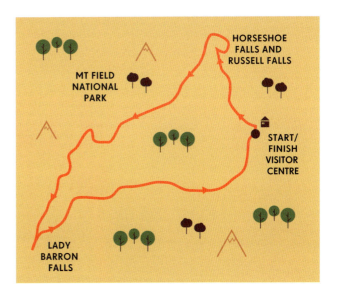

This corner of the 163 sq km (63 sq miles) park is so lush, I can't bring myself to leave. So instead of turning back to the visitor centre with most of the other tourists clustered at the base of the falls, I decide to complete the Three Falls Circuit by continuing on up the steep, slightly slippery trail adjacent to Russell Falls.

In just a few minutes I reach Horseshoe Falls. While smaller than Russell Falls, it's similarly beautiful, tumbling from a natural ampitheatre in two streams that join in a horseshoe-like shape as they flow into a shallow pool dotted with neon green moss-covered rocks. After snapping a few photos, I put my camera away and enjoy the opportunity to take in this surreal scene by myself for a few minutes before the next hiker comes along.

Forming part of the Tasmanian Wilderness World Heritage Area, which covers around a fifth of the state, Mt Field is one of the island's most diverse national parks, shaped by glaciers during the last ice age and offering constantly changing landscapes as you climb to higher altitudes – it's even possible to ski on the snow-dusted slopes of Mt Mawson during the winter months. I get a taste of this changing landscape as I climb out of the cool, verdant valley carved out by the two waterfalls, where moss-encrusted ferns soon become dwarfed by towering swamp gums, the tallest flowering plant on the planet.

This section of the well-marked and maintained trail links up with the Tall Trees Circuit (1km/0.6 miles), created to showcase these giants of the forest, which can grow taller than 100m (328ft) and live for hundreds of years – it's mindboggling to think that the largest swamp gums here were already growing when Dutch explorer Abel Tasman first sighted Tasmania in 1642. There's a clinometer affixed to a viewing platform to help you calculate the height of the trees, if you're so inclined. But I don't need any help to feel small in this otherworldly place, thought to fall within the territory of the Big River people, a palawa (Tasmanian Aboriginal) nation (clan group) whose traditional lands stretch from the Great Western Tiers of Tasmania's Central Highlands to kunanyi/Mt Wellington, which rises up dramatically on the western fringe of Hobart. While there are no Aboriginal artefacts to be found on this particular trail, it's fascinating to learn that evidence of Aboriginal occupation in the national park dates back some 35,000 years.

After the tall trees section, the trail then crosses Lake Dobson Rd before entering a denser section of lush, wet forest. You can opt to call the hike quits at this point and take a short cut back to the visitor centre via Dobson Rd, but having made it this far, I wasn't going to miss out on an opportunity to see Lady Barron Falls, less than a kilometre further along the trail. Located on a separate

THE LAST TASSIE TIGER?

The thylacine captured in the Mt Field region tragically died at Hobart Zoo in 1936, but many refuse to believe the species is extinct, with dozens of sightings recorded over the years. Among the most prolific was a series of images captured by Thylacine Awareness Group of Australia president, Neil Waters. The 2021 'discovery' went viral, but a Tasmanian Museum thylacine expert concluded the animals were most likely Tasmanian pademelons.

Clockwise from far left: greenery-swathed Russell Falls; sulphur-crested cockatoos; eye-popping Mt Field views. Previous page, from left: Horseshoe Falls; looking up in Mt Field National Park

tributary to the other waterfalls on the circuit, its flow tends to be more dependent on rainfall. Luckily for me, Lady Barron Falls is in fine form today, spilling down Lady Barron Creek over a series of small ledges.

The final stretch of the Three Falls Circuit winds back up the gully, tracing the path of Lady Barron Creek before taking me up a steep flight of wooden stairs. After nearly two hours of hiking, I'm not thrilled to discover that the most strenuous section of the trail lies at the end; it's for this reason that some visitors prefer to complete the hike in reverse. But the superb scenery makes up for the short uphill slog.

Mt Field National Park is also known for its abundance of wildlife, with the likes of wallabies, wombats and echidnas commonly seen on trail hikes along with the odd platypus, if you're lucky. The last known wild thylacine (a dog-sized carnivorous mammal better known as the Tasmanian tiger) was captured in the region in 1933, and today the park continues to provide a haven for species that are extinct or endangered on the mainland including the eastern quoll, a native cat-like mammal known for its distinctive coat covered in white spots. Cockatoos squawk in the treetops during my hike, and I make a mental note to visit the park again at night sometime, when glow worms can be seen near Russell Falls. Could this place be any more magical?. **SR**

ORIENTATION

Start/Finish // Mt Field National Park Visitor Centre
Distance // 6km (3.7 miles)
Duration // 2-2.5hr
Getting there // Mt Field National Park is 64km (39.8 miles) or about an hour's drive northwest of central Hobart. Buses run as far as New Norfolk, about half way.
When to go // The trail is navigable year-round; during the winter months there may be a dusting of snow.
What to pack // Bring layers as it can get quite chilly, particularly at Russell Falls.
Where to stay // Tasmania Parks and Wildlife Service run a scenic campsite near the Visitor Centre, by the Tyenna River.
Where to eat // There's hearty cafe fare at the Visitor Centre.
More info // parks.tas.gov.au/explore-our-parks/mount-field-national-park/three-falls-circuit

Opposite: Rainbow Falls, on Springbrook National Park's Warrie Circuit

MORE LIKE THIS
MAGICAL WATERFALL HIKES

MEANDER FALLS, GREAT WESTERN TIERS CONSERVATION AREA, TASMANIA

Another memorable Tassie waterfall hike can be enjoyed an hour's drive southwest of Launceston, in the heart of the dramatic Great Western Tiers Conservation Area. Climbing uphill through beautiful wet forest, the out-and-back trail leads to the base of one of the state's most spectacular waterfalls, which plunges 130m (427ft) over two main tiers. With some steep, rocky and muddy sections to navigate, the trail can be a little challenging for some. Snow and ice can be experienced in winter months, although this can be a plus if you're treated to the spectacle of large icicles forming on the falls. Sturdy shoes and warm layers are a must year-round.

Start/Finish // Meander Falls Rd car park
Distance // 10km (6.2 miles) return
Duration // 6hr
More info // parks.tas.gov.au/things-to-do/60-great-short-walks/meander-falls

WARRIE CIRCUIT, SPRINGBROOK NATIONAL PARK, QUEENSLAND

Warrie is a local Aboriginal language word for 'rushing water', which offers the first clue that there's plenty of waterfall action to be enjoyed on this pretty rainforest trail on the lush Springbrook plateau, an easy day-trip from the Gold Coast. The moderately challenging, well-marked circuit follows the base of The Canyon cliffs to Goomoolahra Falls (look out for the giant spear lilies that grow here) before descending into the mossy green depths of the forest. Crossing several creeks and gullies along the way, the track reaches the 'Meeting of the Waters', where all watercourses draining The Canyon meet, before climbing up the western side of the gorge. Hiking boots are a must, particularly after rain when the trail can get quite muddy.

Start/Finish // Canyon Lookout or Tallanbana Trailhead
Distance // 14km (8.9 miles)
Duration // 5-6hr
More info // parks.des.qld.gov.au/parks/springbrook/journeys#warrie

WHEEL OF FIRE TRACK, EUNGELLA NATIONAL PARK, QUEENSLAND

Named for the distinctive orange flowers that bloom in the surrounding rainforest trees, the Wheel of Fire Track is an ultra-scenic hike in the magnificent Finch Hatton Gorge section of Eungella National Park, west of Mackay, with several spectacular waterfall swimming spots. Around a kilometre along the well-maintained rainforest trail, which is shaded by the canopy for most of the way, the path forks. Here you can cheat and take a short stroll to the beautiful Araluen Cascades, but it's worth pushing on uphill between huge granite boulders to enjoy the superb views of Finch Hatton Creek cascading down through the gorge as you go. At the top there's another waterfall pool, which tends to be several degrees cooler than the swimming area at the Araluen Cascades – perfect for an invigorating dip on a hot summer's day before heading back down the way you came.

Start/Finish // Finch Hatton Gorge car park
Distance // 4.2km (2.6 miles) return
Duration // 1.5-2hr
More info // parks.des.qld.gov.au/parks/eungella/journeys#wheel_of_fire_track

FREYCINET PENINSULA CIRCUIT

Encompassing pristine white-sand beaches, craggy mountain summits and striking coastal topography, this relatively challenging multi-day hike offers all the highlights of Tasmania's Freycinet Peninsula.

'Whose idea was it to do this hike in July, anyway?' I grumble to myself as I fiddle with the poles of my tiny one-person tent, attach one of the guy lines to a nearby she-oak, and rummage in my rucksack for an extra sweater. The sun is dipping behind the craggy silhouette of Mt Mayson, and while we were perfectly warm while hiking that last stretch along the firm sand of Hazards Beach and then climbing over the odd tree in the coastal woodlands to reach Cooks Beach Campsite, the temperature has now dropped into the single digits.

'Where's Jacqui?' I call out to Greg. Heading in the direction of his muffled voice, I find him inside the 19th-century stone hut once used by European whalers and sealers, setting up the camping stove on the picnic table and laying out pouches of our camping food. 'We needn't have bothered carrying all that water,' he tells me. 'I found plenty in the rainwater tanks outside. Jacqui's gone for a swim,' he continues. 'Tell her that dinner will be ready soon; we've got an early start tomorrow.'

'Don't remind me,' I groan. As a trio, we made the unanimous decision to get up at 1am the following day in order to make it up to the summit of Mt Freycinet (620m/2034ft) – the highest mountain in Freycinet National Park – in time for sunrise. I wander out onto the white sand of Cooks Beach, visible from our clearing, and find Jacqui emerging from the sea, wringing out her long blond hair. 'The water's great!' she exclaims. 'You should've joined me!'

I gingerly dip a toe in the surf. It may look like the Caribbean Sea but it's absolutely freezing. Little wonder, given how there

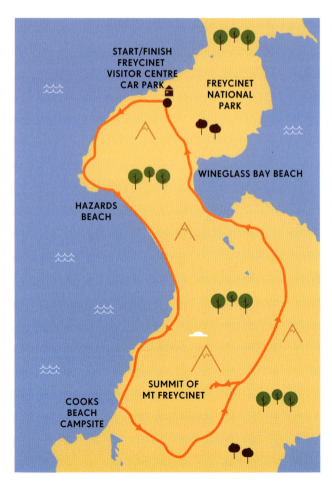

is literally no landmass between Tasmania and Antarctica. But ever since Jacqui has been converted by an Estonian friend – a year-round swimmer – she's been leaping into frigid waters at every opportunity and extolling the benefits of 'ice therapy' for the cardiovascular system.

We can hear Greg shouting even before we get back to the campsite. He's pointing at a dark shape that's flapping away, a ziplock bag in its beak. 'Bloody raven! It's nicked my trail mix!'

'Did you leave your bag unzipped?'

'Of course not.'

'A zipper won't stop them,' Jacqui chimes in, and points at a furry shape streaking across the clearing. 'Wombats and possums might covet our food, but ravens are clever little devils; they've figured out how to unzip a rucksack. Evolution in action.' While Greg and I are well aware of her passion for all creatures furred and feathered, I wish she'd feel less admiration for thieving wildlife.

In the gathering twilight, Greg presents us with steaming bowls of Soya Surprise.

> *"With every sip of my coffee, I feel myself coming back to life as the stars slowly fade, the sky on the horizon begins to lighten and the sea acquires a pearlescent sheen"*

'This certainly tasted better after a hard day's hike,' I comment. 'I wouldn't necessarily make this stuff at home.'

'Are you kidding?' Greg says. 'We're eating like royalty. Though perhaps not quite as well as the Oyster Bay people.' He's referring to the original hunter-gatherer inhabitants of the peninsula, who'd lived here prior to the arrival of Europeans. During our coastal trek earlier on in the day, we tramped along the west side of the peninsula, skirting Mt Mayson and then descended to the firm, wide expanse of Hazards Beach, where we spotted an ancient shellfish midden – the detritus of centuries-old feasts.

We turn in shortly after our own 'feast', and are awoken by the shrill ringing of our alarms, seemingly moments after we'd gone to bed. We pack up in silence and groggily set off back along Cooks Beach. The arc of sand that's blindingly white during the day glints dimly in the light of the full moon. Climbing above the beach, we turn inland, into the dense she-oak forest, crisscrossed with tiny streams and dotted with boggy patches. I stumble over more than one fallen tree and moss-covered rock, and am grateful for the branches laid across the muddiest sections and for the reflectors on trees that tell us that we're on the right track.

TASMANIAN BETTONGS

Besides a wealth of wildlife that inhabits Freycinet National Park – short-beaked echidnas, ringtail possums, sugar gliders, Bennett's wallabies, Tasmanian pademelons, wombats – the Freycinet Peninsula Circuit is one of the few trails in eastern Tasmania where you might be lucky enough to spot Tasmanian bettongs – guinea-pig-sized, adorable marsupials that have become extinct on the Australian mainland. Keep an eye out for southern right whales, dolphins and humpback whales out at sea.

Clockwise from above: black-faced cormorants, Wineglass Bay; a fur seal surveys the Freycinet coastline; the splendid fairywren, an aptly named Freycinet NP resident.
Previous page: Wineglass Bay

Finally up on the saddle between Mt Freycinet and Mt Graham, we find ourselves in a clearing in the blue gum woodland around us, right near the side trail branching off towards the summit of Mt Freycinet.

'Why didn't we camp here?' I ask. 'We could've had all that extra sleep.'

'What, and miss out on my refreshing afternoon swim?' Jacqui counters. 'Besides, this is wild camping only. Did you bring a spade to dig a loo pit in the bush?' I concede that I did not.

The gradient gets considerably steeper, as we clamber over exposed tree roots and use our hands to help ourselves up between giant boulders. The only sounds are that of distant gurgling streams in the forest and our own harsh panting from exertion. Then, finally, we're at the summit, and the forest falls away beneath us. I'm glad that we didn't leave our packs at the saddle, as we wrap up in our sleeping bags and get out our flasks.

With every sip of my coffee, I feel myself coming back to life as the stars slowly fade, the sky on the horizon begins to lighten and the sea acquires a pearlescent sheen, in contrast to the hulking, dark shapes of the Hazards mountain range beyond. As I look out towards Mt Graham and the buttongrass moorland that we are yet to traverse on our way to the white-sand curve of Wineglass Bay – one of Australia's best beaches – and breathe in the scent of banksias and wild peppermint, I realise that I've answered my earlier question. We are the only people in the park and have all this bounty to ourselves. This is why people hike the Freycinet Peninsula Circuit in winter. **AK**

ORIENTATION

Start/Finish // Freycinet Visitor Centre
Distance // 46km (28.6 miles)
Duration // 3 days
Getting there // Freycinet NP is a 2.5-hr drive from Hobart via the Tasman Hwy (A3) and Coles Bay Rd (C302). The nearest town is Coles Bay, 28km (17 miles) from the park entrance. Regular Calows Coaches (calowscoaches.com.au) run daily from Coles Bay to Freycinet Visitor Centre.
When to go // September–November means warm weather without the December–February summer crowds.
What to pack // Insect repellent and all food supplies; there's potable water at Visitor Centre, Honeymoon Bay and Wineglass Bay Walking Tracks car park.
Where to stay // Campsites with composting toilets at Wineglass Bay, Hazards Beach and Cooks Beach.
Tours // Wineglass Bay Tours (wineglassbay.tours) for small-group day-trip Freycinet walks from Hobart; Auswalk (auswalk.com.au) for all-inclusive, pack-free, four-day, self-guided treks, with nightly transfers to luxurious Freycinet Lodge.
More info // parks.tas.gov.au

Opposite, from top: waratah in flower along the Legges Tor trail, Ben Lomond National Park; heady views from the Organ Pipes Circuit trail

MORE LIKE THIS
TASTY TASSIE TRAMPS

TARKINE COAST EXPEDITION

Tramp along the ocean-battered wild coast of the Tarkine – some of the world's oldest temperate rainforest, fringed with extensive coastal heathland – in remotest western Tasmania. Until the completion of the 100km-long (62-mile) Trans Tarkine Track that encompasses part of this coastal trek, guided hikes across Tasmania's frontierland, camping all the way, are the only option for you to access this trackless, pristine wilderness of buttongrass plains, myrtle, pine and leatherwood forests and sand dunes. Starting in the one-horse settlement of Temma, your small guide-led group makes its way to Kenneth Bay along a well-defined coastal trail that ends near Sandy Cape Beach. You then traverse the sandy expanse, fording the shallow sections of Thornton and Wild Wave rivers, and reaching the Sandy Cape lighthouse. A succession of river crossings and traverses along surf-bashed sandy expanses follow until you reach your goal of Pieman River, passing vast shellfish middens left by the Tarkiner people – the Tarkine's original inhabitants.

Start// Temma
Finish // Pieman River
Distance // 58km (36 miles)
Duration // 6 days
More info // tarkinetrails.com.au/tour/tarkine-coast-walking-tours

LEGGES TOR, BEN LOMOND NATIONAL PARK

Bushwalk through meadows of alpine flowers to the craggy alpine plateau of Legges Tor (1572m/5157ft), the second-highest point in Tasmania and one of the highlights of Ben Lomond National Park outside ski season. Kick off this straightforward yet moderately demanding linear hike at the Carr Villa car park. Follow the well-defined trail through eucalyptus forest until it gives way to a vast dolerite scree field. Just west of Misery Bluff that looms above you, you pass through a gap in the stony ramparts as the trail, marked by snow poles, climbs up to the enormous, mostly barren rocky plateau that you're likely to have pretty much to yourself. A gentle uphill meander along the fancifully named Plains of Heaven gets you to the summit. Legges Tor is quite typical of Tasmanian peaks: there are few 'sharp', alpine-style summits here; more often, you tend to find fairly flat dolomite plateaus with a discreet cairn marking the highest point.

Start/Finish // Carr Villa
Distance // 10km (6.2 miles) return
Duration // 4-6hr
More info // parks.tas.gov.au/explore-our-parks/ben-lomond-national-park/carr-villa-to-alpine-village-track

ORGAN PIPES CIRCUIT

Historic stone huts, spectacular rock formations and glorious views of Hobart greet you during this wonderful hike through fragrant bushland on kunanyi/Mt Wellington (1271m/4170ft).Drive up Pinnacle Rd to the car park, then follow a well-defined dirt trail as it ascends steadily through thickets of myrtle, clambering over lichen-covered rocks. Some 30 minutes into the climb, detour to the sandstone outcrop of Sphinx Rock for all-encompassing views of the city and Bruny Island beyond. Crossing a couple of shallow creeks, you pass the Rock Cabin, used by early mountaineers, before continuing along the rugged trail to Junction Cabin and uphill to the caves at the base of Crocodile Rock. The trail merges with a vast scree slope, and you zigzag steeply up, following orange trail markers, to a boulder field. Grab some lunch at the Chalet, where the trail meets the paved road, then proceed to the showstopping Organ Pipes – a russet-coloured dolerite wall that soars above the Tassie capital. Return to the car park via the Sawmill Track and Zig Zag Track.

Start/Finish // Springs car park
Distance // 9.5km (5.9 miles) return
Duration // 4-5hr
More info //parks.tas.gov.au/things-to-do/60-great-short-walks/organ-pipes

MT ANNE

Bring loads of experience, stamina, a stomach for heights and a love for the rough stuff on this classic circuit around the South West's tallest peak.

The southern summer sun beats down relentlessly as I lug my heavy pack up countless steps on the long, dry climb up Mt Eliza. The ascent of Mt Anne's (1423m/4669ft) outlier peak from Condominium Creek is mostly unshaded, thirsty work but the impressive views of flooded Lake Pedder more than compensate for any discomfort.

High Camp, perched inside a scrub band just below Mt Eliza's boulder field, is reached soon enough and I fill my water bottle from the hut's convenient tank. Turning to the southwest, solid, dark clouds stain the distant skyline, but I push on anyway.

The route steepens, becoming a scramble as I pick my way carefully through the massive boulder field, following cairns until I reach Mt Eliza's flattish 1289m (4229ft) summit, where truly magnificent views of Lake Pedder and its islands, the Frankland Range and Western Arthurs are revealed. My route across the exposed Eliza Plateau to the dolerite-capped summit of Mt Anne is clearly visible as I start down a well-used path. Hiding my pack behind a bush, I detour briefly downhill, past several small tarns to the edge of colossal cliffs above Lake Judd. The view along the lake is sublime, with Mt Sarah Jane opposite, Schnells Ridge and Smiths Tarn hogging the foreground, and fabled Federation Peak and Precipitous Bluff riding the far horizon, raw wilderness in all directions.

Recovering my pack, I resume the crossing, Mt Anne looming menacingly larger, until another boulder maze requires a downhill sidle across the western flank of Eve Peak to a rocky saddle and track junction. Again dumping my pack, I follow cairns across the saddle, Lots Wife appearing in the east, a slender thumb of rock rising defiantly above a broken ridge, and uninviting Lake

Timk in 'Tasmanian tiger' country (wild, untracked country with dense scrub) below. Bypassing a small knoll, the cairns lead right and uphill, across more boulders and scree to the base of the sheer summit cliffs. A jagged, airy, at times quite exposed, route ascends right, up and around obstacles, traversing ledges and climbing up small, sharp arêtes, marked by cairns or scrawled arrows, until I reach the blocky, jumbled summit. The 360-degree views complement the day's scenic smorgasbord but the edgy summit isn't a place to tarry, especially with those clouds building, so I carefully retrace my steps, grab my pack then descend the junction's other track a short distance to Shelf Camp. A

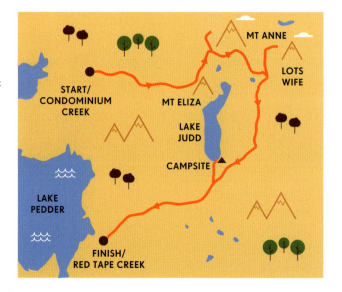

spectacular campsite in good weather, the small, exposed rock slab perched under Eve's northern cliffs has a front-row view of Mt Anne's sensational, sheer eastern face.

The storm hits that night, driving rain, wind and ice, sleep not an option as I reinforce my tent with walking poles. Dawn comes darkly, the blizzard not yet spent but my tent holds, though others camped nearby are not so lucky; snapped poles a reminder of how quickly things can change in the South West. I spend the day in my sleeping bag, making endless cups of tea, snow blanketing everything.

The following morning is clear, the snow already reduced to puddles (it was January) as I pack up and head towards The Notch – the infamous, nasty, gap-toothed saddle, crux of the circuit. I follow a path from camp, descending on ledges before gaining the ridge and dropping steeply into the narrow saddle, huge exposure on either side. Nothing for it but to scramble up the short, near vertical, opposite cliff, thankful my pack is now lighter, otherwise it may have required hauling. I reach the uppermost ledge, satisfied with my progress, then launch into the gnarly traverse under the cliffs of Mt Lot. The route stays high with views of Lake Judd far below and it's slow going winding narrowly in, out, over and around enormous lumps of rock. Another scary sheer climb finally broaches the ridgetop where easier walking prevails to the summit, an excellent lunch spot with Lots Wife, Lake Picone and the Lonely Tarns as backdrop.

Cairns point the way down Lightning Ridge, a long, slow, knee-wrecking, knife-edged boulderfest to the treeline, with stunning views of Lake Judd and the Lonely Tarns off either side. I have mixed feelings leaving the rocky heights, relief tinged with melancholy that the hardest, most extreme and probably most satisfying part of this adventure is already over. Entering the trees, the route turns down a spur separating Lake Picone from Judds Charm before opening onto buttongrass, eventually spilling into the campsite by the latter tarn's outlet creek. I flop exhausted onto a tent platform, laying out my tent and fly to dry and shake my head at Lots Wife, a half-day side trip that I've no longer time or energy for.

Following a deep sleep, it's a brooding morning and feels like rain again as I trudge across the stark buttongrass of the Lonely Tarns, passing small pools and climbing scrubby ridges until finally the narrow path clambers onto a rocky spur of Mt Sarah Jane. Lake Judd is visible momentarily before the track constricts to a steep, boggy scrub tunnel, diving sharply off the plateau. A long, tiring descent follows until I finally cross the Anne River, heading for the invigorating waters of Lake Judd where I rinse off my lethargy and make a final camp.

Rain haunts my last morning as I pack hurriedly, bolting down the track, dreaming of a hot shower. Boardwalks and bridges, rain and rivers blur until I stumble onto the road by Red Tape Creek. Swapping my pack for the old bike I'd stashed nearby, I cycle towards Condo' and my car of dry clothes. **SW**

LAKE PEDDER

Immortalised in the photographs of Olegas Truchanas, the exquisite pink quartzite beach of the original Lake Pedder now lies under 12m (39ft) of water. Pedder's islands are actually mountains, isolated when rivers here were dammed for hydropower in 1972. Protests against the dam ultimately failed, but they kickstarted the Australian environmental movement and raised awareness for later – and successful – anti-dam protests.

Clockwise, from far left:
Mt Anne in the morning sun;
Lots Wife; looking down on
Lake Judd from Mt Anne.
Previous page: Lake Pedder

ORIENTATION

Start // Condominium Creek
Finish // Red Tape Creek
Distance // 24km (15 miles)
Duration // 4-5 days
Getting there // Condominium Creek is 135km (84 miles) from Hobart. Take the B61 past Maydena, then unsealed Scotts Peak Rd for 20km (12 miles). Avoid the 9km (5.6-mile) road-slog from Red Tape Creek by car-shuffling or bringing a bike. Tasmanian Wilderness Experiences (twe.travel) can arrange transport.
What to pack // Be fully self-sufficient and prepared for bad weather: a good tent; warm sleeping bag and clothes; fuel stove; sturdy boots; gaiters; maps; sunscreen; wet weather gear. Bring extra food and fuel, and a short rope for pack-hauling.
Things to know // Sections of this walk are quite exposed.
More info // parks.tas.gov.au (registration and passes); bushwalk.com

*Opposite: Arthurs Pass panorama
from the Avalanche Peak track*

MORE LIKE THIS
ABOVE THE TREELINE

TARARUA NORTHERN CROSSING, NORTH ISLAND, NEW ZEALAND

Close to Wellington, this traditional west-to-east traverse of the Tararua Range is an exceptional multi-day challenge, best attempted between spring and autumn. From Poads Rd, enter dense forest beside the Ohau River. In low water levels follow the Ohau upstream to South Ohau Hut, then ascend the steep Yeates Track to Dora Ridge and Te Matawai Hut. Otherwise, Gable End offers a drier alternative. Climb steeply above Te Matawai onto tussock, past Pukematawai (1432m/4698ft) and over Arete (1505m/4938ft) where a two-bed biv sits sheltered below. Follow the exposed tops south, descending the dicey Waiohine Pinnacles to broad Tarn Ridge before climbing over Girdlestone (1546m/5072ft) and windy Mitre (1571m/5154ft). Descend a long way on rubble, then forest, eventually reaching Mitre Flats Hut where the Barra Track leads to the road.

Start // Poads Rd, Levin
Finish // The Pines, Masterton
Distance // 37km (23 miles)
Duration // 3-5 days
More info // doc.govt.nz; ttc.org.nz

WALLS OF JERUSALEM TRAVERSE, TASMANIA

Good navigation skills are essential for this seldom-travelled cross-country route (best between spring and autumn) across the exposed Central Plateau to the majestic Walls of Jerusalem and beyond. Climb Higgs Track, rising through dense forest to the austere open plateau and Lake Nameless. After Forty Lakes Peak, cairns head for Zion Gate, visible on the horizon though it will take all day just to reach Lake Tyre. Explore the Wall's jewels including Mt Jerusalem, Solomons Throne and Pool of Bethesda before leaving through Jaffa Vale. Pick up a good track by Lake Ball and pass lakes Adelaide and Meston to Junction Lake, where you can exit to the Overland Track via the Never Never or the untracked Traveller Range. Walk out to the Lake St Clair ferry.

Start // Higgs Track, Western Creek
Finish // Cynthia Bay, Lake St Clair
Distance // 65-80km (40-50 miles)
Duration // 7-9 days
More info // parks.tas.gov.au; bushwalk.com

AVALANCHE PEAK & CROW VALLEY, ARTHURS PASS, SOUTH ISLAND, NEW ZEALAND

Jam-pack your weekend with excitement on this breathtaking alpine crossing – best months are November to May. Take the Avalanche Peak Track (1833m/6014ft) from the village to the treeline, where yellow markers continue up tussock then scree to the shingle summit. Enjoy the superb view and note the connecting ridge to Mt Rolleston and the Crow Glacier. Head south from the summit, then traverse scree below the peak's western face to the north-pointing ridge, which is then sidled on its eastern side until rising. Drop off west into Crow Valley at the markers, descending scree to the valley floor, then cross the river and head downstream to Crow Hut. The next day stroll leisurely through forest and river flats to the braided Waimakariri River, which must be crossed several times to reach Klondyke Corner.

Start // Arthurs Pass
Finish // Klondyke Corner, Canterbury
Distance // 17km (11 miles)
Duration // 2 days
More info // doc.govt.nz

KUNANYI/ MT WELLINGTON

Enjoy an energetic, fun-filled day meandering under the Organ Pipes, scrambling through the Lost World and traversing the weather-challenged summit of Hobart's spectacular 'backyard mountain'.

Mountain dew hangs heavy on the undergrowth and light mist obscures the way ahead as I ascend the chill stone steps from The Springs upper car park. Cloaked in silence, the only sounds permeating the dense forest are the whir of a cyclist whizzing suicidally down the wet summit road, somewhere below, and my own laboured breathing. Starting at 680m (2231ft), I'm already halfway up the peak.

Hobart's omnipresent Mt Wellington (kunanyi in Tasmanian Aboriginal palawa kani) rises majestically from sea level for over a vertical kilometre, piercing the clouds and acting as the city's informal barometer. When late afternoon clouds spill over kunanyi, it's time to go home.

The short, steep climb leads to a wide fire trail, which I cross to pick up the Pinnacle Track. I'm alone, too early for the Sunday joggers, too early even for birdlife. The track continues to climb steadily through damp eucalypt regrowth, legacy of decades of previous fires. Altitude is gained quickly and soon I reach another track junction, noting the abrupt, switch-backed left fork, which I'll descend later. Thankfully, my outward route lies along the more inviting, less vertiginous Organ Pipes Track.

Kunanyi is unique for its range of distinct microclimates and vegetation zones – from wet and dry sclerophyll eucalypt forests to alpine heaths and pockets of temperate rainforest – all within easy reach of a capital city. Official and unofficial trails crisscross the mountain and it's a favourite haunt of hikers, mountain bikers, cyclists, birdwatchers, climbers, runners, locals and tourists alike.

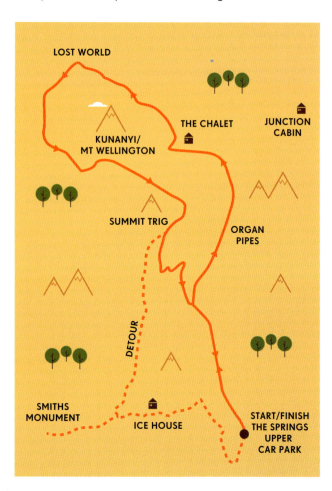

The track now sidles pleasantly along the mountain's eastern flank. Wildflowers like pink mountain berry and Tasmanian waratah replace the regrowth, and honeyeaters and currawongs emerge. From somewhere up high echoes the familiar cry of a yellow-tailed black cockatoo. Small boulder fields create rough bush windows, revealing glimpses of Hobart, the River Derwent and Storm Bay far below, while strange clinks and distant voices filter down from above.

Climbing a little, the path opens onto the massive dolerite buttresses of the Organ Pipes and the source of the mystery voices – rock climbers, laden down with clanking hardware, are inching their way up scary-looking vertical nastiness. I watch enthralled until my neck stiffens, then continue on, wondering how the climbers keep their hands warm. Gnarly snow gums and totemesque pandani now appear and the sun's rays break through the dark horizon's cloud, casting a warming spell over flora and fauna alike. Something darts across the track in front of me, a small, dark blur gone crashing down the side of the hill. Wallaby? Pademelon? Thylacine?

> *"Cloaked in silence, the only sounds permeating the forest are the whir of a cyclist whizzing suicidally down the wet summit road and my own laboured breathing"*

The traverse continues with increasingly better views of the city and Derwent a kilometre below, before eventually a quick, sharp descent ends at a stone picnic shelter, generously known as The Chalet, 1000m (3280ft) above sea level. Back on Pinnacle Rd, I head downhill for 100m (328ft), looking for the Hunter Track on the left. This new path loses altitude quickly as do my spirits, as I know I will need to regain the lost height at some point. A track junction forces out my map: keep left, now on the Old Hobartians Track, still heading downhill. At this rate I'll end up in someone's South Hobart backyard. Finally, after a creek crossing and just before the Old Hobartians wanders off to the right, there's the turnoff left for the Lost World.

This is where the real fun begins. The route is a lively uphill scramble over, under and around massive (and some not-so-massive) boulders. My lost elevation is quickly regained and an element of route-finding focuses my attention as I weave in and out of varied lichen-encrusted obstacles, finally topping out into a large, blocky amphitheatre. The dolerite cliffs of this cut-and-pasted mini Organ Pipes enclose a hemispherical pound of massive fallen rubble piled haphazardly, partly overgrown with vegetation. I pick my way carefully to the ridge on the right of the sheer walls and find a sheltered lunch spot with a view.

👢 LONELY EPITAPH

Weather permitting, consider a scenic detour to John Smith's monument, where the Derwentwater surgeon died in 1858. From the Zig Zag turnoff, follow the South Wellington Track across the dolerite-strewn plateau for 2km (1.2 miles), gradually descending to another junction. Turn right along a rough path for 500m (1640ft) to where the rarely visited monument lies in snowgum forest. Return to The Springs via the historic Ice House and Milles tracks (2.2km/1.4 miles) or backtrack to the Zig Zag.

Clockwise from above: the soaring Organ Pipes; kunanyi/Mt Wellington lookout; trailside colour from the pink mountain berry.
Previous page: sweeping Hobart views from kunanyi/Mt Wellington

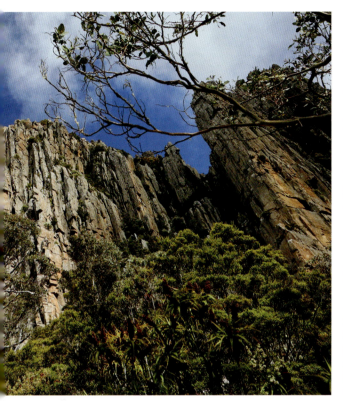

Leading up the ridge, the scant track becomes more defined with height until I clear the cliffs then amble through snowgums to a clearing beside Pinnacle Rd called Big Bend. The map has this point at 1100m (3609ft) – I'd descended 290m (951ft) from the road then climbed 390m (1279ft) back up to it!

Once out of the trees, the wind is howling and I immediately layer-up. Clouds are streaming in from the south as I head up the asphalt, rising above the treeline, the ever more-expansive views east over the city and coastline making up for the wind chill. By the time I reach the platforms of the summit's lookout at The Pinnacle it's starting to sleet and I reel off a couple of quick snaps before heading for my exit route. The top of kunanyi/Mt Wellington is actually a large exposed, rocky plateau of fragile alpine heath and bog, wide open to the frigid southwesterlies blowing in from the Roaring Forties and Antarctica.

Visibility is low as I scurry past the massive Broadcast Australia TV transmitter looking like some giant wizard's wand embedded in the mountaintop. The temperature has plummeted and it feels like snow as I reach the Zig Zag Track, my down elevator. The rocky path drops off the eastern face and with an immediate loss of altitude I leave the near-blizzard above and behind, the route descending steeply, weaving through the dolerite cliff-line, until finally reaching the junction I'd noted hours earlier. Already some 300m (984ft) lower, I peel off a few layers for the final easy stroll back to The Springs. As they say, it's all downhill from here. **SW**

ORIENTATION

Start/Finish // The Springs upper car park, Pinnacle Rd, Hobart
Distance // 11km (7 miles)
Duration // 4hr
Getting there // The Springs is 13km (8 miles) from Hobart on Pinnacle Rd. Metro bus routes 448/449 run from City Interchange to Fern Tree then walk 1.6km (1 mile) uphill to The Springs via Fern Glade and Radforth tracks.
What to pack // Bring water for the day; snacks; good footwear; rain jacket; warm sweater; hat; sunscreen; Wellington Park Recreation Map (TASMAP)
Things to know // Weather on the summit is notoriously fickle with high winds and temperatures at least 10°C (50°F) lower than at sea level. A sunny day can change into a whiteout or blizzard instantly.
More info // wellingtonpark.org.au; parks.tas.gov.au; tastrails.com

Opposite, from top: Olivers Rd, snaking up Mt Roland; valley views from Gertrude Saddle

MORE LIKE THIS
WALKS WITH ALTITUDE

MT ROLAND, TASMANIA

Dominating the landscape of North West Tasmania, the daunting, rugged and often cloud-obscured mass of Mt Roland (1234m/4048ft) is easily conquered in one vigorous day; hike between spring and autumn for the best conditions. From the car park on O'Neills Rd, climb gently along an old 4WD track which progressively steepens. Cross a small creek, taking the left fork at a track junction to begin a long sidle along the skirts of neighbouring Mt Vandyke. The track narrows after bridging O'Neills Creek, climbing steeply to an obvious saddle at the valley's head. Turn left at the next junction for a leisurely stroll across a buttongrass plateau to the distant summit trig, where a final boulder scramble will reveal breathtaking 360-degree views. Or a total whiteout. Retrace your outward route or return via Mt Vandyke.

Start/Finish // O'Neills Rd, Gowrie Park
Distance // 15km (9 miles)
Duration // 4-6hr
More info // sheffieldtasmania.com.au

GERTRUDE SADDLE, FIORDLAND, NEW ZEALAND

A spectacular day walk (best from November to May) leads up the insanely beautiful (and avalanche-prone) Gertrude Valley from just below Homer Tunnel. The imposing sheer walls of the Darran Mountains tower above the marked trail as it crosses dry, rocky creeks and small vegetation bands before emerging onto open tussock. Follow cairns and markers up ledges by the valley headwall, crossing an icy creek and climbing slabs up to Black Lake which is as cold as it looks. Whio (blue duck) are sometimes found here. Chains lead up further slabs on the right to eventually reach the saddle (1410m/4626ft), revealing incredible views into the Gulliver Valley and surrounding snow-capped mountains. Rare tuke (rock wren) frequent nearby boulders and those with a head for heights will want to continue upwards towards Barrier Knob.

Start/Finish // Gertrude Valley car park, Milford Rd
Distance // 7km (4 miles)
Duration // 6-8hr
More info // doc.govt.nz

FEATHERTOP TO BOGONG TRAVERSE, VICTORIA

Not for the fainthearted, but perfect for hikers looking to head cloudwards, the Feathertop to Bogong Traverse is an incredible multi-day hike that crosses Victoria's Bogong High Plains and scales the summit of the state's highest peak, Mt Bogong, and second-highest, Mt Feathertop. Your legs will ache, your knees will shake and you'll work up a sweat as you tough it out over the five to six days of mountain climbs, river crossings, frigid temperatures and altogether punishing terrain. But it'll certainly be well worth it for the amazing views as you take in the magical high country scenery, where brumbies gallop and wildflowers bloom in spring. You'll also be rewarded for your efforts with some interesting history and the chance to stay in historic huts along the route.

Start // Diamantina Hut, Mt Hotham
Finish // Mountain Creek, Tawonga South
Distance // 77km (48 miles)
Duration // 5-6 days

LAKE RHONA

Ascend into the remote mountains of the Tasmanian Wilderness World Heritage Area to find an unexpected lake and alpine beach.

Great beaches are nothing out of the ordinary on Tasmania's coastline, but to find one high in the mountains of the South West Wilderness is extraordinary. But as we stand on the slopes of the Denison Range, deep inside Franklin-Gordon Wild Rivers National Park, a lake lies pooled below us. Its water is as dark as stout, and along one of its edges, a crisp white beach runs in an arc beneath 400-metre-high (1312ft) cliffs. It's like finding a little piece of Wineglass Bay punched into the mountains. We have arrived at Lake Rhona.

Every place has certain spots it likes to keep hidden from the outside world. In Tasmania, Lake Rhona has long been one of those veiled places. But sometimes secrets are too beautiful to stay hidden, and in recent years this alpine lake – so defiantly beautiful in the harshest of locations – has been outed to the world. For walkers, Lake Rhona has gone mainstream.

On a low range of hills pinched between the Florentine and Gordon rivers, we set out walking for the lake, descending for half an hour to the bank of the Gordon River. There is no bridge across this waterway, which is one of Tasmania's largest rivers, just a fallen tree that, as if by design, spans the river from bank to bank. To cross the river means to cross this log.

If water levels are high, the river flows over the log, closing off access to Lake Rhona. This day, things are marginal. Water pours over the top of the tree, but reaches only to the top of our boots. It's passable, even if we can't see the tightrope of wood through the darkness of the tannin-stained water. We inch across the river, searching with our toes for the log beneath.

Through the bush that lines the river, we step out into a classically Tasmanian scene. Mt Wright and the Denison Range rise ahead, with the land between the river and the mountains laid out flat, forming a buttongrass plain known as the Vale of Rasselas. The coming few hours will be spent stepping and splashing through this plain.

Buttongrass plains, which cover more than 10,000 sq km (3861 sq miles) of Tasmania, are notoriously muddy, with each tussock of grass like an island in a sloppy black pit. Stepping through this uniquely Tasmanian environment is like an act of faith. You might just sink to your ankles, or you might plunge in knee-deep or hip-deep. I once sank to my chest in the mud.

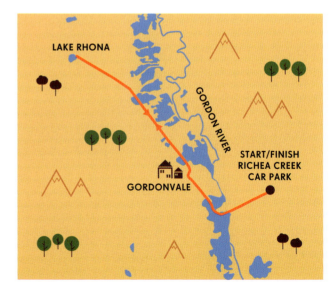

We have our lunch on a patch of grass in Gordonvale, the site of a long-abandoned home now littered with rusting farm implements, and continue north through the Vale of Rasselas, creeping closer to a prominent ridge that drapes down from Reeds Peak in the Denison Range.

Naturally we are mud-coated when we arrive at the base of this quartzite ridge, which leads like a steep escalator up to Lake Rhona. It's a 400-metre (1312ft) ascent from the plain to the shores of the lake, but in boots heavy with mud the climb feels like twice that.

Progress is slow as we ascend through an apocalyptic landscape. In 2019, a bushfire tore through this area, reaching to the very edge of Lake Rhona. To protect the lake from the approaching blaze, national park firefighters took the unusual step of installing a line of sprinklers around its shores, successfully preventing the fire from engulfing the lake, though the land around it remains scorched

In this barren mountain surround, it seems fanciful to think that a lake and a beach could be here somewhere, until we rise over a shoulder of the ridge and there it is – Lake Rhona, laid out below, as smooth as tin and as brown as amber. In minutes, we're down on its shores, stepping onto a beach where no beach rightly belongs. Tents colour its sands like confetti, and the cliffs tower overhead. If you've never been sure about whether you're a mountain or a beach person, this place is the perfect compromise.

We drop our packs and set up camp on the sand. By evening the lake has stilled to a mirror-like finish, and the morning will be even more spectacular, with the rising sun bathing the surrounding peaks in orange light. I slip out of my tent at dawn, lie back on the sand and watch a perfect day hatch.

This lakeside beach is an easy spot at which to while away a day, but there are also places that beckon beyond. The Denison Range is a stunning piece of natural architecture, a line of bare mountains inset with a string of lakes – Rhona is just the showpiece lake. Stand on the lake's beach and the range looks daunting, but the way to its top is surprisingly straightforward.

After backtracking a few hundred metres, an unmarked trail runs up a ridge beside the lake, ascending through magnificent alpine gardens as Lake Rhona shrinks below.

I scramble to the top of 1290m (4232ft) Reeds Peak and neighbouring Great Dome, amid flourishes of flowering scoparia, a ferociously scratchy alpine plant that conversely blooms like a florist shop every summer.

As I return from the peaks, I wander to the cliff edge, where Lake Rhona appears, far below where I stand. It's a scene as magnificent as any in Tasmania – this singular mountain lake with its beaming white smile of a beach.

I step back from the cliff edge and begin the descent off the range. An afternoon on the beach, mountain-style, beckons. **AB**

GORDONVALE

The rusted farming relics around Gordonvale hint at a former human presence in the wilderness. In the 1930s, an osmiridium miner from nearby Adamsfield, one Ernie Bond, bought a lonely piece of land here, built a home and planted fruit trees. Becoming known as the Prince of Rasselas, Bond was renowned among passing bushwalkers, serving them up wallaby stew, garden veggies and even homebrew beer.

Clockwise, from far left: the Lake Rhona surrounds in bloom; Tasmania's endemic eastern spinebill; forested hills in Franklin-Gordon Wild Rivers National Park. Previous page: Lake Rhona

ORIENTATION

Start/Finish // Richea Creek car park
Distance // 30km (18.6 miles)
Duration // 2-3 days
Getting there // The only access is by private vehicle. The trailhead is 40km (24.9 miles) from Maydena, along Florentine Rd to Terry Walsh Rd.
When to go // Summer is the best time for this hike.
Where to stay // Camping is the only option along the trail.
Things to know // Access to the lake is dependent on water levels in the Gordon River. After rain, the levels can rise and cover the log across the river, making it impassable. Carry extra supplies in case you have to wait a day or two for the river level to drop. A permit is required to walk to Lake Rhona; register through the Parks and Wildlife Service website.
More info // parks.tas.gov.au

*Opposite, from top: Dove Lake,
overlooked by Cradle Mountain;
looking down on Lake Judd
from Mt Lot*

MORE LIKE THIS
LAKESIDE HIKES

ROTOMAIREWHENUA/BLUE LAKE, SOUTH ISLAND, NEW ZEALAND

This tiny lake near the southern edge of Nelson Lakes National Park is claimed to have the world's clearest water, making it a compelling destination. The 80km (49.7-mile) Travers Sabine Circuit passes within reach of the lake, providing an accessible approach, though it can also be reached out and back over Travers Saddle. Once over the saddle, the circuit descends to West Sabine Hut, where the Rotomairewhenua/Blue Lake route diverges, climbing at times steeply to the lake. Blue Lake Hut is set back from its shores, presenting the chance to stay a night in this little mountain paradise, though because of the water's clarity, hikers are requested not to swim or wash in it. If one mountain lake isn't enough, continue south for another 1km (0.6 miles), climbing to larger Rotopōhueroa/Lake Constance, one of the biggest truly alpine lakes in New Zealand.
Start/Finish // Lake Rotoiti
Distance // 92km (57 miles)
Duration // 6-7 days

DOVE LAKE, TASMANIA

Famously the mirror in which Cradle Mountain is admired, this high lake also doubles as the framework for one of Tasmania's 60 Great Short Walks. The straightforward hike laps the lake, delivering the trademark view of its boatshed, built in 1940 by the national park's first ranger, with Cradle Mountain rising above. There are equally impressive views from Glacier Rock on the opposite side of the lake (and from myriad other spots along the track) and the trail passes through a magnificent stand of temperate rainforest, called the Ballroom Forest. Along the lake's southern shores, the track passes directly beneath the imposing summit cliffs of Cradle Mountain. In autumn, the slopes above the trail blaze red, yellow and gold as the native deciduous fagus turns in colour.
Start/Finish // Dove Lake car park, Cradle Mountain-Lake St Clair NP
Distance // 6km (3.7 miles)
Duration // 2hr
More info // parks.tas.gov.au/explore-our-parks/cradle-mountain/dove-lake

LAKE JUDD, TASMANIA

Ringed by some of Tasmania's most dramatic peaks – Mt Anne, Mt Eliza, Mt Lot – Lake Judd was long one of the state's great mud slogs, until a bushfire prompted a change. Closed for two years after a 2019 fire, the track to the lake was reborn as a boardwalk at the end of 2021. The walk follows the finish of the Mt Anne Circuit, in reverse, curling between Schnells Ridge and Mt Eliza. After 6km (3.7 miles), the lake walk branches away from the circuit, crossing a line of low ridges to arrive at the shores of the ice-carved lake. There's little room to explore once you're here – just a tiny patch of open shore boxed in by thick bush – but there's a Gothic grandeur to the cliffs and peaks that rise from the lake's opposite shore.
Start/Finish // Red Tape Creek
Distance // 16km (9.9 miles)
Duration // 4-6hr

THE THREE CAPES TRACK

Weave through dense forest above pounding surf and soaring dolerite cliffs to taste the wilderness of Australia's Tasman Peninsula on an epic but achievable four-day trek.

The welcoming committee on the Three Capes Track was quite something. Tree martins swooped in salute, gobbling kelp flies alongside towering cliffs. New Zealand fur seals bobbed in the coves, waving hind flippers above the waves. And a juvenile sea eagle stood to attention on a stump, peering along its fearsome bill as stern as any royal sentry.

It was a dramatic transition from the bustling precincts of Port Arthur Historic Site. At that atmospheric spot, a Victorian-era penal colony where the most hardened convicts once toiled, I joined hikers boarding a small boat for the 75-minute voyage to the trail's official start. Easing away from the looming penitentiary, we rounded the eerie Isle of the Dead – where more than 1200 transportees lie buried, thousands of kilometres from home – and admired those birds and seals before being dropped alongside the cobalt waters of Denmans Cove.

Here begins one of Tasmania's newest and most alluring treks. The Three Capes Track is an accessible introduction to wilderness

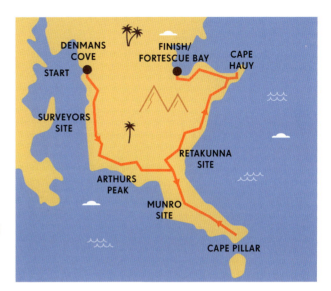

walking, somewhere between rufty-tufty camping trails and the gourmet lodge-to-lodge packages such as those on Maria Island and the Bay of Fires. Over 46km (29 miles) and four days, walkers encounter sea cliffs, aromatic eucalypt forest and leech-infested rainforest, windswept heath and two of the three titular capes (the other, Cape Raoul, is visible but not visited, though it will be included in a mooted route extension). Accommodation is in three custom-built cabin sites, with simple, comfy bunkrooms and well-equipped kitchen and toilet blocks – bring a sleeping bag and food, but none of the other paraphernalia required on a hardcore plunge into Tasmania's more-remote wildernesses.

The walking and landscapes, though, are epic enough from the off. From gorgeous Denmans Cove I traced the path through ghostly gum woods, Port Arthur Bay just discernible through the spooky mist. On that first day I tramped a gentle 4km (2.5 miles) to Surveyors, the first of the three cabin sites, each with different but appealing views. That night I munched dinner on the open deck, gazing across heath grazed by Bennett's wallabies, west to the craggy columns of Cape Raoul, and east to the hump of Arthurs Peak – the next day's main challenge.

"That night I munched dinner in the open, gazing across the craggy columns of Cape Raoul and the hump of Arthurs Peak"

The Three Capes Track could generously be described as undulating. There are no huge summits to conquer, but instead a rolling trail, sometimes on well-maintained dirt or rocky paths, elsewhere along springy wooden boardwalks. The second day's hike led initially through more eucalypt forest, where first a wallaby then a bronze skink darted off the path ahead, to a curious sculpture – the first of some 37 *Encounters on the Edge* studding the trail. Each was created especially for the track, and reflects an aspect of the area's human or natural heritage. *Punishment to Playground* is a bench filled with snorkel masks, fishing reels and golf clubs, a nod to the changing function of nearby Point Puer; today a golf course, until 1849 it was the site of a boys' prison. A little further on came a pile of large, smooth wooden cubes: *Who Was Here?*, a reminder to look for the square poos of snuffling wombats.

Through scrub and forest scented with eucalypt and tea tree I climbed, to be rewarded with a new vista to Cape Pillar, the next day's objective. Habitats morphed almost minute by minute: stands of stringybark and mossy forests; cliffs where signs indicated nesting sea eagles; more heath and dense woods where yellow-tailed black cockatoos squawked overhead.

That night at Munro cabin, I peered along the coast to cape number three, Hauy, and listened to surf pounding the cliffs and wind howling through the treetops. The weather was turning fast

THE LONELIEST LIGHTHOUSE

Atop Tasman Island off Cape Pillar perches Australia's loftiest lighthouse. Thanks to sheer dolerite cliffs reaching 300m (985ft), construction proved an epic challenge: it was nearly 40 years after the initial survey that the prefabricated cast-iron lighthouse first glowed in 1906. Life on this storm-lashed rock was harsh; Jessie Johnston, the first keeper's wife, dubbed it 'Siberia of the south', and communications to the Tasmanian mainland were initially limited to signal flags. The light was automated in 1976.

Clockwise, from top: Cape Raoul; a Bennett's wallaby peers from the bracken; the pillars of Cape Hauy. Previous page: approaching the destination at Fortescue Bay

– as it does in Tassie – but it failed to turn back overnight, and next morning I set out through thick cloud and stinging mizzle. The third day is an out-and-back from Munro along the narrow peninsula to Cape Pillar, traversing a path lined with trees bent by fierce winds that scream around the cape. Shapes and sounds were rendered soft and deceptive by the mist: a flash of brown might have been a wallaby hopping off the trail, the calls of birds blending with a chorus of frogs in a nearby billabong.

Nervously I clambered up the sheer-sided ridge named the Blade to reach the cape itself, where the cloud lifted just long enough to reveal a dizzying drop and Tasman Island beyond, the lighthouse-capped, desolate lump of rock dangling off the end of the peninsula. Then the clouds descended once more, and I tramped back to Munro to pick up my pack for the short leg to Retakunna cabin, that last night's stop.

Some creatures, of course, love rain – and on my last morning I had unwelcome encounters with several. In the wet forest below Retakunna battalions of leeches wiggled, latching on to my bare knees till rivulets of blood trickled down my shins. No matter. The mossy, ferny forest is magical enough to counter any parasite loathing. Soon I re-emerged on to the cliffs, soul salved by views back to Cape Pillar and across to Mt Fortescue, the final haul.

Cape Hauy itself, an hour's detour from the main track, was a suitably epic finale: pillars erupted from the spume, tempting rock climbers who tackle the aptly named Totem Pole. For me, though, the end was in sight – figuratively and literally: Fortescue Bay, where I baptised my weary feet in the warm waters lapping the sand. Three capes, two legs: one spectacular introduction to the Tasmanian wilderness. **PB**

ORIENTATION

Start // Denmans Cove
Finish // Fortescue Bay
Distance // 46km (29 miles)
Getting there // The four-day package starts and ends in Port Arthur, and includes a boat to the trailhead and return bus from Fortescue Bay. Port Arthur is 95km (59 miles; 90-minute drive) from Hobart, Tasmania's capital, a little less from Hobart Airport. Daily buses run by Tassielink (tassielink.com.au), Gray Line (grayline.com.au) and Pennicott Journeys (pennicottjourneys.com.au/three-capes-track) serve Port Arthur from Hobart.
Tours // The trek is available self-guided; book through the official website (threecapestrack.com.au). The fee includes transport to and from the trailhead and end point, as well as accommodation and a guide book. Guided tours are available with Tasmanian Walking Co (taswalkingco.com.au/three-capes-lodge-walk).
When to go // The warmer months (November to April) offer better, though far from guaranteed, weather.

Opposite: walk to Figure 8 Pools on the Royal National Park's Coast Track

MORE LIKE THIS
COASTAL MULTI-DAY TREKS

THE COAST TRACK, ROYAL NP, NEW SOUTH WALES

Tracing the dramatic wind- and sea-sculpted sandstone cliffs of Royal National Park, just south of Sydney, this moderately challenging trail pairs panoramic coastal views with some of the prettiest swimming spots on the NSW south coast. It's possible to knock off this hike in a single (long) day, but most people opt to take two, pitching a tent at the North Era bush campsite, 18km (11.2 miles) along the trail. This allows plenty of time for cooling off at the likes of Wattamolla Beach and the made-for-Instagram Figure 8 Pools in the warmer months, admiring the wildflowers that blanket the coastal heathland in spring, and watching humpback whales bounce along the coast during winter. Look out for the heritage shacks at South Era on day two.

Start // Beachcomber Ave, Bundeena
Finish // Otford Lookout, Otford
Distance // 26km (16.2 miles)
Duration // 2 days
More info // nationalparks.nsw.gov. au/things-to-do/walking-tracks/ the-coast-track

HAKEA TRAIL, FITZGERALD RIVER NP, WESTERN AUSTRALIA

Another ruggedly beautiful coastal hike lies in Western Australia's Fitzgerald River National Park, 419km/260 miles (or around 5.5 hours' drive) southeast of Perth. Weaving through coastal heathland, along powder-white beaches and over rocky headlands, the Hakea Trail – named after the striking royal hakea plant that is prevalent in this area – boasts dreamy Southern Ocean views with every step. It's possible to cover the distance in a single day if you're super fit, but spreading the full hike over two days will connect you more deeply with your spectacular surroundings. There's a peaceful waterside campsite with barbecue facilities at Hamersley Inlet, roughly halfway, where black swans are known to gather.

Start // Cave Point
Finish // Quoin Head
Distance // 23km (14.3 miles)
Duration // 1-2 days
More info // parks.dpaw.wa.gov.au/ site/hakea-trail

MAMANG TRAIL, FITZGERALD RIVER NP, WESTERN AUSTRALIA

Fitzgerald River National Park lies almost equidistant between Albany and Esperance on WA's south coast. That makes this out-and-back coastal trek, typically a two-day trip, a prime whale-watching opportunity. Winter (June onwards) is whale season here and also when the temperatures are at their most manageable, although any period between March and November is ideal. The trail starts from Point Ann on soft sand before the terrain becomes rockier and more arduous after Lake Nameless. You'll need to carry your own food and water and pay park fees. You can camp at Fitzgerald Inlet before turning around for the 15km (9.5 mile) hike back the way you came, hopefully having spied some spouts out to sea.

Start // Point Ann
Finish // Fitzgerald Inlet
Distance // 31km (19.2 miles)
Duration // 13hr
More info // trailswa.com.au/trails/ mamang-trail/

STRZELECKI PEAKS

Scale the highest mountain on Tasmania's largest offshore island, climbing to views over Bass Strait and a constellation of other islands.

On the summit of the Strzelecki Peaks, I feel a bit like a dinghy in an ocean storm. Wind gusts buffet the mountain and my feet are planted like anchors, holding me to the rock against this blustery assault. It's a fairly standard day atop the highest mountain on Flinders Island.

Emerging directly out of Bass Strait, the Strzelecki Peaks cap an island that is straddled by the line of the notorious Roaring Forties – the winds that blow across the 40th parallel south. Windy days are as common as wallabies on the island, but the reward for climbing this blowy 756m-high (2480ft) mountain is one of the finest coastal views in Tasmania.

My drive to the start of the walk is through a cavalcade of wildlife – wallabies and wombats grazing the fields around the base of the mountain as eagerly as the cattle. I'm running later than planned, delayed by an unusual stand-off – a snake sunbaking between the front door of my accommodation and my car.

At the trailhead, surrounded by farmland, the mountain looms large. Its slopes are a piebald patchwork of forest and bare granite, but quickly it's gone from view as the trail steps immediately into a tunnel of tea tree. A stream pours down beside the trail, running so perfectly along the line of a granite slab that it resembles a mining water race.

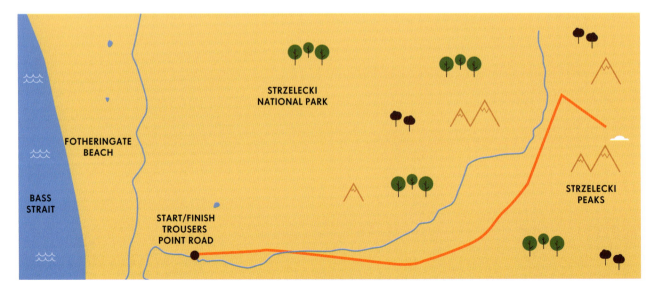

It will be a few hours before I stand on the summit, admiring its vast outlook, but ultimately my greatest memory of the mountain will not be the view. Instead, it will be the variety of bush – the ascending scale of ecosystems – on the slopes. As the trail begins its steepening climb beside a high line of granite – a foretaste of things ahead – the bush is dry and open. It stays this way for a while, creeping up the slopes without variation, at least until the trail dips to cross a deep gully wrinkled into the mountain.

Suddenly, the slopes are covered in tall ferns and the ground is sprinkled with paper daisies. Regal, multi-limbed eucalypts stand tall and wide, their branches looking like something out of a prehistoric fantasy film as they reach over me.

Soon, these impressive trees are below me as I continue up the mountain named after Polish explorer Paweł Strzelecki, the man who named Australia's highest peak, Mt Kosciuszko, and who, in 1842, scaled this Flinders Island mountain while sailing aboard the *Beagle* with Charles Darwin.

Through breaks in the trees, I stand eye to eye with the granite walls that are like plates fitted onto the slopes. Boulders perform balancing acts worthy of a circus performer, and clouds speed overhead like warning signs about the windy conditions to come. The trail appears to be climbing towards one pass on

"I ascend like a primate, hands and feet on the rock, scrambling towards the summit"

the mountain, but soon it turns, cutting beneath Strzelecki's enormous summit cliffs and into another new environment. Damp, ferny glades now line the trail, dripping after recent rain, and the walk becomes like a mossy tunnel. The tree cover breaks open around large granite boulders, revealing views down to the coast.

There's an accidental appearance to the landscape – boulders placed here and there, bald spots of rock seemingly pasted onto the mountain – and as I come to the base of the summit cliffs, I wriggle through gaps between boulders, emerging inside an overhang notched into the cliffs. Below me, the wind-pruned trees stand almost at right angles, slicked back and stunted by the prevailing winds. It's like a bonsai garden tended by nature.

At the end of another short, steep climb, I step up onto a ridge and into blasts of wind so strong that I feel as though I too might start to grow sideways if I stood here long enough.

The summit now rises immediately ahead of me, with the island rolled out flat below, framed in beaches and the brilliantly coloured shallows of the sea.

TROUSER TALK

From the summit of the Strzelecki Peaks, the most prominent part of the view is Trousers Point, the hook-shaped headland at its foot. Sounding more like a clothes store than a geographic feature, the point is said to have taken its name from one of two unconfirmed 19th-century stories. In the first, a sailor on a ship that broke its moorings leapt from the deck onto the rocks sans his trousers; in the second, a box of trousers from a wrecked ship washed ashore here.

Clockwise, from top left: emerald pastures below Strzelecki Peaks; shoreline and peak views at Trousers Point; Strzelecki Peaks loom above the Flinders Island flats; along the trail to the peaks. Previous page: surveying the scene at Trousers Point

After a short descent into a damp pass, the final climb begins, and it's the day's most telling moment. A granite slab rises out of the bush like a stone wall. Climbing it is a bit more than a walk and a bit less than a rock climb, and I ascend like a primate, hands and feet on the rock, scrambling towards the summit, using small notches and flakes in the rock for holds.

The final moments of the climb are along a short and exposed summit ridge. I pass a family taking shelter behind a boulder, huddled out of the wind, which blows with its typical ferocity. And yet the sun shines on, and it's still probably the least windy day I've experienced on the mountain in my four climbs over the years.

A few more steps and I'm atop the Strzelecki Peaks. I am, for the moment, the highest thing in Bass Strait.

Over the tops of the peaks that run along the range, neighbouring Cape Barren Island appears to the south and, beyond it, the distant shores of northeast Tasmania, some 60km (37.2 miles) away. Below my toes is Trousers Point, bookended by two of Flinders Island's most beautiful beaches, and offshore from the point is pyramidal Mt Chappell Island, infamously home to the world's largest tiger snakes.

I stand absorbing the view, even as the wind tries to blow me from the summit. I will eventually succumb, giving in to this force and retreating down the mountain, but not for a while yet. **AB**

ORIENTATION

Start/Finish // Trousers Point Rd
Distance // 6km (3.7 miles)
Duration // 5-6hr
Getting there // Sharp Airlines flies to Flinders Island from Melbourne, Hobart and Launceston. There is no public transport on Flinders; a hire car is essential. The trailhead is a 15km (9.3-mile) drive south from the main town, Whitemark.
When to go // Summer and autumn are the best times to be walking on the Strzelecki Peaks. Spring is the windiest season.
What to pack // Anticipate very different conditions atop the mountain than on the coast. Carry warm, windproof clothing.
Tours // Tasmanian Expeditions (tasmanianexpeditions.com.au) runs a six-day Flinders Island Walking Adventure trip that includes a climb to the summit of the Strzelecki Peaks.
More info // visitflindersisland.com.au

Opposite, from top: Cloudy Bay,
Bruny Island; Mt Killiecrankie,
Flinders Island; wombat at Point
Lesueur, Maria Island

MORE LIKE THIS
TASMANIAN ISLAND HIGHS

MT MARIA, MARIA ISLAND

Standing 711m (2332ft) above the sea
around it, Mt Maria is the tallest peak
on Maria Island, the island national park
off Tasmania's east coast. Beginning in
Darlington, the former convict settlement
where ferries from Triabunna now dock,
the long day walk combines a few of the
island's trademark natural features. Setting
out through Darlington's grassy clearings,
which are typically dotted with wombats,
it soon passes the swirling sandstone
patterns of the Painted Cliffs. Turning up
the slopes on the Inland Track, it passes
through dry woodland before picking
through boulder fields and making a final
scramble onto the summit. The scene from
the summit is an aerial overview of the
island: McRaes Isthmus immediately below,
looking as thin as dental floss from this
height; Point Lesueur and its convict relics
to the east; and Darlington to the north.
Start/Finish // Darlington
Distance // 16km (9.9 miles)
Duration // 7-8hr
More info // parks.tas.gov.au/explore-
our-parks/maria-island-national-park/
mount-maria-track

MT MANGANA, BRUNY ISLAND

Bruny Island's tallest peak is a bit of a
misnomer – it's not that tall, rising to
just 571m (1873ft) – but it does provide
a surprisingly lofty perspective over the
island and parts of southern Tasmania.
The walk begins kindly, setting out
from high on the peak's shoulder, 430m
(1410ft) above sea level. The course is
straightforward, with the track heading
directly up the mountain's northern ridge,
never too steep, never totally gentle. The
path forms a corridor through temperate
rainforest before arriving at the summit,
which appears messy at first, with a
helipad and communications tower and
no views, but a path to the right leads to
a boulder field with views over Cloudy
Bay and Labillardiere Peninsula and
west to the mountains of Tasmania's
Southwest wilderness.
Start/Finish // Coolangatta Rd
Distance // 4km (2.5 miles)
Duration // 2hr
More info // brunyisland.org.au

MT KILLIECRANKIE, FLINDERS ISLAND

The Strzelecki Peaks' companion mountain
on Flinders Island is Mt Killiecrankie, a
great grey lump of rock plugged between
Killiecrankie Bay and The Dock. The walk
begins along the 2km (1.2-mile) length of
Killiecrankie Beach, reaching almost to
the beautiful little cove (with a striking sea
arch) at Stackys Bight before turning off
the coastal route and beginning up the
316m-high (1036ft) mountain. The ascent
passes through Diamond Gully, named for
the local gems – Killiecrankie diamonds,
which are actually a semi-precious topaz
– that are prized by fossickers. The summit
has typically broad views over the north of
Flinders Island and its long beaches. From
the summit, you can return along the same
route, or turn the walk into a longer loop,
descending to the rock-strewn bay at The
Dock and following the rugged coastline
back to Killiecrankie.
Start/Finish // Killiecrankie
Distance // 10km (6.2 miles)
Duration // 4-6hr

SOUTH AUSTRALIA & NORTHERN TERRITORY

ULURU
BASE WALK

Circling Uluru on foot is a soulful experience, and one of the best things you can do anywhere in central Australia.

On the road in from Yulara, I was struck by the sheer presence of this remarkable rock that stood implacably upon the horizon. Bathed in the soft pink light of early morning, it seemed to rise from the surrounding desert like an apparition, as unlikely here in the deserts of central Australia as it was austere and beautiful. This was Uluru, and I found it impossible to take my eyes off this vast and magical thing. The idea of walking all the way around it on that first visit gave me pause, just as it has done every time since.

From a distance, it was the scale of Uluru that held my gaze. Uluru is, after all, the world's largest single-rock monolith. (Mt Augustus in Western Australia is larger but contains a number of rock types.) Uluru is 3.6km (2.2 miles) long and its highest point is 348m (1142ft) above the base (or 867m/2844ft above sea level). Two-thirds of Uluru actually lies beneath the sand.

Up close, Uluru was another thing altogether. From the Mala car park, one starting point among many for the Uluru Base Walk,

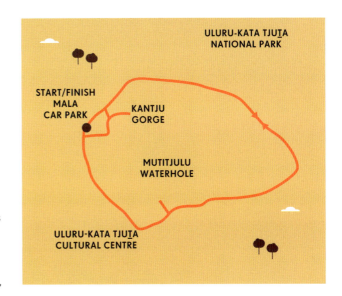

it was the texture of the rock that fascinated. In places, Uluru's sandstone carapace undulated like waves cast in stone, caught in the act of crashing upon a desert shore. Elsewhere, vertical lines marked the path of rains that have cascaded down off the high places over millennia past. And small canyons and caves, fissures and pockmarks, told a story of the relentless winds and sun that have weathered Uluru since it was formed hundreds of millions of years ago.

The car park was yet to fill with the tour buses that would arrive throughout the day. The sun, still low in the eastern sky, was yet to beat down upon the trail. I set out, serenaded by birdsong as the trail passed beneath the eucalypts that press close against the base of Uluru's western flank.

The trail traced the outline of the rock, drawing near, so close in places that I could reach out and touch the red sandstone, which was still in shadow. Sections of Uluru's base, including many of its caves, are off-limits to visitors, part of a network of sites that are sacred to the Anangu people. These sites were clearly marked, and, if anything, the prohibitions only reinforced my sense of the privilege of visiting, of the trust placed in visitors by Uluru's Traditional Custodians. And besides, there was more than enough beauty to go around without needing to transgress upon sacred ground.

Between two such sites, the trail led into a deep, V-shaped cleft in the rock. Known as Kantju Gorge, it was a dramatic introduction to Uluru's steep, steep walls, suddenly overhead. It was dizzying,

> *"Kantju Gorge was a dramatic introduction to Uluru's steep, steep walls. It was dizzying, claustrophobic even. The gorge and its eucalypts felt like a secret world"*

claustrophobic even. The gorge and its eucalypts felt like a secret world, one in which it was easy to feel small, in profound contrast to the red-rock walls towering above me.

A few hundred metres to the northeast, the path drifted slowly away from Uluru's base, then turned east, running parallel to Uluru's north face. With red sand underfoot, it felt like true desert. Shade was meagre, and I was grateful to be walking before the sun was too high in the sky: perhaps more than any other section of the walk, this is one to avoid in the heat of the day. Even so, the path's distance from Uluru, although just a few hundred metres away at its furthest point, allowed me to take in the broad sweep of the rock, and I was once again lost in the scale. It filled the horizon. Vertiginous slopes of smooth rock. Uluru's deep red offset by the incredible blue of the desert sky. Mysterious caves and clefts. Seen from any perspective, but especially from here, Uluru had gravitas and great beauty.

Where Uluru narrowed at its easternmost point, the Uluru Base Walk again got up close and personal with the rock, looping

TRADITIONAL OWNERS

Uluru is sacred to the Anangu (Pitjantjatjara), but it was only 'discovered' by European explorers in 1873, when surveyor William Gosse passed through the area and named it Ayers Rock. It was handed back to its Traditional Owners in 1985, then immediately leased to the Australian Parks and Wildlife Service for 99 years; the Anangu still take an active role in managing today's Uluru-Kata Tjuta NP.

From left: Uluru-Kata Tjuta wildlife – sand goanna and thorny devil lizard; magical Mutitjulu Waterhole, a sacred site of the Anangu people; outback windmill near Uluru. Previous page: Uluru at sunset

ORIENTATION

Start/Finish // Mala car park
Distance // 10.6km (6.6 miles)
Duration // 3-4hr
Getting there // Ayers Rock/Connellan Airport is the gateway airport to Uluru, with flights from major Australian cities with Qantas (qantas.com), Virgin Australia (virginaustralia.com) and Jetstar (jetstar.com). If you're driving, the gateway town is Yulara, which is 447km (277.7 miles) southwest of Alice Springs along the sealed Stuart and then Lasseter highways.
When to go // April-October are the best months, though start early to avoid the hottest parts of the day. Daytime temperatures can be dangerously high November-March.
What to pack // A hat; sunglasses; plenty of water.
Tours // You can book Indigenous cultural tours and ranger-led guided walks at Yulara's Tour and Information Centre.
More info // parksaustralia.gov.au/uluru

south and then southwest. It was impossible to get lost – my all-consuming reference point was never far away – but the same couldn't be said of Uluru's stories; interpretative panels told Dreaming or Tjukurpa stories of how Uluru came into being, and of the plants and animals that lived here.

Close to two-thirds of the way around, a side trail led beneath the trees, past river red gums and through green grasses to Mutitjulu Waterhole. The miracle of water in the desert was a thing of great wonder. But more than that, this is a sacred pool, and the interplay of light and colour and shadow was nowhere more beautiful along this walk than it was here.

As the loop closed, the crowds ebbed into the background, the tree's canopy thickened, and the path hugged closer to the base of the rock. This was – and usually is – the quietest stretch of the whole trail. There was an intimacy with Uluru here that I found nowhere else along the trail. Great fallen boulders lay strewn along the path, and caused me to cast anxious glances to points higher up. The horizon disappeared, crowded out by the dull green of eucalypts. Birds were more plentiful, too, as were their songs.

I returned gradually to the world and its noise, to the clamour of car parks and human chatter. I was back where I began, and I turned to look for one last time at Uluru. I gave an involuntary gasp: so dramatic was its grandeur that I felt as if I were seeing it again for the first time. **AH**

Opposite, from top: red walls and
a lush valley at King's Canyon;
Valley of the Winds wildflowers

MORE LIKE THIS
NORTHERN TERRITORY
RED-ROCK ROUTES

KINGS CANYON RIM WALK

Prepare yourself for some of the best views in the outback when you set out on the Kings Canyon Rim Walk. The initial section is steep and strenuous, and easily the most difficult section of the trail. But having done the hard work, you get to enjoy a hike that circles the canyon rim. From so many vantage points, you'll stand atop the cliffs and look out over (and down into) a chasm unlike any other in central Australia. Along the way, you'll descend wooden stairs into a side valley known as the Garden of Eden, which is awash in lush ferns and ancient cycads with a shaded pool at the valley's innermost reaches. Returning to the rim, you'll pass gigantic beehive-shaped domes which the Luritja Indigenous people identify as men in the creation stories. The views along this section of the walk, just before your descent, are some of the most dramatic of the entire walk.
Start/Finish // Kings Canyon main car park
Distance // 6km (3.7 miles)
Duration // 3-4hr

VALLEY OF THE WINDS WALK

Walking into Kata Tjuta's Valley of the Winds is like entering a vast natural cathedral, a hidden world locked away from view by the stunning rock walls of what was once known as the Olgas. The walk in from the car park climbs to a narrow portal with stunning views down into the heart of the range from Karu Lookout. From here, the trail twists and climbs beneath dizzying rock walls of the deepest red, before climbing further to the Karingana Lookout. Along the way, and beyond as the trail descends again and loops back towards Karu, you'll enjoy views of many of the 36 weathered domes that make up this remarkable natural collection of rocks; 'Kata Tjuta' means 'many heads' and possesses great significance for the local Anangu (Pitjantjatjara) people. See if you can spot Mt Olga, the highest point (546m/1791ft above sea level), which rises 200m (656ft) higher than Uluru.
Start/Finish // Kata Tjuta main car park
Distance // 7.4km (4.6 miles)
Duration // 2-4hr
More info // parksaustralia.gov.au/ uluru/do/walks/valley-of-the-winds

BARUWEI LOOKOUT & LOOP

There are many vantage points for taking in Katherine Gorge in Nitmiluk National Park, but none more accessible, nor more spectacular, than the walk to the Baruwei Lookout and returning via a longer loop. You could just climb to the lookout and back (1.8km/1.1 miles, one hour one-way): the views from the summit are easily the most beautiful of the entire walk. But completing the full loop is worth the extra walking time, with excellent views out over the Katherine River as you go. Much of the Baruwei walk traces the storyline (or songline) of the creation ancestor of the local Jawoyn Indigenous people.
Start/Finish // Nitmiluk National Park Visitor Centre
Distance // 4.8km (3 miles)
Duration // 2hr

WALK
THE YORKE

Get a taste of this mega trail that traces Yorke Peninsula's coastline for a whopping 500km (311 miles) as it passes endless ocean vistas, historical ruins, lighthouses and plenty of wildlife.

When it comes to 'epic', surely anything spanning 500km (311 miles) earns instant qualification – I introduce this colossal hike that circumnavigates the boot-shaped Yorke Peninsula. A two-hour drive southwest from Adelaide, Walk the Yorke (WTY) was unveiled in 2016 as a means to showcase the region's magnificent beaches, cliff-top lookouts, wildlife and laidback coastal communities.

If you plan on doing WTY's entire 500km trail, count on it taking anywhere from 20 to 30 days. Beginning at the top of the 'boot', Port Wakefield is where you'll make your way down past mangroves, beaches and saltpans to reach the 'heel' around Edithburgh for clifftops, lighthouses and marine wildlife sanctuaries. It then 'arches' past beaches and bays to curl around the 'toe' for national parks, dramatic seascapes and long beach walks. Passing Corny Point, you'll reach the top of the 'foot' at Point Turton with coastal reserves and rocky headlands, from where it makes its way up the 'shin' to finish at Moota Bay.

However be aware that outside the townships, this is a remote wilderness hike; one where reliable drinking water access is an issue, so unless you have someone to arrange water drops, it's best to tackle its 16 'hero walks' individually.

So I am here to do the 'toe' of the boot, one of WTY's most popular sections that goes from Marion Bay to Gleesons Landing via Dhilba Guuranda-Innes National Park. It's 61km (38 miles) one-way (95km/59 miles return) that'll take me four days.

Leaving my car at the seaside town of Marion Bay, I follow the yellow trail markers leading me out from civilisation. First impressions here are memorable as I make my way along a cliff-top trail offering sublime ocean views before entering Dhilba Guuranda-Innes National Park. Co-managed by the Narungga Traditional Owners, this is one of Yorke's premier attractions, drawing in folk for its beaches, wildlife, shipwrecks and historical ruins.

At Stenhouse Bay I spot the first of many kangaroos and emus before reaching a photogenic lookout over turquoise waters and a heritage-listed jetty, where locals, I'm told, are here to fish for shark, of all things. There are also interesting remnants from its gypsum mining days, including historical graves and a rusty old locomotive.

A further hour's walk brings me to tonight's campsite at Cable Bay Beach. I don't hang around long, as soon as I set up my tent I'm off on a 30-minute walk to visit Spencer Lighthouse.

Dating to 1975 and made of concrete, it's not quite what I had in mind, but what it lacks in history and romance, it makes up for with the sweeping vistas across Kangaroo Island and Althorpe Island.

On the return trail I encounter more emus before I'm off on another off-trail jaunt along the Inneston Historic Walk. Sunset's a wonderful time to visit the 19th-century ruins of this gyspum mining town, that includes an old school, bakery and restored miners' cottages – some converted into accommodation. But it's at the old post office where I get a lovely surprise – encountering a group of tammar wallabies. Once widespread, they became extinct on the mainland in the 1920s until being reintroduced a few years ago, so it makes a wonderful end to the day.

The next morning begins with a rousing ocean swim, before making my way along the mallee-lined road en route to visit the *Ethel* shipwreck. Though not always visible, today I'm fortunate to see its rusty iron bones embedded in the sand where it ran aground in 1904. It's just one of many shipwrecks (85 to be precise) that have met their demise along this treacherous coast; you'll see another one here 50m (164ft) out to sea – the boiler of the *SS Ferret*.

From here it's back on the tarmac to reach West Cape – the tippy toe of the boot – where there's another lighthouse. This one's from the 1980s and made of stainless steel, so it's even uglier, but again the views don't disappoint.

TAMMAR WALLABY

With kangaroos, emus and marine fauna, Dhilba Guuranda-Innes NP offers plenty of wildlife – but most are here to see the tammar wallaby, Australia's smallest. Extinct on the mainland since the 1920s, they were reintroduced here in 2004 – as were critically endangered brush-tailed bettong marsupials in 2021, as part of the Marna Banggara (Great Southern Ark) project to develop a safe haven for threatened species.

Clockwise, from top left: roos are frequent hikemates on the Walk the York trail; Spencer Lighthouse; the rusting wreck of the Ethel. Previous page, from left: Dhilba Guuranda-Innes National Park coastline; Stenhouse Bay

Pondalowie Bay's next, a popular surf beach and campground on Yorke's southwest coast, and from here it's another 7km (4.3 miles) to arrive at tonight's campsite at Shell Beach. Here a short scramble across the rocks leads me to its pristine rock pools. It's a popular stop with the Instagram set, but today, luckily, I'm the only one here and immediately strip off to plunge into glass-clear waters resembling an aquarium exhibit. Returning to my campsite I discover the rain tanks are bone dry, a reminder to everyone to pack enough drinking water – which fortunately I have.

The next day's 30km (18.6-mile) hike has me exiting the national park and trudging along its west coast beaches. Climbing dunes and atop cliff-top trails the views here are glorious but the soft sand's tough going. So by the day's end I'm happy to reach my campsite at Daly Head surf beach.

The final day begins with a leisurely one-hour walk along the beach to reach the finishing line at Gleesons Landing. Well, sort of, as I still have to get back to Marion Bay. But rather than retracing my steps along the sand, I'm taking the inland 'shortcut' through the national park along Marion Bay-Corny Point Rd. And though I wouldn't describe this long, sweaty 34km (21-mile) leg as the highlight, the prospect of a cold beer and a bed is enough of a motivator to get me over the line. I'm back by 4pm, finishing off what's been a wonderful four-day adventure. As for the other 400km (249 miles) of the boot? After this taster, that's well and truly on my to-hike list. **TH**

ORIENTATION

Start/Finish // Marion Bay (via Gleesons Landing)
Distance // 95km (59 miles)
Duration // 4 days
Getting there // Marion Bay is 284km (176 miles) southwest of Adelaide. Yorke Peninsula Coach (ypcoaches.com.au) run buses from Adelaide to Port Wakefield, Moonta Bay, Edithburgh and Hardwicke Bay; you'll need a car for southern areas.
When to go // Mar-Nov (unreliable drinking water in summer).
What to wear // All-weather gear; sturdy boots; hat; fly net.
What to pack // Hiking tent and camp supplies; drinking water; filtration system; swimwear; insect repellent, sunscreen.
Where to stay // There are 19 basic campgrounds; not all have rainwater tanks. Towns have lodges/B&Bs and caravan parks.
Where to eat // Carry your own food outside the towns.
Things to know // Book permits ahead at yorke.sa.gov.au; or parks.sa.gov.au for Dhilba Guuranda-Innes National Park.

*Opposite: picture-perfect coastal
pillars on the Cape Raoul Track*

MORE LIKE THIS
CLIFFTOP CAPERS

SEAL ROCKS COASTAL RESERVE, KING ISLAND, TASMANIA

Remote, rugged and romantic is this tiny windswept pastoral island that bobs in the middle of Bass Strait halfway between Tasmania and the mainland. Its rich maritime history of shipwrecks and lighthouses can be explored on the King Island Maritime Trail, but for natural beauty, head to Seal Rocks coastal reserve. Here you can embark on the Copperhead Walk that takes in rugged steep cliffs through coastal heathland overlooking Seal Rocks, all the while taking in the force of the Roaring Forties that blast in from these tempestuous wild waters. Further along is a calcified forest where you'll find hundreds of ancient forest limestone pillars that jut from the landscape to provide an otherworldly sight.

Start/Finish // Seal Rocks car park
Distance // 6km (3.7 miles)
Duration // 2hr
More info // kingisland.org.au

ELLISTON COASTAL TRAIL, SOUTH AUSTRALIA

Sitting northwest of South Australia's triangular-shaped Eyre Peninsula is this beautiful ocean-side walk that winds around a scenic and rugged coast overlooking the beginning of the Great Australian Bight. Starting off at the lovely surf beach of Little Bay, here you can pay your respects to the Aboriginal Traditional Owners while taking in the sobering history at the *Recognition Sculpture*, a memorial dedicated to events of a 19th-century massacre. The trail winds around viewpoints at Wellington Bay to the idyllic seaside town of Elliston that overlooks Waterloo Bay and its heritage-listed jetty. Passing around Salmon Point takes you along its cliff-top trail that extends for 6.5km (4 miles) to the finishing point at Cape Finniss, a rocky headland that forms the start of the wonderfully named Anxious Bay. The trail is well signed, with plenty of stops offering interesting information covering local history and wildlife ecosystem.

Start // Little Bay Surf Break
Finish // Cape Finniss
Distance // 13.6km (8.5 miles)
Duration // 6hr return
More info // ellistoncoastaltrail.com.au

CAPE RAOUL TRACK, TASMANIA

One for lovers of pristine coastal wilderness, this spectacular cape walk follows a well-maintained 7km (4.4-mile) trail. Starting out from south of Stormlea, around two hours from Hobart, the path begins among native bushland of eucalypt and tea tree as it slices through this western section of Tasman National Park. Not long after, the forest opens to views out to Shipstern Bluff before you make your way along Cape Raoul plateau, passing coastal banksia to enjoy wonderful views out to the southernmost cape of the Tasman Peninsula. The finishing point at its southern end rewards with astonishing views of unique 200m-tall (656ft) dolerite pillar formations that rise dramatically from the sea. Keep your eyes peeled and if you're lucky you'll spot seals from the lookout.

Start // Stormlea Rd
Finish // Cape Raoul
Distance // 14km (8.7 miles) return
Duration // 5hr
More info // parks.tas.gov.au/explore-our-parks/tasman-national-park/cape-raoul

KANGAROO ISLAND WILDERNESS TRAIL

Skirting the west coast of Kangaroo Island in Flinders Chase National Park, this is one of Australia's most rewarding multi-day hikes, with ample opportunities to spot wildlife.

The Cape du Couedic lighthouse slowly comes into view as we make our way along the clifftops. The sea churns wildly at the base of the cliffs below – a change from the slow, serpentine perambulations of the Rocky River that we've followed down to the coast from where the Cup Gum campsite used to be before the fire. Little remains of the cup gums in question, though green shoots are rampant upon the flame-blackened ground, and a couple of wallabies that were grazing there bound away as we pass.

Up ahead, Rich has stopped walking. He appears to be looking at something intently. 'What is it?' I call out to him, but he doesn't

hear me. It's too blustery and exposed up here, with the wind whipping our hair and clothes as if they were sails. Coming up behind Rich, I can see that just in front of him there's a small cairn. Our guide looks surprisingly pensive – quite a change from the easy-going, wise-cracking guy that we've been getting to know over the past couple of days. 'My great-great-uncle almost died on those rocks below,' Rich tells me by way of explanation, nodding at the churning white froth just out to sea and the dark jagged reef. I raise my eyebrows in question. 'It was a passenger ship from Glasgow, the *Loch Sloy*. They were on their way to Adelaide; the crew were looking for the light on Cape Borda, in the northwest

corner of Kangaroo Island. 'This lighthouse' – he gestures at the whitewashed sentinel in the distance – 'hadn't been built yet.'

I nod, urging him to continue.

'They overshot it in the dark,' Rich continues. 'They were only 300 yards from shore when they hit the reef. It was completely dark. My great-great-uncle, an apprentice – he was only eighteen at the time – was washed ashore. Him and three others, but one of the survivors died from their injuries. Then they scaled these cliffs, and spent several days wandering around, living off limpets and dead penguins until they finally made it to the lighthouse and were rescued.'

'That's a heck of a story.'

'Isn't it? Mind you, many Aussies got here in a roundabout way. At least my relative was luckier than the passengers of the *Loch Vennachar* – a sister ship that got smashed nearby, at West Bay. No one survived; the sharks and the sea got 'em.'

I'm glad that Fiona isn't nearby to hear it; while my nine-year-old niece has shown considerable enthusiasm for land-bound wildlife that we've seen so far, she's so terrified of sharks that nothing could induce her to go near the water during our seemingly endless trudge along the wide, dune-backed sandy expanse of Maupertuis Beach. Sinking into the soft sand with every step proved quite hard-going, even for an energetic outdoorsy kid used to hiking, but when I tried to convince her to walk with me along

"We spot a kangaroo with a joey in her pouch on the forest trail, my niece's first exotic wildlife encounter outside a zoo"

the firmer wet sand by the water's edge, she refused, as if a great white was poised to leap out of the water and drag us to a watery doom. I blame my sister: Charli may have introduced Fi to wildlife documentaries at too tender an age.

Rich and I catch up with Fiona and Charli at the lighthouse and we follow a winding boardwalk down towards an ancient rock bridge.

'What's that smell?' Fiona wrinkles her freckled nose.

The olfactory evidence of their presence becomes potent before we even see them, but soon enough we spot large dark shapes sunbathing on the rock below.

'Look!' Fiona points excitedly as a seal surfs onto the flat rock below the arch on the crest of a wave, while smaller shapes – seal pups – frolic in the rock pools. Further out to sea, sleek grey fins indicate the presence of a small pod of dolphins.

'It's a shame we haven't seen any whales,' Charli tells me. 'It's the wrong time of year for that. But we're definitely lucky with wildlife sightings.'

AFTER THE FIRES

Kangaroo Island's 2019/2020 bushfires were the most devastating in its recorded history, with almost half of the island's 4405 sq km (1700 sq miles) affected. A large chunk of the Ravine des Casoars Wilderness Protection Area in Flinders Chase NP was burned, as well as the Kelly Hill Conservation Park, with considerable habitat and wildlife loss. Basic park infrastructure has been rebuilt and wildlife is returning to the recovering grounds.

Clockwise, from top left: the aptly named Remarkable Rocks; spot fur seals on the Kangaroo Island coast; carnivorous fan-leaved sundew near Black Swamp on the Wilderness Trail. Previous page: sunset at Cape du Couedic lighthouse

I concur. Our first day's hike took us into the bush, along a zigzagging boardwalk through the Black Swamp, dotted with crimson bursts of flowering banksias, then down a dirt trail lined with tiny red sundews, carnivorous plants that, as Charli the naturalist explained to her daughter, dissolve the insects that land on them and consume them. While, much to Fiona's disappointment, we never spotted any telltale bubbles in the watering holes that announce the presence of the shyest of Australia's creatures – the platypus – we did spot a kangaroo with a joey in her pouch on the forest trail, my niece's first exotic wildlife encounter outside a zoo.

The sun is setting by the time we're back at the lighthouse, along with a gaggle of selfie seekers. A part of me is irritated that they've all just driven up here and didn't have to get here the hard way, hiking along the coast like us, but when Rich beckons us over to our shuttle to catch a ride to our guesthouse for the night, I realise that I don't mind not camping one bit.

We make an early start the following day. The trail runs inland, into a copse of tea trees, before teasing us with glimpses of Sanderson Bay and finally emerging atop a dome-like, burnt-orange granite cliff, with rock formations on it twisted into artistic abstract forms.

'They are called Remarkable Rocks,' Rich tells us, and we agree that the rocks are indeed remarkable, before ducking back into the newly sprouting bush. **AK**

ORIENTATION

Start // Rocky River Campground
Finish // Kelly Hill Conservation Park
Distance // 61km (37.9 miles)
Duration // 5 days
Getting there // The park entrance is 110km (68.4 miles) west of Kingscote via the South Coast Rd or the Playford and West End hwys. Kangaroo Island is reached by ferry from Adelaide.
When to go // The park is accessible year-round. Warmest weather is November-March; come June-August for orchids.
Where to stay // Until park lodgings are rebuilt, hikers must stay in accommodation provided by licensed operators.
Tours // Inspiration Outdoors (inspirationoutdoors.com.au); Primal Adventures (primaladventures.com.au); Trek Tours Australia (trektoursaustralia.com.au).
More info // parks.sa.gov.au

*Opposite, from top: Stirling Range
sunrise from the Bluff Knoll trail;
hike Gippsland shores on Victoria's
Wilderness Coast Walk*

MORE LIKE THIS
NATIONAL PARK
WILDERNESS WONDERS

BLUFF KNOLL, WESTERN AUSTRALIA

Ascent of this popular peak is a rite of passage for Western Australians, and delivers 360-degree views over the hills of the Stirling Range National Park as well as the Porongurup range and Mt Manypeaks. From the car park, it's a straightforward yet demanding climb to the flat granite summit of Bluff Knoll (1095m/3592ft) – or Pualaar Miial as it's known to the Noongar people, who believe that the summit is home to spirits that live in the often-enveloping mist. You first descend to the creek before climbing steadily up the well-defined trail along the slope through thickets of eucalyptus and banksia. Budding botanists should keep an eye out for the surprisingly hardy Queen of Sheba orchid en route. You eventually emerge on the saddle, where the trail swings sharply to the left. Mind your footing on the steep steps leading up to the summit, as there are sheer drops in places.

Start/Finish // Bluff Knoll car park
Distance // 6.8km (4.2 miles) return
Duration // 3-4hr
**More info // trailswa.com.au/trails/
bluff-knoll/print**

BALD HEAD, WESTERN AUSTRALIA

Just a short drive from Albany, this fantastic (and little-known) peninsula hike is not as famous other attractions in Torndirrup National Park, but it's no less stunning for it. From the end of Murray Rd (ignoring the turnoff for Misery Beach), this easy-to-follow yet occasionally steep and rugged trail runs along the narrow ridge of the Flinders Peninsula, a granite finger jutting out into the waters of the Southern Ocean. The first part is a stiff ascent to the top of Isthmus Hill, followed by a relatively gentle descent, then another steady uphill on a packed limestone trail up to Limestone Head before a long descent along exposed granite and boardwalk sections to the very tip of the peninsula. Along the way, there are unobstructed views of the granite cliffs and the greenery-clad slopes running down towards the big blue on either side of you; there's also a terrific Albany cityscape on your way back.

Start/Finish // Murray Rd trailhead
Distance // 12.5km (7.8 miles) return
Duration // 5-7hr
**More info // trailswa.com.au/trails/
bald-head-walk-trail/print**

WILDERNESS COAST WALK, VICTORIA

This epic multi-day trail takes in swathes of far-east Gippsland's wild coast in Croajingolong National Park, encompassing ocean-battered stretches of sand, hidden coves and wildlife-rich coastal landscapes. While trekkers with limited time may access the trail with a 2WD at Bemm River, Thurra River, Wingan Inlet, Shipwreck Creek and Mallacoota Inlet, it's well worth hiking the full length of the coast to appreciate the pristine natural habitats you pass through. Some days, you'll have the wild shoreline entirely to yourself as you alternate between trudging along deserted, wave-battered beaches, crossing sand banks, hiking through coastal and cliff-top tea-tree forest, with rugged cliff and beach vistas peeking through the greenery, and bisecting open heathland. The trail incorporates dirt footpaths, old management trails, stretches of boardwalk and open expanses of sand; fording (or swimming across) some narrow rivers is required, and in some sections you need scrambling and good wayfaring skills.

Start // Sydenham Inlet
End // Wonboyn
Distance // 100km (62 miles)
Duration // 8-10 days
**More info // parks.vic.gov.au/places-to-
see/parks/croajingolong-national-park/
things-to-do/walk-the-wilderness-coast**

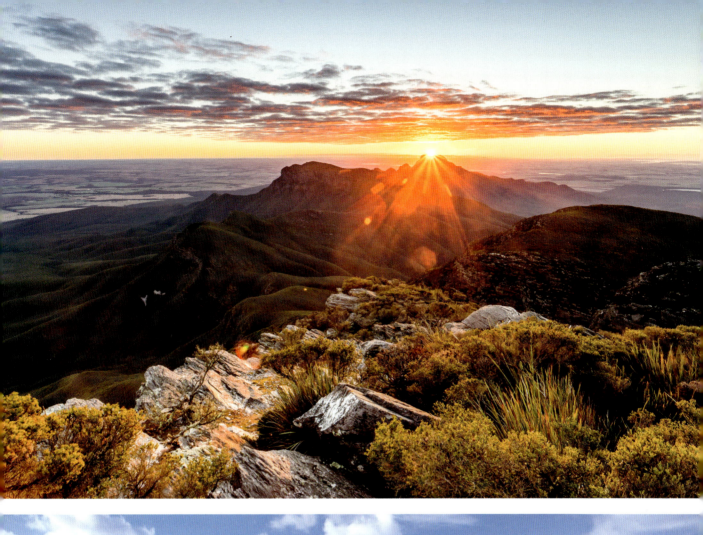

THE LARAPINTA TRAIL

The Larapinta Trail is an outback epic, bucking and weaving along the ridgeline of the West MacDonnell Ranges from one glorious canyon to the next.

To hike the Larapinta Trail from Alice Springs to Mt Sonder is a true outback epic, a traverse of one of the most beautiful mountain ranges anywhere in Australia's Red Centre. At one end, Alice Springs, the largest town for more than a thousand kilometres in any direction. At the other, a stirring panorama extending over two parallel ridgelines of red rock and out into the endless desert horizon beyond. And everywhere in between – this is one beautiful walk.

This is the land of the Arrernte Indigenous people, and their stories shadowed me as I set out from Alice Springs. They also kept me company all along the route. In Arrernte Dreaming stories, on their journey across the land, three caterpillars created the West MacDonnell Ranges, the East MacDonnells, and – in between the two – Mparntwe (the site of what is now Alice Springs). In many places, it was easy to see the resemblance between the mountains, which form the backbone of Tjoritja/West MacDonnell National Park, and the caterpillars of these intriguing stories.

For the first-time hiker, it's a landscape that fires the imagination. In places, the great, bouldered summits that unfurl across an east-west trajectory looked less like caterpillars than the vertebrates of a dragon's back. Elsewhere, I sensed a nod to geological aeons past in the reptilian, almost prehistoric cast to the landforms.

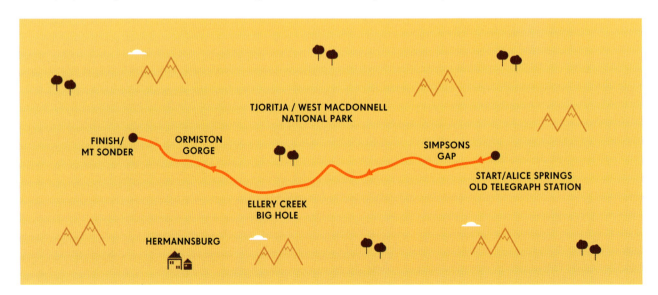

TJORITJA / WEST MACDONNELL
NATIONAL PARK

FINISH/
MT SONDER

ORMISTON
GORGE

SIMPSONS
GAP

START/ALICE SPRINGS
OLD TELEGRAPH STATION

ELLERY CREEK
BIG HOLE

HERMANNSBURG

Leaving Alice Springs, I found myself almost at a run. Loud at first, the noise of road trains rumbling along the Stuart Hwy, receded into the background. Soon enough, the sounds of civilisation dulled and became distant. An awareness grew that I had left the city.

The first day's walk – nine hours, nearly 25km (15.5 miles) – bridged those two worlds. By early evening, my arrival at Simpsons Gap brought with it excitement and peace in equal measure. One of the great defiles for which the West MacDonnells are renowned, Simpsons Gap was eucalypts and black-footed rock wallabies and sheltered pools beneath steep cliffs. On one side, the desert stretched deep into the north. On the other, a more sheltered world rested between the two main branches of the range.

If day one was about leaving the city behind, day two and the days that followed were all about immersion as I followed the contours, gaining altitude and descending into dry valleys. The roads that carried day-trippers and their vehicles were well away to the south, no longer even a distant presence. The only other people I saw were occasional fellow hikers.

The hike soon took on its own rhythm. I rose with the sun, and hiked hard and early. This enabled me to rest, or to walk at a more leisurely pace, in the hottest part of the day. Later, as the day

"Hugh Gorge, where I swam beneath the stars after a day of walking beneath the intense sun, felt like a lost world of life-giving water"

cooled, evenings brought gentle breezes, a special kind of quiet magic filled with silence and stars and the curious awareness of Australia's small marsupials just beyond the circle of light.

These simple pleasures were the undoubted nightly highlights of the trek. But each day brought new and unimagined gifts. At Birthday Waterhole it was the diamond doves and zebra finches at sunset as they came down to drink. Hugh Gorge, where I swam beneath the stars after a day of walking beneath the intense sun, felt like a lost world of life-giving water.

From the highs of Razorback Ridge, down through Ellery Creek and Serpentine Gorge, each landmark seemed more beautiful than the last. But if I had to pick a favourite view of all, it would be from Counts Point, on day eight of 12, between Serpentine and Ormiston gorges. From there, I looked down upon a valley entirely enclosed by steep mountain slopes. It was a world unto itself, seen only by those who walked the trail. Beyond, the views swept out across the layers of red summits, extending into the very heart of Australia.

By this stage of the journey, I couldn't help but feel that the Larapinta Trail was undergoing something of a sustained crescendo, with one astonishing view after another. So many of these coalesced around Ormiston Gorge, where the cliffs seemed higher and the valleys deeper. Ghost gums and sandy beaches, waterholes and whistling kites – little wonder that Ormiston is the most celebrated of all the gorges of the West MacDonnells.

Ormiston also draws some of the richest birdlife anywhere along the trail. The cries of a pair of whistling kites echoed off the high cliffs, and more doves and finches came down to drink and chatter in the near branches. I even caught a glimpse of the rufous-crowned emu-wren amid the spinifex. At sunset a dingo gave the camp a wide berth and continued on its way.

Upon leaving Ormiston Gorge the next morning, I knew that I was into the final section of the trail, that there were fewer than 50km (31 miles) still to go. I walked from Ormiston to the usually dry Finke/Larapinta River, one of the outback's great seasonal waterways, a place of gushing torrents after rains and heavy-going soft sand the rest of the time; when I passed through, it was very much the latter.

On the final night, I slept in Redbank Gorge, another of the West MacDonnell's signature canyons. Wishing the Larapinta Trail would never end, I lay awake deep into the night beneath great silhouetted outcrops, scarcely moving so as not to disturb the silence.

On day 12, all that remained was to climb on weary legs to the highest point of the Larapinta Trail, the summit of Mt Sonder (1380m/4528ft above sea level). The views seemed to go on forever. **AH**

WILDLIFE OF THE WEST MACS

The West MacDonnell Ranges are a great place to spot native Australian wildlife. Red kangaroos and dingoes are commonly seen close to sunrise and sunset when few people are out and about. Sightings of black-footed rock wallabies are common throughout the range. Rich birdlife is another highlight, from raptors such as whistling kites and peregrine falcons to desert specialists like the spinifex pigeon, Australian ringneck and the western bowerbird.

Left to right: Simpsons Gap pools; Larapinta Trail marker. Previous page, from top: on the trail into Simpsons Gap; Mt Sonder sunrise

ORIENTATION

Start // Alice Springs Old Telegraph Station
Finish // Mt Sonder
Distance // 223km (138.6 miles)
Duration // 12-15 days
Getting there // Alice Springs Airport has regular flights from Australian cities with Qantas (qantas.com) and Virgin (virginaustralia.com). By road, Alice Springs is 1534km (953 miles) from Adelaide, 1496km (930 miles) from Darwin.
When to go // April to September are the best months, but start early to avoid the hottest parts of the day. From November to March/April, daytime temperatures can be dangerously high.
What to pack // Hat; sunglasses; camping gear; ample water.
Tours // Trek Larapinta (treklarapinta.com.au) runs multi-day guided walks along part or all of the Larapinta Trail.
More info // larapintatrail.com.au

Opposite, clockwise from top: Giles Track views, Watarrka National Park; Amphitheatre rock art, Nitmiluk National Park; hike between waterfalls on the Jatbula Trail

MORE LIKE THIS
CHALLENGING TREKS
IN THE NORTHERN TERRITORY

GILES TRACK,
WATARRKA NATIONAL PARK

If you've fallen for Kings Canyon and long to explore beyond the crowded canyon trails, Giles Track, which runs along the southern flank of the George Gill Range, will give you a taste of blissful outback isolation. Named after Ernest Giles, one of the most successful of the 19th-century explorers who roamed the outback, it's a suitably rugged experience, taking you into areas of Watarrka National Park that only a fraction of the park's overall visitors ever experience. It's ideal for hikers of moderate experience and fitness, and its highlights, such as Kathleen Springs and Reedy Creek, are those sections of trail that enter into the shadow of the mountains, where water fills sheltered pools in the otherwise arid landscape.

Start // Kathleen Springs
Finish // Kings Canyon main car park
Distance // 22km (13.7 miles)
Duration // 2 days

JATBULA TRAIL,
NITMILUK NATIONAL PARK

The gorges of Nitmiluk National Park are the geological echoes of the Arnhem Land Escarpment, and they provide some of the best hiking in the Top End and surrounds. Along the Jatbula Trail, you'll leave behind the crowds of Katherine Gorge and launch into a wilderness of waterfalls, idyllic waterholes and utterly magnificent scenery. Highlights include Biddlecombe Cascades, Crystal Falls, the Amphitheatre and Sweetwater Pool. The trail follows an ancient songline of the Indigenous Jawoyn peoples and is filled with significance; before setting out, talk with one of the Indigenous rangers at the visitor centre to learn more. The track climbs the escarpment, and is a challenging trail all the way to Leliyn (Edith Falls). The trail is for experienced hikers only and is open from May to September. Jatbula can only be walked in the one direction, and you must walk in a minimum party of two.

Start // Katherine Gorge
Finish // Leliyn
Distance // 66km (41 miles)
Duration // 5 days
More info // jatbulatrail.com.au

JAWOYN VALLEY,
NITMILUK NATIONAL PARK

This fabulous walk will show you the best of Katherine Gorge scenery, but take you beyond the crowds and into the lightly trammelled trails of the Nitmiluk National Park backcountry. You'll get a taste of the gorge scenery for which the park is famous at 8th Gorge, which is itself reason enough for taking this trail. You'll find yourself stopping often, sometimes because this is a strenuous trail, but more often to admire the views, especially in the vicinity of the gorge. But it's the Jawoyn Valley that really adds depth and perspective to your hike, with fascinating galleries of ancient rock art in many of the rock shelters that line the valley.

Start/Finish // Nitmiluk National Park Visitor Centre
Distance // 39km (24 miles)
Duration // 2-3 days

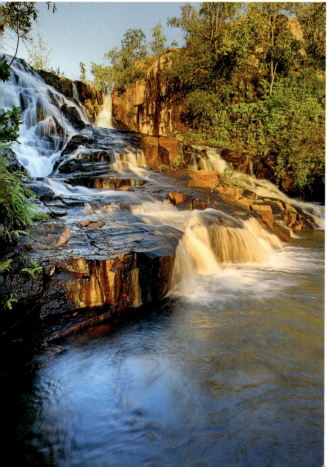

THE ARKABA WALK

The guided Arkaba Walk combines epic wilderness with eco-friendly luxury, from starlit swags to sleeping in a heritage homestead, all to the backdrop of South Australia's Flinders Ranges.

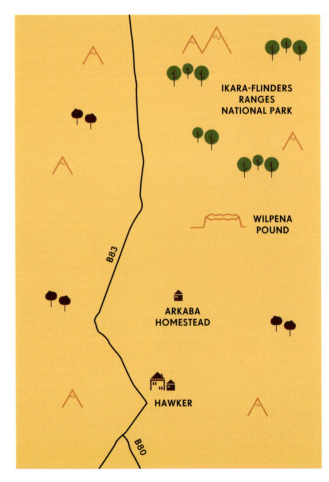

Burrowing into my outdoor swag bed on the first night of the Arkaba Walk, I sense I'm not alone. Something warm and furry has crept in beside me. It's a relief to realise it's just a fluffy, sheepskin-covered hot-water bottle – kindly secreted there by our guide – and is not a random marsupial.

Passionate field guides lead the way and have all of our dining and glamping needs covered on this incredible trek. We're hiking for three days across South Australia's stunning Flinders Ranges, but we're doing it in style. We're carrying backpacks and water, but we don't have to lug heavy tents and food. Operated by Wild Bush Luxury, the Arkaba Walk is perfect for those who like a good trek, escaping into remote countryside, but enjoy a few creature comforts along the way.

An iconic Australian adventure, the Arkaba Walk starts and finishes at Arkaba Homestead, a former sheep station turned boutique eco-lodge. Most of the walk unfolds on 60,000 acres (24,281 hectares) of Arkaba's privately owned land. It's a unique chance to experience the outback in a small group without a soul in sight, yet is far more accessible from a major city than touristy Uluru. Arkaba is also involved with bold conservation efforts across its vast property, eliminating introduced feral animals such as foxes, cats and goats that decimate local wildlife and vegetation. The team works to protect native species and plants in its sanctuary, reduce the impact of sheep farming on the bush, and supports a colony of rare yellow-footed rock-wallabies. A proportion of guest fees goes towards this biodiversity conservancy and rewilding.

My four fellow walkers have driven five hours north from South Australia's capital, Adelaide, to reach Arkaba. The route runs through the famed Clare Valley, perfect for sampling riesling at winery stopovers. I catch the six-and-a-half-hour bus ride instead, rolling through arable flatlands past snoozy small towns. At Hawker, Arkaba's team picks me up for the 15-minute transfer to the homestead, ready for the next morning's trek.

Jaw-dropping geological wonder Wilpena Pound marks the start of the trek, a short drive away. A vast natural amphitheatre fringed by mountains with tall, dry trees dotting its core, it looks like a meteorite has struck earth leaving a yawning crater. In fact, this ancient rock bowl was formed by the land uplifting over millennia, dazzling proof of the power of Mother Nature. Our first day's 13km (8-mile) hike takes us across the basin of the breathtaking Pound, before we climb the ridge edge and drop down to Black Gap, our inviting campsite.

A mob of emus huddle together nearby. They're a truly kooky looking bird, with their bug eyes, spiky hair, shaggy feathers and skinny legs. Our guide shows us to our simple swag beds, set on standalone wooden platforms and angled towards views of forest and the majestic Pound. Covered by a canopy, each comes with a roll of canvas 'swag' bedding, which can be

"The delicate, shifting colours of the rocky hillsides are stunning, especially the pinks, purples, mauves and reds as sunrise or sunset lick the surrounding peaks"

stuffed with soft blankets and a pillow. It's semi-alfresco but as snug as a tent, and suits this arid hot-by-day, cool-by-night climate. Drovers of old were partial to swags but they'd be shocked to see our sleek updates, and amazed by the gourmet three-course dinner hosted in a lantern-lit dining tent. We sip hearty South Australian red wine – local like all the produce – around the flames before hitting our swags. Sleeping under the huge outback sky is magical, with innumerable twinkling stars visible in the profound darkness.

A copper bowl of heated rainwater beckons when I clamber from my cocoon at dawn, a pampering touch for washing my face. Afterwards, I shower in a secluded corrugated iron booth nearby, redolent of the film *Mad Max*. A pulley tips a bucket of warm water over me, while I peek out at the pristine landscape surrounding the camp.

WILPENA POUND

Part of Ikara-Flinders Ranges NP, Wilpena Pound is known to the local Adnyamathanha Indigenous people as Ikara ('meeting place'). According to Aboriginal beliefs, it was created when two giant Dreamtime serpents carved the landscape in their wake; their coiled, petrified bodies formed the enclosure. Cradled by mountain ranges on the desert's edge, the 800-million-year-old basin is 17km (10.5 miles) long by 8km (4.9 miles) wide, and 1171m (3841ft) at its peak

Clockwise, from top left: looking down into the Wilpena Pound basin; all the shades of red en route to the Arkaba Walk; Ikara-Flinders Ranges birdlife – red-capped robin and red-rumped parrot. Previous page: Wilpena Pound

ORIENTATION

Start/Finish // Arkaba Homestead
Distance // 43km (26 miles)
Duration // 3 nights/4 days
Getting there // It's a 5-hour drive from Adelaide to Arkaba.
When to go // Mid-March to mid-October. The walk only operates in Australia's cooler seasons, avoiding summer.
What to pack // Boots; light layers; hat; sunscreen (backpacks, water, toiletries and walking poles provided).
Where to stay // The all-inclusive Arkaba Walk is hosted by Wild Bush Luxury (arkabawalk.com), with two nights in swag camps and a third at Arkaba Homestead.
Things to know // Detailed route maps are reserved for guests, as Arkaba Walk falls mainly on private land. Trespass is not allowed, including from the nearby Heysen Trail.
More info // wildbushluxury.com

Rugged yet romantic with endless horizons, the Flinders Ranges unfold over the next two days of our trek, which weaves from lofty hilltops to lowly creek beds. Each day is around a 15km (9-mile) walk, taking up to seven hours. Kangaroos are an enchanting sight, with three species – big reds, smaller western greys and stocky euros – plus more compact wallabies calling the Flinders home. I'll never forget the giant, twisted river red gum trees by the dry creeks, with their camouflage-patterned, two-tone bark. The delicate, shifting colours of the rocky hillsides are stunning, too, especially the pinks, purples, mauves and reds as sunrise or sunset lick the surrounding peaks.

Birdlife is another highlight, as our guide picks out the cries of the tiny willie wagtail and red-capped robin (and you can't miss the laughing kookaburra and noisy galahs). We spy falcons and a soaring Wedge-tailed eagle, and learn to distinguish between elegant and red-rumped parrots, as well as a host of animal droppings. It's a fairly demanding walk, but our mixed-age group copes well, encouraged by inspiring insights from our knowledgeable guides.

Alluring Arkaba Homestead, founded in 1851, offers an indulgent retreat for our last night, filled with touching mementoes of its sheep-farming past. No wifi or TV distracts us, but by now that's just the way we like it. **SD**

Opposite, from top: spy the
Three Sisters on the Echo Point
to Scenic World hike; Rangitoto
from Milford Beach

MORE LIKE THIS
RAVISHING ROCKS

COASTAL WALK, MORNINGTON PENINSULA, VICTORIA

Around 90 minutes' drive south of Melbourne, the Coastal Walk hugs the Mornington Peninsula's surf-lashed, southern side, offering an inspiring eight-hour trek along sandy beaches and gravel tracks linking two striking geological features. Part of Mornington Peninsula National Park near Bass Strait, it's best tackled over two days. Start at looming, wave-eroded Pulpit Rock, a short walk from Cape Schanck Lighthouse, formed by millions of years of volcanic activity (its base is dubbed Devils Desk). The route then bears west, passing Gunnamatta, Rye, Sorrento and Portsea ocean beaches, with spectacular cliff-top vistas, rugged rocks, dunes and coastal scrub along the way. Impressive rock arch London Bridge marks the walk's end. Beware of changing tides and only swim when beaches are patrolled along this dangerous coastline or cross to the sheltered bayside. Keen beans can extend the walk to Port Nepean National Park to explore heritage military and quarantine buildings.
Start // Pulpit Rock, Cape Schanck Lighthouse
Finish // London Bridge, Portsea Ocean Beach
Distance // 30km (18.6 miles)
More info // visitmornington peninsula.org

ECHO POINT TO SCENIC WORLD, NEW SOUTH WALES

Get up close to the landmark rock stack The Three Sisters in New South Wales' Blue Mountains. A 90-minute drive west of Sydney, this two- to three-hour hike is short but dramatic. From Katoomba, in the Blue Mountains National Park, the looping trail starts at Echo Point Lookout. Admire panoramic views of The Three Sisters, backed by blue-tinged escarpments. The trio's highest turret is 922m (3024ft). In Aboriginal legend, this unusual sandstone formation represents three sisters turned into stone. Take the Three Sisters Walk beside the visitor centre to the 1909-built Giant Stairway, which leads to the Jamison Valley floor below. Descending its 998 vertiginous steel-and-stone steps you'll pass below the Sisters. Stroll along flat Federal Pass track through eucalypts and rainforest to Scenic World, where you can ride the historic, super-steep Scenic Railway up to their cafe or ascend the heart-pumping Furber Steps. Return to Echo Point via Katoomba Falls on the view-blessed, 2.1km (1.3 mile) Prince Henry Cliff walk.
Start // Echo Point Lookout, Katoomba
Finish // Scenic World, Katoomba
Distance // 4.7km (3 miles) one-way
More info // nationalparks.nsw.gov.au; scenicworld.com.au

RANGITOTO SUMMIT TRACK, NORTH ISLAND, NEW ZEALAND

A 25-minute scenic ferry ride from downtown Auckland, on New Zealand's North Island, this easy day-trip trek heads up dormant volcano Rangitoto, which occupies its own little island in the Hauraki Gulf. Rangitoto is the youngest and largest volcano in Auckland's volcanic field, emerging from the sea about 600 years ago. Its distinctive, symmetrical cone is a local icon. It takes around two hours to complete the 7km (4.3-mile) round trip hike to the summit, starting from Rangitoto Wharf. A signed track leads you on a gentle climb through rugged lava fields and the world's largest pohutukawa forest to the 260m (853ft) peak. From the top, admire gorgeous views of New Zealand's largest city, emerald islands and the sparkling blue ocean. Detour to fascinating black lava caves on the way down. There's no drinking water or snacks so bring your own and wear sturdy shoes as the trail is uneven.
Start/Finish // Rangitoto Wharf
Distance // 7km (4.3 miles)
More info // newzealand.com/int/ rangitoto-island

THE HEYSEN TRAIL

Following a prodigious 1200km (746 miles) along South Australia's geological backbone, the Heysen Trail stands unrivalled as the country's longest (and arguably most diverse) marked hiking trail.

Like many kids growing up in South Australia's Barossa Valley wine region, riding my bike to school was a treasured ritual. Every day I would lean patiently against the post at the end of my street, waiting for the morning traffic to clear. My hand would rest on a reflective red arrow pointing towards the distant amber ranges. This marker was a real curio for a 12-year-old cycling devotee – very few interests could be found within pedalling distance. Whatever mysteries the marker signified lay unexplored beyond the hills.

Two decades later, after ditching the wheels and embracing Australia's diverse bushwalking landscapes, I arrived back in South Australia bubbling with hiking spirit. The Heysen Trail – named after Hans Heysen, the renowned landscape artist – had remained at the doorstep of my childhood home, quietly awaiting my return. Finally, my time had come; the wild, as they say, had called. The following two months would be spent hunting red arrows and discovering lands beyond the hills.

The 5.5-hour drive north to the northern Heysen trailhead at Parachilna Gorge (buses can deliver through-hikers to either end of the trail) did little to suppress weeks of unchecked anticipation. Though a final weather-beaten sign warning trekkers to be 'well equipped and experienced' injected some realism into this first-time long-haul solo hiker.

Any residual butterflies faded over the first fuss-free kilometre. Twisted peppermint gums lined a snaking crimson creek bed, blunting the region's potent winter sun. This dappled runway led me to the forested outskirts of Ikara-Flinders Ranges National Park, where a brood of kangaroos foraged on the leafy

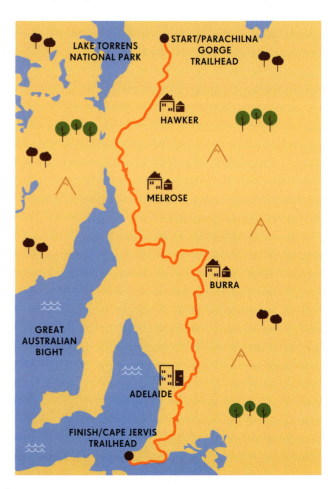

undergrowth (show me a more authentic long-distance launching pad and I'll eat my sweaty hat).

The pathways over and around the razorbacked ABC and Heysen ranges and through the gum-lined Aroona and Bunyeroo valleys were stunning in their semi-arid beauty. The trail down the amphitheatric Wilpena Pound – Ikara to the local Adnyamathanha people – and across Willochra Plain delivered a rustic medley of saltbush flats, shady creek beds and magical golden-hour bluffs.

In the historic rail town of Quorn, my hiker's hunger and I launched a schnitzel crawl into the state's mid-north. My trail diet of dehydrated dahl, scroggin, porridge, tuna, ANZAC biscuits and billy tea wasn't cutting it. With a trouser-size already lost after eleven days, deep-fried dinners became a civilisation staple – guilt-free calories are, in fact, real. Huzzah!

After two weeks navigating bushland, the trail south of Goyder's Line (a surveyed phenomenon demarking rainfall suitable for growing crops) heralded an abrupt transition. Manicured paddocks replaced wilderness; I had entered the flat agricultural channel east of the Flinders Ranges. Over much of the next four weeks, I would be engulfed in pastoral green.

> *"Time felt both abundant and redundant. Life had been simplified to its essentials: walking, eating, sleeping and pondering the world's peculiar intricacies"*

By the time I entered Melrose, in the shadow of imposing Mt Remarkable (960m/3150ft), my mind had synced entirely with the trail. Daybreak had become my alarm; birdsong my Spotify playlist; the horizon my Netflix viewing. Twenty-kilometre days were routine; passing hikers were few. Time felt both abundant and redundant. Life had been simplified to its essentials: walking, eating, sleeping and pondering the world's peculiar intricacies.

The sight of vineyards outside Australia's oldest copper mining town, Kapunda, signalled my imminent Barossa homecoming. The twilight panorama of my childhood hometown, Tanunda, required a second take. Rolling fields and old-growth vines rippled with life: it was as though I saw the valley through new eyes. After six weeks absorbing the simplicity of nature – morning dew on spider webs, the medicinal bouquet of eucalyptus, dusk's mesmerising hush – I appreciated familiar details that I'd once overlooked.

As with all happy reunions, hugs were offered liberally, and sentimentality was indulged – but time was soon the enemy. On leaving, I stroked the signposted trail marker that had piqued my curiosity years earlier. Then, inhaling deeply, I stepped toward the radiating Barossa Range. My time to explore its secrets had arrived.

South Australia's corrugated agricultural terrain rose into the Adelaide Hills – a dense nest of conservation parks and

FRIENDS OF THE HEYSEN TRAIL

Australia's hardworking trail volunteers are the lifeblood of its bushwalking community; the Friends of the Heysen Trail embody this dedicated workforce. Since 1986, its members have been found straightening posts, mending fences, replacing markers, re-routing tracks, slashing weeds, plumbing tanks and constructing shelters the length of this epic route. Without these dutiful trail angels, Heysen hikers wouldn't enjoy the variety of quality bushwalking experiences offered today.

Clockwise, from above: the author hiking the Heysen near Willochra Plain; South Australia vines; rapeseed in bloom along the route; Southern Ocean coastline at Newland Head, near the end of the Heysen Trail. Previous page: Fleurieu Peninsula

coniferous plantations. My legs burned at the apex of Morialta Conservation Park, overlooking Adelaide's sprawling cityscape. I had reached peak civilisation – but I knew the crowds would thin quickly as I continued south.

I shed a euphoric tear when I finally reached the vast Southern Ocean. Finally, after 55 days, my battle-wearied boots had carried me to the southern fringes of the Fleurieu Peninsula. Sea spray permeated my nostrils, expanded my lungs and willed me forward. Surrounded by mottled mallee scrub, golden beaches and oceanfront reserves, the climactic four-day tramp to Cape Jervis disappeared in a blink. The finish line emerged before I could really make peace with the Heysen's conclusion and my newfound inner perspective.

Through 17 towns; 40 free walk-in campsites, shelters and reconditioned huts; 23 national and conservation parks; and the Country of seven Traditional Owners, a Heysen Trail through-hike should not be underestimated. The trek tests physical and mental fibre, demanding self-sufficiency, planning, training and unavoidable pain. But those who dare are generously compensated. Few hikes capture Australia's remarkable natural diversity like the Heysen. The arid outback gateway to the north; ancient ranges, fertile countryside and expansive forests through the centre; and striking craggy coastline to the south – it's an Australiana pilgrimage.

The benefits of taking a break from society are considerable. Long-distance through-hikes stoke independence and daring, tapping into primal instincts and dormant intuition. Everyone should probe life's existential questions once in a while; the Heysen might just conjure some answers. **JW**

ORIENTATION

Start // Parachilna Gorge
Finish // Cape Jervis
Distance // Approx. 1200km (746 miles) including spurs
Duration // 50–60 days
Getting there // From Adelaide, the southern trailhead at Cape Jervis is a 1.5-hour drive (102km/63 miles) south. Driving north to the Parachilna Gorge terminus takes 5.5 hours (487km/303 miles). Transfers are available.
When to go // May-June offers the best conditions for hikers heading north; August-September is better for walking south.
What to pack // Clothing; food; shelter; fuel; hiking equipment; first aid: be prepared with a fully-loaded kit.
Where to stay // The trail provides 200-plus accommodation options, including free huts, shelters and campsites.
Tours // The Friends of the Heysen Trail offer day, weekend and week-long walks (heysentrail.asn.au/walks).
Things to know // The trail is closed to hikers during Fire Danger Season, generally November to April.
More info // Keep up to date with trail developments at heysentrail.asn.au

Opposite, from top: hike the Clare Valley countryside on the Lavender Federation Trail; Wild South Coast Way shoreline near Victor Harbor

MORE LIKE THIS
BEST-OF-THE-REST HIKES IN SOUTH AUSTRALIA

LAVENDER FEDERATION TRAIL

Beginning on the banks of the Murray River one hour (72km/45 miles) east of Adelaide, the Lavender Federation Trail offers an alternative snapshot into regional South Australia. Named for the Heysen Trail's architect, Terry Lavender OAM, the route connects quaint villages, billowing hillsides and the world-class Clare Valley wine region: rambling England's Cotswolds with an Aussie tinge. This two-week trek heads west from Murray Bridge, skimming Monarto Safari Park (watch for one of Australia's largest lion prides), then veers over the all-seeing Mt Beevor (503m/1650ft). From the summit, unspoilt views span the broad Murraylands towards the distant Southern Ocean. Your journey north tracks past spring-time wildflowers, hidden gorges and pioneering ruins from a bygone era. And to finish? Few trails enjoy a culinary climax like that on offer in Clare, where award-winning rieslings, regional produce and generous hospitality await your weary bones.

Start // Murray Bridge
Finish // Clare
Distance // 325km (202 miles)
Duration// 2 weeks
More info // lavenderfederationtrail. org.au

ALLIGATOR GORGE RING ROUTE

In the heart of Mt Remarkable National Park, Alligator Gorge offers one of the most iconic walks in the Flinders Ranges. A series of rugged rock-hops, hearty climbs and ancient geology make this four-hour circuit a favourite for bushwalkers. After journeying the 3.5 hours (293km/182 miles) north of Adelaide, hike out of the adjacent car park in an anti-clockwise direction – this ensures all major highlights are saved for the end. A gentle fire track rises steadily until Ring Route Track (detour here for a dazzling panorama of Spencer Gulf), then descends via a series of waterworn quartzite platforms. The creek bed is eventually engulfed by a chiselled ochre canyon through The Narrows. Keep an eye on conditions and prepare for knee-deep wading following a downpour. National Park vehicle entry fees apply.

Start/Finish // Alligator Gorge car park
Distance // 8.9km (5.5 miles)
Duration// 4hr
More info // walkingsa.org.au/walk/ find-a-place-to-walk/alligator-gorge- ring-route-hike

WILD SOUTH COAST WAY

The Heysen Trail's southern bookend, running east to west along the Fleurieu Peninsula coastline, delivers a masterclass in windswept walking. Open year-round, this four- to five-day expedition has received recent upgrades, an extension into historic Victor Harbor, and a fancy new name: the Wild South Coast Way. Chaperoned by views of Kangaroo Island, the path south from the Cape Jervis trailhead crosses rocky shorelines and dipping gullies before swerving inland through the dramatic Deep Creek Conservation Park. The passage across Tunkallila Beach enjoys anonymity, with 4km (2.5 miles) of largely inaccessible oceanfront – a refuge for dolphins and fur seals to surf the shoreline. Take time here to relax – you'll need your energy for the notoriously steep climb up the eastern flank. The final days include a series of grasslands, granite bluffs, meandering shoreline tracks, and, eventually, a civilised stroll into Victor for hot cinnamon doughnuts.

Start // Cape Jervis
Finish // Victor Harbor
Distance // 80km (50 miles)
Duration// 4-5 days
More info // parks.sa.gov.au/park- management/wild-south-coast-way

QUEENSLAND & WESTERN AUSTRALIA

THE SCENIC RIM TRAIL

Taking you deep into one of the world's most significant rainforests, Queensland's newest multi-day hike can be as luxe or as adventurous as you like.

Sometimes I have to pinch myself that I grew up with the world's largest subtropical rainforest in my backyard. An ancient wilderness protected by 41 national parks and reserves straddling the New South Wales/Queensland border, the Unesco World Heritage-listed Gondwana Rainforests of Australia are known for their rich biodiversity, providing habitats for more than 200 rare or threatened plant and animal species. I'm always looking for an excuse to spend more time in this special place, so when I heard that a new four-day hiking trail in this subtropical dreamscape was in development, I mentally laced my boots.

The brainchild of the Turner family, owners of the Spicers Retreats boutique hotel group, the Scenic Rim Trail traces a rainforest-clad ridgeline in Queensland's Main Range National Park on Gondwana's northwestern fringe. Linked by three architect-designed eco-lodges, the Spicers' version is a luxurious, guided four-day experience. A five-day option, including a koala walk at Spicers Hidden Vale near the trailhead, is also available.

But the Scenic Rim Trail isn't just for walkers with deep pockets. As part of the deal with the Queensland Parks and Wildlife Service, the undulating trail is also publicly accessible, with three basic campgrounds located along the one-way route, hiked from north to south. Requiring you to carry all food and camping equipment, the independent option is a decidedly more adventurous affair. But with camping fees costing just AU$6.85 per night, it's also an absolute bargain.

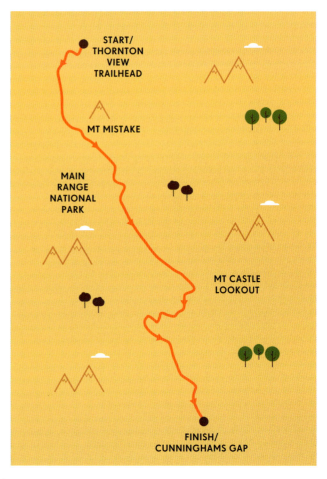

START/
THORNTON
VIEW
TRAILHEAD

MT MISTAKE

MAIN
RANGE
NATIONAL
PARK

MT CASTLE
LOOKOUT

FINISH/
CUNNINGHAMS GAP

The Spicers option, I learned, brings new meaning to a hiking experience. Independent hikers can't miss the abandoned relics from the region's logging days that dot the trail, but my two expert guides Ellie and Hayden brought this pioneer heritage – as well as the region's little-known Aboriginal history – to life with their evocative commentary. Rather than hampering the hike, the 'Black Summer' bushfires that affected parts of the trail in late 2019 (delaying its opening until mid-2020) also created meaningful talking points along the way.

Guided groups (capped at 12 guests) are also treated to a luggage shuttle service, making the hike more accessible to walkers who may not be able to carry a heavy load. Not exactly hike-fit myself following months homebound by Australia's coronavirus lockdowns, I was particularly grateful to be carrying only a light day-pack on day one, which begins with a long, uphill climb to the ridgeline through a eucalypt forest on a Spicers-owned property, where bright green epicormic growth was rapidly engulfing trees blackened by the fires of the previous summer. After the heavens opened upon us during a vertigo-inducing ladder climb at the top, I was even happier to be welcomed to Spicers Mt Mistake Farmhouse later that afternoon with a glass of bubbles. I could get used to this type of hiking, I thought, as I readily accepted a top-up.

> *"Taking us through a waterfall wonderland, the third day was my favourite – despite the horror of removing my gaiters in the afternoon to discover that a leech had been snacking on my shin"*

The landscape changed so abruptly the next morning as we entered the national park, it felt like stepping through a magic wardrobe into a Narnia-like fantasy land. As we peeled off one by one to maximise the benefits of *shinrin-yoku* – a Japanese term meaning 'forest bathing' – I allowed my real-world stress to melt into the verdant tangle of green.

Home to plant and animal species relatively unchanged from their ancestors in the fossil record, the otherworldly rainforest backdrop is the indisputable star of the Scenic Rim Trail. But on the Spicers' experience, the accommodation comes a close second.

Designed to have the smallest possible environmental footprint without compromising on comfort, the two off-grid 'eco-camps' that housed us for the next two nights comprised a string of cosy sleeping cabins connected by a central walkway to a communal lounge and dining room where, after each long day on the trail, we were treated to sumptuous dinners that left camp-stove meals for dead.

EXTEND YOUR HIKE

Spicers Retreats also hosts two- and three-day guided hiking experiences in the southern section of Main Range National Park, just across the Cunningham Hwy, that can be tacked on to the four- or five-day experience. Guided day walks include a vigorous climb to the summit of Mt Mathieson, with glamping accommodation at Spicers Canopy. Top off each day with a relaxing soak in the outdoor hot tub – and a decadent three-course dinner showcasing local produce.

Clockwise, from above: Gondwana Rainforests canopy; Scenic Rim overnight amid the eucalypts; wildlife of the Gondwana – satin bowerbird and orchard swallowtail butterfly. Previous page: Scenic Rim views in Main Range National Park

Almost identical in design, the two eco-camps are tucked well off the main trail, which adds around 10km (6.2 miles) to the standard 47km (29-mile) route. Though with creature comforts at the public camps limited to a composting toilet and a rainwater tank, independent hikers deserve the short cut.

Taking us through a waterfall wonderland, the third day on the trail was my favourite – despite the horror of removing my gaiters in the afternoon to discover that a leech had been snacking on my shin. This is an Aussie rainforest after all, and getting intimate with its creepy crawlies is all part of the adventure.

Native wildlife and birds prove to be more difficult to spot along the trail, with the dense foliage providing the perfect camouflage. Though I was thrilled to spot two beautifully patterned carpet pythons and a skittish wallaby along the way, along with a rainbow of butterflies.

Scrambling up to the Bare Rock (1168m/3832ft) lookout on day four, a gorgeous spot to enjoy our wholesome packed lunch while soaking up the views across the rolling farmlands below, we encountered the first people outside our group since beginning our journey. It was the first hint that civilisation wasn't far away and, sure enough, the faint hum of traffic gradually grew louder as we began our descent into Cunninghams Gap, where a highway linking the Darling Downs to Brisbane weaves through the bottom of the valley.

As we neared the bottom, part of me didn't want to leave our rainforest cocoon. But after ripping off my gaiters at the end of the trail to find another leech preparing to tuck into its own lunch, I was suddenly glad to retire my hiking gear – until my next tramp, at least. **SR**

ORIENTATION

Start // Thornton View Trailhead, Thornton
Finish // Cunninghams Gap, Cunningham Hwy
Distance // 47km (29.2 miles)
Duration // 4 days
Getting there // The trailhead is 110km (68.4 miles) or a 1.5-hr drive southwest of Brisbane. Arrange a drop-off, or do a car shuffle with a fellow hiker.
When to go // April to September, when conditions are cooler and dryer. Spicers offers a different route from December to February that avoids the worst of the summer heat.
What to wear // Hiking boots with ankle support and light, long-sleeved clothing.
What to pack // Gaiters; heavy duty insect repellent.
Where to stay // Spicers Hidden Vale, Grandchester.
Where to eat // Homage Restaurant, Spicers Hidden Vale.
Tours // Book Spicers Retreats' Scenic Rim Trail hikes at spicersretreats.com/scenic-rim-trail
More info // parks.des.qld.gov.au

Opposite, clockwise from top: catch some cascades on the Twin Falls Circuit, Springbrook National Park; stream lily in flower, Lamington National Park; hiking the Lamington trails

MORE LIKE THIS
RAINFOREST RICHES

TWIN FALLS CIRCUIT, SPRINGBROOK NP, QUEENSLAND

When time is short, this gorgeous hike in the Gold Coast hinterland offers a great taste of the Gondwana Rainforests. The best way to experience the walk is by following the trail in an anti-clockwise direction, starting from either the Tallanbana Trailhead or the Canyon Lookout. Signposted along the way, it's a fairly easy route that passes behind two stunning waterfalls and among ancient brush box trees. Want more? This trail forms part of the Warrie Circuit, a 14km (8.7-mile) trek that takes five to six hours to complete. Sturdy footwear is recommended for both trails, which can get slippery behind the falls, even when it looks dry.
Start/Finish // Tallanbana Trailhead or Canyon Lookout
Distance // 4km (2.5 miles) return
Duration // 2hr

COOMERA CIRCUIT, LAMINGTON NP, QUEENSLAND

The Coomera Circuit is a blockbuster day-hike offering some knockout scenery: rainforest-covered cliffs, verdant forest and some ravishing cascades, including the Coomera and Yarrabilgong waterfalls, which plunge into a 160m-deep (525ft) gorge. It's one of the most breathtaking walks in the Binna Burra section of southeast Queensland's Lamington National Park. Kicking off from the Binna Burra upper day-use area, it's recommended to follow the trail in an anti-clockwise direction. You'll leave the Border Track after 1.9km (1.2 miles) to ascend along the edge of the Coomera Gorge. As you follow the path of the Coomera River, keep your eyes peeled for the chance to see the bright blue-and-white Lamington spiny crayfish. There are a few river crossings before rejoining the Border Track and returning to the trailhead.
Start/Finish // Binna Burra upper day-use area
Distance // 17.4km (10.8 miles) return
Duration // 7hr

BRINDLE CREEK WALKING TRACK, BORDER RANGES NP, NEW SOUTH WALES

Don't forget to pack your swimwear for this beautiful walk in the high country of northern NSW – there are plenty of places to take a dip along the way, including Evan Falls. The Brindle Creek Walking Track follows a creek line through misty rainforest and is a highlights reel of the most spectacular scenery of the Border Ranges National Park: you'll pass ancient, looming Antarctic beech trees and massive hoop pines, and have the chance to spot the lovely helmholtzia lillies that thrive in the damp, moist air. Pack a picnic to enjoy at the Antarctic Beech Picnic Area, where bandicoots and pademelons might be your lunch guests. Leave plenty of time to return, retracing your steps to the Brindle Creek Picnic Area.
Start // Brindle Creek picnic area
Finish // Antarctic Beech picnic area
Distance // 6km (3.7 miles) one-way
Duration // 3-4hr

THE CAPE TO CAPE TRACK

One of Australia's finest overland hikes is this glorious coastal odyssey leading through WA's pristine southwest to take in dramatic ocean vistas, wildlife encounters and springtime wildflowers.

Normally it's the endpoint where hikers are rewarded with glorious all-encompassing, life-affirming views. Yet here I am, not even having taken a single step along Western Australia's epic 125km (78-mile) Cape to Cape Track, and I'm already being treated to the astonishing sight of frolicking humpback whales from atop Cape Naturaliste Lighthouse. With six days ahead of me, I can't help but wonder if I've peaked too early. But this aptly named hike – which spans from Cape Naturaliste to Cape Leeuwin – is bookended by two extraordinary viewpoints, so it's safe to assume an equally dramatic finish awaits.

As hard as it to drag myself away from this memorable sight, it's time to set off along the first 11km (6.8-mile) leg. I'm taking advantage of the free designated hiking campsites, so I head out with my tent and portable gas cooker. I've timed my run for mid-spring not only for the whale migration, but also for southwest WA's famous wildflower blooms.

Starting out along the cliff-top ridge, the wheelchair-friendly path snakes its way through low-lying heath to offer sweeping coastal views out over the Indian Ocean. At Wilanup Lookout I stop to see if I can spy more whales. Humpbacks aren't the only visitors to these waters, with southern right whales, dolphins and seals also regularly spotted, but no luck this time. Continuing further south brings me to Sugarloaf Rock, a hulking photogenic landmark that sits among crashing surf and where red-tailed tropicbirds plunge spectacularly in search of lunch.

Here the boardwalk trail finishes up to become an undulating gravel path that follows the contours of Leeuwin-Naturaliste Ridge and its namesake national park. And though Cape to

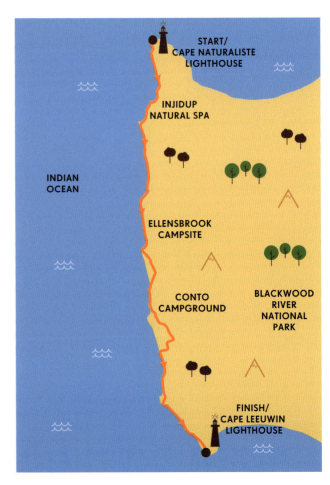

Cape is a relatively new trail (opening in 2001), this limestone ridge is one that's been traversed for some 45,000 years by the Indigenous Wardandi people.

Approaching my camp at Mt Duckworth, I pause to watch local surfers carve it up at the world-class Three Bears break, and arrive to set up my tent just before sunset.

Waking to the racket of cockatoos, day two's 23km (14.3-mile) walk begins with more bouquets of wildflowers as the path dissects lowland scrub before opening to ocean views and limestone cliffs. After 45 minutes the trail skirts the laidback beach town of Yallingup and then onto Smiths Beach with turquoise waters, bone-white sands and ochre lichen-flecked granite formations. It continues among rolling dunes to reach Canal Rocks, where I spot a glistening New Zealand fur seal basking in the sun. Passing Wyadup Bay, the next stop is Injidup Natural Spa, a scenic rock pool that tempts for a quick splash. But I continue ahead to a sheltered string of beaches before taking the final 5km (3.1-mile) stretch through more wildflower trails to arrive at Moses Rock and its ripper surf beach and campsite among peppermint woodland.

On day three the single-track leads through coastal scrub before another beach walk and up among the clifftops for stupendous views. One of today's highlights is the towering Wilyabrup Cliffs, where I take the stairs down to view them from the beach as folk abseil down its cliffface. Moving

"I've timed my run for mid-spring not only for the whale migration, but also for southwest WA's famous wildflower blooms"

along I pass Margaret River's famous surf beaches and the seaside hamlet of Gracetown, before continuing among flower-filled landscapes contrasted with dramatic seascapes and spectacular limestone formations. Rounding out the 19km (11.8-mile) day I pass Meekadarabee Falls to arrive at Ellensbrook campsite before 5pm.

Day four begins among jarrah forest before rejoining the coastal ridge. Passing the spectacular white sands of Kilcarnup Beach and the limestone cliffs at Cape Mentelle, I arrive at the mouth of Margaret River – Cape to Cape's halfway point. In winter you'll have to wade across waist deep (if you can cross at all), but today I'm able to time my run with the incoming tide to continue on to the coastal township of Prevelly. The path winds back inland among a forested stretch of impressive grasstrees and wildflowers before the ocean reappears as I pass by coastal heath. Crossing Boodjidup Brook I reach a 300-stair descent and am thankful I'm not coming the other way. I'm back again along soft sand to arrive at the blinding white sands of Redgate Beach, before taking lunch at Bobs Hollow, a scenic shelter

WILDFLOWERS

If Cape to Cape's coastal wilderness wasn't spectacular enough, come spring (August to November) a dazzling new layer of beauty is added as native wildflowers pop in a multitude of colours. From flowering shrubs and trees to endemic orchids and everlastings, there are some 8000 species to tick off your list. To get to know your cowslips from cockies tongues, bring along a wildflower booklet available from local tourist info centres.

From far left: hiking the Cape to Cape at Margaret River; surfing Three Bears break near Sugarloaf Rock; sulphur-crested cockatoo. Previous page: spot humpback whales and dolphins from lofty Cape Naturaliste Lighthouse

among limestone cliffs. From here it's a three-hour trek to Conto Campground, a national park campsite that needs to be booked in advance. Here I'm treated to some of the best cliff-top views of the trip, and where I'm very fortunate to spot a pod of dolphins pass by.

The penultimate day starts out with a beautiful walk amid the towering karri trees of Boranup Forest before returning to a single-track at Boranup Beach for a 7km (4.3-mile) stretch to Hamelin Bay. I witness the cool sight of local resident stingrays gathering to feed in the shallows. It's another hill climb through dunes overlooking Foul Bay (nicer than it sounds) before reaching Cosy Corner and its spectacular blowholes. Further ahead I get my first glimpse of my final destination, Cape Leeuwin lighthouse, from where it's a 45-minute walk to Deepdene Campsite.

And that brings us to our final day. I start along a wild stretch of surf beach, before scrambling over boulders and wading shin-high through river crossings, and then I reach the home straight along Augusta Sea Cliffs. I admire the stalactite-like formations at Quarry Bay, before passing the limestone-encrusted Leeuwin Waterwheel, and then the magical moment arrives: Cape Leeuwin Lighthouse. The largest lighthouse (c.1895) on mainland Australia, and what a fitting finale it is to stand at Australia's most southwesterly point with a sense of satisfaction of having completed this wonderful wilderness coastal hike. **TH**

ORIENTATION

Start // Cape Naturaliste lighthouse
Finish // Cape Leeuwin lighthouse
Distance // 125km (78 miles)
Duration // 5-8 days, or broken into individual sections
Getting there // Cape Naturaliste is 263km (163 miles) southwest of Perth. Transwa (transwa.wa.gov.au) and Southwest Coach Lines (southwestcoachlines.com.au) run buses between Perth and the Cape's gateway town, Dunsborough.
When to go // All year; Aug-Nov for wildflowers and whales.
What to pack // All-weather hiking gear; sturdy boots; hat; hiking tent; camp supplies; water filter; bug spray; sunscreen.
Where to stay // There are four free hiking campsites, plus paid campgrounds, and accommodation in the townships.
Where to eat // Eat in the townships or cook campsite meals.
Things to know // Bring ample water: rainwater tanks can run dry.
More info // capetocapetrack.com.au

Opposite, from top: Cape Woolamai's red-rock Pinnacles; Point Cartwright Lighthouse in Mooloolaba, endpoint of the Caloundra Coastal Walk

MORE LIKE THIS
OCEANSIDE HIKES

CALOUNDRA COASTAL WALK, QUEENSLAND

Showcasing Caloundra's string of glorious white sandy beaches is this scenic Sunshine Coast walk overlooking sparkling azure waters. Starting out at the aptly named Golden Beach, you'll gaze out over the sheltered waters of Moreton Bay Marine Park where Bribie Island sits out on the Pumicestone Passage famous for birds, dolphins and dugongs. Follow the beach promenade to loop around Bullock Beach and Happy Valley before arriving on the inviting sands of Kings Beach with its rock pools and oceanfront saltwater pool. Dicky Beach and Wurtulla Beach are next where cafes, fish and chips and breweries lure in passers-by. You'll then pass the surf beach of Kawana before the trail skirts Pacific Blvd to reach Point Cartwright Lighthouse in Mooloolaba. Keep an eye out for migratory humpback whales that are regularly spotted from July to late October.
Start // Golden Beach
Finish // Mooloolaba
Distance // 25km (15.5 miles), one-way
Duration // 6hr, one-way

CAPE WOOLAMAI CIRCUIT WALK, VICTORIA

Hidden away on the southeast of Victoria's famed Phillip Island is Cape Woolamai and its scenic walking trails through beautiful coastal landscapes. And with its dramatic windswept cliff-tops, big surf and wildlife encounters, it's very much in the same mould as Cape to Cape, perhaps with the exception of the warmer weather. The trail starts out along the east side of Cape Woolamai to take you by rugged beaches and historical remnants from its 19th-century granite quarry. Be sure to keep an eye out for wallabies, whales and the shearwater colony that make the epic journey to and from Alaska each year. Next you'll pass Phillip Island's highest point at the Beacon (112m/367ft) before continuing along the cliff trail for another spectacular lookout over the Pinnacles with its craggy sci-fi-looking rock formations. Returning via the west coast, enjoy the views of Cowrie Bay and its lefthander before finishing at Cape Woolamai beach with more great surf and an ocean-side kiosk for a well-earned milkshake.
Start/Finish // Woolamai Surf Beach
Distance // 8.5km (5.3-mile) loop
Duration // 3hr
More info // visitbasscoast.com.au/cape-woolamai-walks

BUSHRANGERS BAY TRAIL, VICTORIA

If you enjoyed Cape to Cape's cliff-top coastal views and remote lighthouses, then you'll love Cape Schanck's Bushrangers Bay. Located on the southernmost tip of Victoria's Mornington Peninsula National Park, this 2.6km (1.6 miles; one-way) wilderness trail starts at Cape Schanck's beautiful 19th-century lighthouse. Climb up on a guided tour while looking out for whales and views over the volcanic plug of Pulpit Rock that sits out at sea. The walk takes you eastwards along a spectacular basalt cliff path offering great views over Bass Strait and its rocky bays. Leading through coastal banksia woodlands, it then loops around to beautiful Bushrangers Bay with wilder ocean panoramas, remote beaches and unique rock formations. If you want to keep going, you can opt for the Two Bays Walking Track, which runs 26km (16.2 miles) from Cape Schanck to the seaside town of Dromana.
Start/Finish // Cape Schanck Lighthouse
Distance // 5.2km (3.2 miles) return
Duration // 2hr
More info // visitmorningtonpeninsula.org/PlacesToGo/Walks.aspx

THE K'GARI/FRASER ISLAND GREAT WALK

Make the journey across to this island wilderness escape to walk among ever-changing landscapes of native shaggy forest, stunning freshwater lakes, rugged beaches and memorable wildlife encounters.

As I board the barge for the short journey from Queensland's Rainbow Beach to Fraser Island (K'gari), it's clear there are two types of visitors here – those with 4WDs and those with hiking boots. It's the latter I belong to as I prepare to tackle the world's largest sandy island on foot. While this epic hike can be broken down into individual sections, I'm here to do the entire Great Walk in one go. It's a 90km (56-mile), seven-day, self-sufficient adventure that follows the steps of the Butchulla people, the Traditional Owners, who've roamed K'gari for some 50,000 years.

Translating as 'paradise', the World Heritage-listed K'gari is a different kind of paradise to Queensland's tropical island cliché. Forget the palm trees and poolside cocktails; this here is your true rugged outdoor wilderness.

The island has two points of arrival. Those coming from Hervey Bay arrive at Kingfisher Bay to the west; others arrive at the southern tip where I disembark at Hook Point. From here most hikers arrange transport to the official starting point at Dilli Village, but my pack's straight on my back as I wave goodbye to the 4WD brigade and take off along the forested inland path for this first 'unofficial' 25km (15.5-mile) leg. After a few hours the undulating forest track opens up to grasstrees and Jabiru Swamp, where I stop to take lunch at the first hikers' campsite. It's then on through banksia and coastal shrub to arrive at Dilli Village campground by 4pm, and after pitching my tent I immediately head to the beach. Heeding the local's strong advice not to swim – due to both sharks and rips – I don't dare to venture past my knees.

The next day marks the official start of the hike and continues deeper into the island's interior through twisted trees and bushy

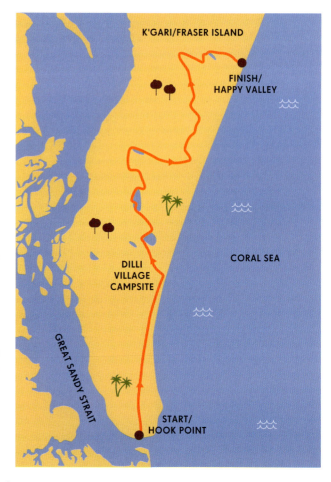

K'GARI/FRASER ISLAND

FINISH/ HAPPY VALLEY

DILLI VILLAGE CAMPSITE

CORAL SEA

GREAT SANDY STRAIT

START/ HOOK POINT

foxtail ferns. After 6.3km (4 miles), I make my first stop at the freshwater Lake Boomanjin. This is the world's largest perched lake (meaning it's fed by rainwater and not any other system), and makes a wonderful stop for morning tea and a bracing dip in its tea-coloured waters. From here I enter a patch of ancient rainforest where staghorn ferns, palm lilies and towering kauri offer me my first true glimpse of K'gari's biodiversity. After 7.2km (4.5 miles) I arrive at the beguiling Lake Benaroon to take lunch under the shade of a paperbark tree. Making good time, I sneak in another swim (how could one resist a lake as beautiful as this?) before continuing to Central Station. I skirt the blue waters of Lake Birrabeen, with its chalky white sands and melaleucas, before joining the old logging road through endemic forests of brushbox and towering satinay to reach Lake Jennings. Passing K'gari's central dunes, the trail continues among eucalyptus, kauri, palms and strangler figs before reaching tonight's campsite at Central Station.

The following day starts along a boardwalk meandering through the rainforest to cross the tranquil Wanggoolba Creek, with its white sandy floor and glass-clear waters. The track heads along the dune ridge into another eucalypt forest from where emerges the superb Basin Lake. Ringed by white sand, it's a real stunner and I'm fortunate to have the place to myself for my morning swim, save for a white-bellied sea eagle that soars above.

A further two-hour hike brings me to Lake McKenzie. With its pristine, crystal-clear waters meeting fetching soft white sands, it's all so utterly perfect it looks Photoshopped. As if that's not magical enough, I spot my first dingo trotting alongside the lake. This here's my campsite for the evening, and after setting up my tent I return to take in a superb sunset to close out the day.

On day four I loop around Lake McKenzie through picturesque rainforest before heading into shady woodland over dunes,

DINGOES

K'gari's dingoes are the island's most famous residents and are believed to be Australia's purest bred population. You can be certain to encounter them at some point, and it's advised to never feed them and always give them a wide berth – especially during breeding season (March to May) and weaning season (September to October) when they can be on the feisty side. If you're a solo hiker, a trusty 'dingo stick' (ie any old trailside stick) can come in handy as protection.

Clockwise from above: tea-tree tannins colour the Lake Boomanjin waters; wild K'gari – kookaburra and a beachgoing dingo.
Previous page: lovely Lake McKenzie

where I see a massive goanna strutting ahead. And if I thought Lake McKenzie was spectacular, Lake Wabby is even better. Encroached by thick forest and a massive sand dune tumbling to its shore, it's truly a unique sight. And here I do what most tourists do: I trundle down to plunge into its emerald waters.

With another 16.2km (10 miles) to my campsite to go, I return to the ridge trail to pass the desolate Badjala Sandblow, where I see more dingoes making their way through the sparse vegetation. Passing dry woodland I then enter a beautiful corridor of rainforest where I don't need a map to know that I've arrived at the Valley of the Giants. These are some of the biggest trees on the island. I crane my neck to look up towards massive 70m-tall (230ft) satinays, kauri and brushbox – some that date back 1000 years. And the best bit is my campsite's right among them.

The last day begins with a delightful walk through a lush valley of intertwined vines, banksia and grasstrees before joining the old logging track past Bogimbah Creek to arrive at Lake Garawongera. I take time to enjoy its beautiful white sands and paperbark trees before the forested track turns to sand as I reach the finishing point at the coastal settlement of Happy Valley. And like a welcoming gift, I'm fortunate to see humpback whales offshore as I enjoy a cold beer and reflect on what truly was a Great Walk. And like that, my pre-booked island taxi arrives to take me down the 75 Mile Beach road to where the barge awaits to take me back to the mainland. **TH**

ORIENTATION

Start // Hook Point
Finish // Happy Valley
Distance // 90km (56 miles)
Duration // 5-8 days
Getting there // Flights land at Hervey Bay, 300km (186 miles) north of Brisbane; catch a barge from here or Rainbow Beach.
When to go // March to December
What to pack // All-weather hiking gear; sturdy boots; hat; hiking tent; camp supplies; water filter; bug spray; sunscreen.
Where to stay // As well as designated hike-in campsites, there are lodges in Dilli Village and Happy Valley. Book through parks.des.qld.gov.au/camping
Where to eat // It's self-sufficiency outside the townships.
Tours // Fraser Island Hiking (fraserislandhiking.com)
Things to know // Pre-book rides with Fraser Island Taxi Service (www.fraserservice.com.au), the only transport option.

Opposite, from top: a sundown surf at Noosa Heads; Dripstone Beach, Casuarina Coastal Reserve

MORE LIKE THIS
SHORESIDE STROLLS

CASUARINA COASTAL RESERVE, NORTHERN TERRITORY

Making up part of Darwin's 1500-hectare Casuarina Coastal Reserve is this foreshore coastal walk that takes in the city's finest beaches and famous Timor Sea sunsets. Add in pubs, crocs, WWII relics and a nudist beach and you've got yourself a very Darwin-themed trail. At low-tide you could walk all the way along the beach from Rapid Creek to Buffalo Creek (if you're prepared to risk the crocs, that is), otherwise the shared sealed cyclist-pedestrian path from Nightcliff to Casuarina Beach is the way to go. It starts along a promenade lined with palms and namesake casuarina trees to pass grassy areas ripe for picnics. From here it opens up to ocean views before reaching Darwin's only jetty as you cross over Rapid Creek footbridge where locals fish for barra. At Dripstone Cliffs you'll encounter ruins of WWII observation posts dating to 1939, and then finish up at Darwin Surf Life Saving Club with its inviting cafe.

Start // Casuarina Drive, Nightcliff
Finish // Casuarina Beach
Distance // 6km (3.7 miles) one-way
Duration // 2hr
More info // nt.gov.au/leisure/parks-reserves/find-a-park/find-a-park-to-visit/casuarina-coastal-reserve

THURRA RIVER DUNES WALK, VICTORIA

While K'gari/Fraser Island may be up north and Victoria's Croajingolong National Park in East Gippsland is way down south, the scenery is surprisingly similar. Along with its pristine coastal hinterland of rugged, isolated surf and bushland, Thurra River is famous for its dunes that soar 30m (98ft) high to provide wonderful views over Bass Strait. The walk here leads through coastal scrub and banksia before hitting unmarked sandy trails that'll lead you to the dunes. The descending return leg has you splashing your way past the beautiful clear tannin-coloured waters of Thurra River to lead you back to your campsite. This region was affected by the 2020 bushfires, so check the conditions before setting out.

Start/Finish // Thurra River campground
Distance // 4km (2.5 miles) return
Duration // 2hr
More info // parks.vic.gov.au/places-to-see/sites/thurra-river

NOOSA HEADS COASTAL TRACK, QUEENSLAND

Just south of K'gari/Fraser Island on the mainland lies Noosa, one of Queensland's premier holiday destinations. As well as stunning beaches, you'll find some wonderful walks through coastal hinterland national park. Starting out from Noosa Heads, this coastal trail follows a beach boardwalk past white powdery sands to lead onto a shady, well-built track overlooking the exquisite Little Cove Beach. Entering the national park you'll be treated to spectacular coastal vistas at Boiling Pot, Granite Bay and Hell's Gates, a mix of rocky headlands interspersed with picture-perfect beaches with shimmering aquamarine waters. Pause at Dolphin Point to see if you can spot any out there, or otherwise, if lucky, migrating humpbacks that pass through June and November. Here the path becomes an unsealed track as it winds around dramatic coastal viewpoints that lead south down over cliff edges overlooking Alexandria Bay and Devil's Kitchen.

Start/Finish // Noosa Heads main beach
Distance // 10.8km (6.7 miles) return
Duration // 4hr
More info // parks.des.qld.gov.au/parks/noosa/journeys/coastal-walk

DAINTREE RAINFOREST CIRCUIT

Feel the ancient energy of the Daintree Rainforest on an accessible tramp in one of the World Heritage Site's most magical corners, where living dinosaurs still roam.

How incredible are rainforests? Immersed in these verdant cathedrals of life, I find it impossible not to be awed, not only by their raw natural beauty but also by the crucial role these biodiversity powerhouses play in supporting life on earth.

This awe was magnified when I stepped into Tropical North Queensland's Daintree Rainforest for the first time. For the Daintree is no ordinary rainforest. Stretching for some 70km (43.5 miles) from Mossman Gorge north to the Bloomfield River, this magnificent tangle of greenery is the world's oldest continually surviving tropical rainforest. A real-life Jurassic Park, it's home to descendants of plants and animals that shared this coastal wilderness area with the dinosaurs, including the formidable cassowary, a large flightless bird with dagger-like talons you wouldn't want to find yourself on the receiving end of.

Today, a 735 sq km (284 sq miles) expanse of the Daintree is protected by Daintree National Park, which is split into two sections. The heart of the Daintree lies in the Cape Tribulation section north of the Daintree River, reached by car ferry. But the more accessible Mossman Gorge section, just a 20-minute drive from Port Douglas, is just as beautiful.

I had assumed that such an iconic national park would be laced with hiking trails, so I was surprised to discover that there are only a handful of mostly short public walks in the Daintree. But I quickly learned that a long hike isn't necessary to experience the wonder of this special place, maintained for millennia by a number of Traditional Owner groups, particularly the Eastern Kuku Yalanji people, who took official ownership of the park in 2021.

In the Mossman Gorge section, the Rainforest Circuit is one of the Daintree's most popular trails. Visiting this section of the park begins with a 2km (1.2-mile) shuttle bus ride from the Indigenous-run Mossman Gorge Centre (which runs every 15 minutes), from where the elevated, 660m-long (0.4 mile) Baral Marrjanga Track leads me through the rainforest to a spectacular lookout over the Mossman River. Many visitors don't make it past this popular crocodile-free swimming spot, where gin-clear water cascades over huge granite boulders. It's tempting to join the dozen-odd people splashing around in the rock pools on this sultry afternoon, but I leave my boots on for now, keen to hike deeper into the World Heritage Site first.

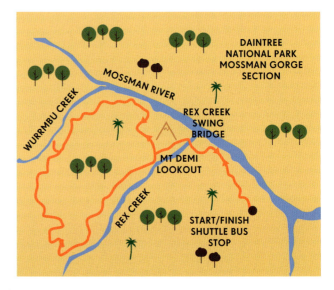

"Breathing in the clean rainforest air, I feel instantly more relaxed – the Daintree is the ultimate natural mood booster"

Crossing a suspension bridge just beyond the swimming area, I take a minute to enjoy the view of the rainforest-covered peak of Manjal Dimbi (Mt Demi) from a lookout right before the Rainforest Circuit trailhead. Weaving alongside Rex Creek before looping back alongside Wurrmbu Creek, the well-maintained dirt path is impossibly lush thanks to the steep mountain ranges rising up behind the gorge, which trap moisture from the nearby ocean, ensuring frequent rainfall. Breathing in the clean rainforest air, I feel instantly more relaxed. There's some science behind this, with research finding that a chemical released by trees and plants called phytoncides can help to reduce stress. With more than 3300 plant species found in the Daintree, it's the ultimate natural mood booster.

With some stairs and obstacles such as tree roots to navigate, the Rainforest Circuit – combined with intense, year-round humidity – may be challenging for small children and mobility restricted visitors. But for me it's an easy meander that I could have completed in less than an hour had I not made frequent stops to read the information panels detailing the rainforest's ecological and cultural importance, marvel at unusual fungi sprouting from the forest floor, and admire the lush mosses and ferns dripping from the ancient rainforest trees lining the path. Several short side trails lead to a rock shelter possibly once used by the Kuku Yalanji, a giant strangler fig, and several creek access points. I'm tempted to have a quiet dip at one of them, but opt instead to stay dry for now.

Along the way I spot patches of the forest floor disturbed by wild pigs – a key threat, along with climate change, to the Daintree's survival – and hear rainforest birds chattering away in the canopy. My wildlife sightings, however, are limited to butterflies. The wider Wet Tropics Area may be home to more than 700 species of vertebrate animals – including 35% of Australia's mammal species alone – but it's not easy to spot the creatures of the Daintree, who are the ultimate masters of camouflage.

There was one particular critter, however, that I really hoped to see. Known as Jalbil in the Kuku Yalanji language, the Boyd's forest dragon is essentially a living dinosaur. Growing to about 16cm (6.3in) long and sporting an impressive array of facial spines, this relic of the Jurassic era is known to cling to rainforest tree trunks in the Mossman Gorge area. But as hard as I looked, these striking agamids, which can change colour to regulate their body temperature, eluded me. Luckily, I was visiting Mossman Gorge with Aaron Port, a Kuku Yalanji guide from Walkabout Cultural Adventures, who has deep knowledge of the rainforest passed down over generations – including a knack for spotting these elusive lizards. Sure enough, when we meet up at the end of the Rainforest Circuit for a swim, Aaron locates a Jalbil hidden in plain sight on a tree trunk right beside the trail. Prone to remaining fixed to their resting spot upon the approach of danger, the dragon sat perfectly still as we marvelled at this incredible species, the proverbial icing on a superb rainforest hike. **SR**

Clockwise, from far left: cassowary in the Daintree forest; Mossman Gorge rainforest pool; clear waters at Mossman Creek. Previous page: strangler fig at Mossman Gorge

ORIENTATION

Start/Finish // Mossman Gorge Centre
Distance // 3.4km (2.1-mile) circuit
Duration // 1-2hr
Getting there // There's parking at the Mossman Gorge Centre, 80km (50 miles) north of Cairns.
When to go // It's generally safer to swim in the Mossman River during the dry season (April-October).
What to pack // Don't forget your swimwear.
Where to stay // Enjoy a night at recently reopened Silky Oaks Lodge on the banks of the Mossman River.
Where to eat // Sample traditional rainforest foods at the Mossman Gorge Centre's Mayi Cafe and Restaurant.
Tours // The Mossman Gorge Centre also offers Indigenous-led Dreamtime Walks on trails used by Kuku Yalanji since time immemorial.
More info // mossmangorge.com.au; parks.des.qld.gov.au

Opposite, from top: Jindalba
Boardwalk, Daintree National Park;
look out for crimson rosella parrots
on the Murray Scrub Walking Track,
Toonumbar National Park

MORE LIKE THIS
LUSH RAINFOREST CIRCUITS

JINDALBA CIRCUIT TRACK, DAINTREE NATIONAL PARK, QUEENSLAND

In the Cape Tribulation section of Daintree National Park, the Jindalba Circuit Track takes hikers deep into dense lowland rainforest at the base of Mt Alexandra (Jindalba means 'foot of the mountain' in the Kuku Yalanji language). Cassowaries are known to roam this corner of the Daintree, and you might also be lucky enough to spot musky rat-kangaroos foraging on the forest floor and Bennett's tree-kangaroos hanging out in the canopy. While it's not a long track, the dirt path is rocky in places, and there are a few creek crossings, so sturdy shoes are recommended. For an easier walk, take a stroll on the 650m (0.4-mile) Jindalba Boardwalk, which makes a loop inside the Jindalba Circuit Track.

Start/Finish // Jindalba day-use area
Distance // 3km (1.9-mile) circuit
Duration // 1.5hr
More info // parks.des.qld.gov.au/ parks/daintree/journeys/jindalba-circuit-track

MURRAY SCRUB WALKING TRACK, TOONUMBAR NATIONAL PARK, NEW SOUTH WALES

Like the Daintree, the lush Gondwana Rainforests of Australia date back to the birth of the continent some 180 million years ago. Around a 2-hour drive west of Byron Bay in northern NSW, lesser-known Toonumbar National Park forms part of this lush World Heritage Area. Immerse yourself in this ancient wilderness on the Murray Scrub Walking Track, an easy stroll through forests of Bangalow palms and huge strangler figs. Listen out for the calls of rare songbirds as you near the highlight of the walk: an incredible stand of old-growth red cedar trees towering over you. For the best chances of spotting wildlife such as the red-legged pademelon, come on a hot day after rain, when wildlife activity peaks.

Start/Finish // Murray Scrub car park
Distance // 5.5km (3.4-mile) loop
Duration // 2-3hr
More info // nationalparks.nsw.gov.au/ things-to-do/walking-tracks/murray-scrub-walking-track

QUEEN MARY FALLS CIRCUIT, MAIN RANGE NATIONAL PARK, QUEENSLAND

Less than a 2-hour drive southwest of Brisbane, Main Range National Park also forms part of the Gondwana Rainforests. Among its most scenic short trails is this circuit in the Queen Mary Falls section of the park, near the town of Killarney. If you want to go easy on the legs, it's best to follow the trail in a clockwise direction. The walk kicks off along a ridgeline dense with eucalyptus trees, so don't forget to look up to try and spot koalas. The views up here take in the rainforested gorge and the waters of Spring Creek, diving 40m (131ft) over the falls and creating a magical display of rainbows in the mist. If it's a steamy Queensland summer day, you'll be keen to follow the trail to the valley floor where the waterfall mist provides a refreshing cool-off.

Start/Finish // Queen Mary Falls picnic area
Distance // 2km circuit (1.2 miles)
Duration // 40min
More info // parks.des.qld.gov.au/ parks/main-range/journeys/queen-mary-falls-circuit

THE BIBBULMUN TRACK (WALPOLE)

Sample the best of WA's South West on this ramble from idyllic sheltered inlets through ancient karri and tingle forests to a remote coastal 'wilderness'.

Under an ashen sky the relentless Southern Ocean batters the granite rocks of desolate Aldridge Cove. The wind is howling and the spray drenching as I locate a small plaque dedicated to a walker who never made it home. On a good day, some would choose to swim here, but it's a lonesome spot and the feeling of isolation, exposure and my own fragility is both oppressive and exhilarating. I stay high on the granite and feel the power of the elements until my face is raw and my hair full of salt. Only then do I return to my pack.

I'm in Nuyts Wilderness, an off-piste area adjoining the Bibbulmun Track near Walpole in Western Australia's wild South West. The Bib', WA's longest official walk, runs 963km (598 miles) from Kalamunda in the Perth Hills to Albany on the continent's ragged bottom edge. Modelled on the US Appalachian Trail, the relatively undemanding route (it's not a wilderness walk) links purpose-built campsites, existing campgrounds and the odd small town via a network of forestry roads, single-file footpaths, old 4WD fishing tracks and sandy beaches. Designed for through walkers, most campsites are spaced roughly a short day's walk apart and contain three-sided shelters, toilets and water tanks. The official route is well-marked by bright yellow Waugal – a symbolic representation of the

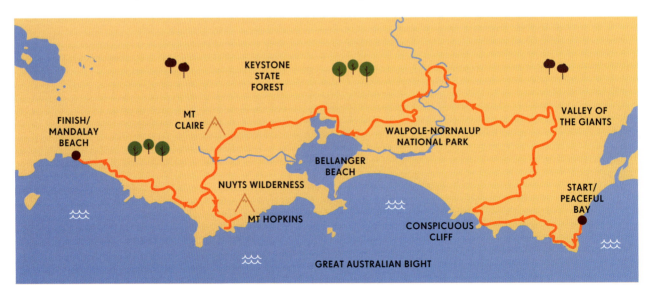

Rainbow Serpent, rather apt given the number of reptiles active in the warmer months.

Having only a week, I'd opted for a section of the Bib' on Wagyl Kaip Boodja around Walpole, combining both coastal and forest scenery. Six days ago, dropped at Peaceful Bay, a sleepy campground with a sheltered beach and ubiquitous fish and chips shop, a leisurely afternoon start saw me heading south along brilliant white sand hemmed by shallow turquoise waters. Climbing onto the coastal heath, the track provided dazzling views over the granite coast and wild Southern Ocean, each step revealing a new hidden cove or rocky headland, though whitecaps hindered whale spotting.

Turning inland, the route joined a 4WD track before reaching Rame Head where I'd chosen my cosy tent over a shelter full of school kids. The next day had involved climbing, first over the limestone Conspicuous Cliff with its incredible views, down to the adjacent beach, then a slow grind up into the magnificent karri and tingle forests of the Valley of the Giants, where massive ancient trees ringed the secluded (and thankfully empty) Giants campsite.

Walpole's forests are among the tallest on earth and day three had begun with a mesmerising stroll 40m (131ft) high in the canopy along the Tree Top Walk, followed by a ground-level appraisal of

the heavily buttressed bases of the red tingle, a striking eucalypt that grows exclusively in Walpole. Staying under the tall trees, I'd arrived at the lovely Frankland River campsite, spending a sunny afternoon on the riverbank.

Day four and more forest walking led to the Giant Tingle (another buttressed behemoth) before the route descended to the coast, arriving at Coalmine Beach where I spent the night in the privately run campground, choking at the price.

Collecting the rest of my food and fuel from the Walpole visitor centre, I'd then left town, the route meandering past empty holiday rentals before finally heading back into the forest and more karri and tingle action on the soggy climb to Mt Clare. The uninspiring, low granite slab summit and nearby dank shelter had soured my mood. I'd contemplated pushing on but the weather was tanking so I'd settled for a gourmet cookup with my new supplies and necked the local vino decanted from my water bladder.

Away early the next morning, I descended quickly through the forest to the Deep River suspension bridge. The vegetation changed rapidly, trees shrank then disappeared, replaced by wildflowers – kangaroo paws, chorizemas, dryandras – before sandy coastal heath studded with grass trees and yet another 4WD track. At a boot cleaning station the Bib' and its Waugals turned right but I stayed on the unsigned vehicle track and entered Nuyts Wilderness.

'Wilderness' here refers to a lack of signage and facilities, as the easily followed wheel ruts lead across the open heath directly to the coast. Mt Hopkins (205m/672ft) stood off to the east, a collection of granite boulders on a hilltop begging to be bagged. I relished the newfound sense of freedom after the strict regimentation of the Bib' and the scenery didn't disappoint – if not true wilderness, it was certainly wilder. Only a few kilometres from the busy Bibbulmun, Nuyts receives barely a trickle of visitors.

With my pack regained, I head down the spur to Thompson Cove, and set up camp by a copse of blackened trees. Badly burnt in recent times, the area's regrowth is now quite thick and it's a bush bash to the beach, a much nicer swim option than Aldridge Cove. With the afternoon still young, I head towards Mt Hopkins on a rough path that becomes progressively more overgrown. At 3km (1.8 miles) from camp, it takes about an hour but the summit views of the surrounding uninhabited coastline, inland lakes, remote islands and fragile ecosystems are the highlight of the trip so far, and I return to camp rejuvenated, falling asleep to the sound of the roiling sea.

Back among the Waugals the next morning, I take a quick side-trip to Hush Hush Beach with its steep cliffs, then push on, bypassing Long Point shelter, before several undulations drop me onto the fabulous Mandalay Beach, where I dawdle up the shining sand, processing what I've seen over the last week. And hoping my lift is waiting for me in the car park. **SW**

BIBBULMUN NOMENCLATURE

Noongar – the Indigenous inhabitants of southwestern Australia.
Bibbulmun – refers to the Noongar sub-group who once occupied the lands the trail traverses.
Boodja – a Noongar word for country.
Wagyl Kaip – southern Noongar clans whose lands range west from Point D'Entrecasteaux to Fitzgerald River.
Waugal – the Rainbow Serpent, a Creation being from the Dreaming.

Left, from top: towering red tingle eucalypt, Walpole; a fabulous finish for the Bibbulmun Track at Mandalay Beach Previous page: Aldridge Cove, Nuyts Wilderness

ORIENTATION

Start // Peaceful Bay
Finish// Mandalay Beach
Distance // 105km (65 miles)
Duration // 6-8 days
Getting there // TransWA buses connect Walpole to Perth and Albany. Naturally Walpole Tours offer trailhead transfers.
When to go // Year-round. Early spring for wildflowers (beware snakes); winter is mild and wet, summer hot and flyblown.
What to pack // Bibbulmun Track Map 7 (Walpole) covers the entire route. Take lightweight gear; rain jacket; gaiters; sleeping bag; compass; fuel stove. A tent, mosquito dome or bivvy bag will be needed where shelters are absent.
Things to know // Walpole visitor centre sells stove fuel and trail maps, and can arrange accommodation and transport.
More info // bibbulmuntrack.org.au; parks.dpaw.wa.gov.au; bushwalk.com

*Opposite, from top: kea parrots
on Arthur's Pass, Three Passes trail;
hike to aptly named Blue Lake on
the Te Araroa Trail*

MORE LIKE THIS
WALKING THE WILDERNESS

TE ARAROA TRAIL (NELSON LAKES TO LEWIS PASS), SOUTH ISLAND, NEW ZEALAND

Expand your hiking skills on a section of one of the world's greatest long distance tramps. This modified snippet from the 3000km (1864-mile) Te Araroa connects the mountain majesty of Nelson Lakes to the gentle open valleys of the St James Walkway. From West Bay follow the road to Mt Robert then pick up the marked track to Speargrass Hut. Sidle endless beech-cloaked ridges to Sabine Hut on Lake Rotoroa. Follow the Sabine upstream to Blue Lake where poles lead above the tree-line, past Lake Constance and over 1870m (6135ft) Waiau Pass, infamous for terrible weather. Once in the Waiau it's easy open walking and you can join the dots via Waiau, Christopher and Ada Pass huts to pop out at the picnic shelter at Lewis Pass.
Start // West Bay, St Arnaud
Finish // Lewis Pass
Distance // 95km (59 miles)
Duration // 8-10 days
More info // doc.govt.nz; teararoa.org.nz

THE THREE PASSES, CANTERBURY, SOUTH ISLAND, NEW ZEALAND

Excellent backcountry skills are required for this historic pounamu route crossing the Main Divide from Arthur's Pass to the wild West Coast. Walk up the Waimakariri River from Klondyke Corner, crisscrossing the east-flowing braids to Carrington Hut. Ascend steep Taipoiti Gorge then climb Harman Pass to the Ariel Tarns, a picturesque alpine bowl at the foot of permanently snow-covered Whitehorn Pass. Only attempt Whitehorn in good weather. A long scree descent leads to humble Park Morpeth Hut on the fast-flowing Wilberforce. Zigzag up Browning Pass to moody Lake Browning, then descend into the Arahura Valley, where Harman Hut appears in the distance. Traverse soggy Styx Saddle before emerging from the forest at Grassy Flat Hut. A long wet slog along the west-flowing Styx eventually brings the road-end.
Start // Klondyke Corner, Arthur's Pass
Finish // Lake Kaniere Rd, Hokitika
Distance // 53km (33 miles)
Duration // 4-6 days
More info // doc.govt.nz

KANGAROO ISLAND WILDERNESS TRAIL, SOUTH AUSTRALIA

Though the Kangaroo Island Wilderness Trail suffered significant damage in the 2019/2020 bushfires, infrastructure has since been rebuilt and the island is in recovery mode, with wildlife starting to return. It remains one of the best multi-day hikes in Australia, combining the rugged scenery of the Southern Ocean coastline with the botanical beauty of the Flinders Chase National Park. The trail hugs the west coast of the island and is accessible year-round, but the best time to come is during winter (June to August) to see beautiful orchids in bloom. It kicks off on day one at Rocky River, and over the course of five days hikers are taken through a diversity of habitats: past platypus waterholes; stunning cascades; breathtaking ocean views; the famous Cape du Couedic Lighthouse; the Remarkable Rocks. You finish up at the Kelly Hill limestone caves.
Start // Rocky River campground
Finish // Kelly Hill Conservation Park
Distance // 61km (37.9 miles)
Duration // 5 days
More info // parks.sa.gov.au/parks/ flinders-chase-national-park

THE THORSBORNE TRAIL

Sun, swims and short walking days are the lures on this four-day beach hop along the tropical shores of Australia's largest island national park.

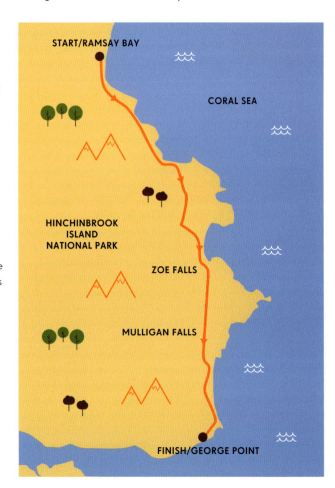

Beneath mountains that rise more than 1100m (3610ft) direct from the Coral Sea, waterfalls pour into cooling pools. Coconut palms angle over white-sand beaches and there's not another person in sight. It could be an idyllic scene from an exclusive tropical resort, were it not for the weight of my boots and the backpack on my shoulders.

I'm hiking on the Thorsborne Trail, which hugs the beach-lined east coast of Hinchinbrook Island, Australia's largest island national park, afloat off the Queensland coast midway between Cairns and Townsville. The morning ferry from Cardwell has dropped me in behind Ramsay Bay – the Thorsborne's northern trailhead – and I'm now walking south through the coral-littered sand.

The tone of the walk is set early, switching from beach to bush to beach, a pattern that will persist for the next four days. Ramsay Bay becomes the well-named Blacksand Beach, followed by a stark few minutes as the trail makes one of its few climbs of note, rising over the low shoulder of Nina Peak. A short side trail ascends to the top of this 312m (1024ft) peak, which is the Thorsborne's one true lofty vantage point. Stretching out below me are the long sweep of Ramsay Bay and the smaller beaches of Nina Bay and Little Ramsay Bay. Behind Ramsay Bay, channels run through the mangroves like veins through the land. This mass of mangroves – considered to be Australia's most diverse mangrove community – is visual evidence of an island with two very different personalities. The ocean coast traversed by the Thorsborne Trail is cut straight from the tropical-island playbook – beaches, palms, waterfalls – while the inside coast, along narrow Hinchinbrook Channel, is a wild soup of crocodiles. There are croc warning signs along the ocean beaches as well, but the fearsome animals are rarely sighted; no attacks have been reported here.

START/RAMSAY BAY

CORAL SEA

HINCHINBROOK ISLAND NATIONAL PARK

ZOE FALLS

MULLIGAN FALLS

FINISH/GEORGE POINT

"As I float in the pool, heat draining from my body, its resident fish nibble at my toes. It's a spa treatment from nature"

Like so many hikes, the best parts of the Thorsborne Trail may be its camps. On Little Ramsay Bay, less than 7km (4.3 miles) from where I set out, I pitch my tent in the sand and soak away the day's heat in a lagoon behind the beach. The island's highest mountains tower over the camp, and I cook and eat on the beach, where the only lights are my head torch and the stars.

The new day brings so many things, as is customary on Hinchinbrook. As I continue south towards Zoe Bay, there are rapid transitions in the bush. One minute I'm in rainforest, the next in a paperbark swamp and, just as soon again, back among mangroves. This one island is so many places. An opportunity to go for a swim presents in Banksia Creek, and in this heat a swim is never turned down. Another swim awaits at Zoe Bay, where I will camp this second night. It's not an ocean swim – crocodile warning signs caution against that bit of stupidity – but in a gorgeous pool at the base of Zoe Falls, about 15 minutes' walk inland from camp. Its clear waters are the most inviting sight of the day, and as I float in the pool, heat draining from my body, its resident fish nibble at my toes. It's a spa treatment from nature.

Dawn arrives the next morning as a red brush, painting first the mountaintops and then the beach, where a reef shark cruises the shore. This day's walk is one of the trail's shortest – 7km (4.3 miles) to Mulligan Falls – but arguably also the toughest. I begin back past Zoe Falls – another day, another swim – where the Thorsborne Trail's most sustained climb begins, ascending more than 200m (656ft). It's steep at first, scrambling beside the waterfall, at the top of which there's plunge pool after plunge pool with views over the treetops into Zoe Bay, now far below – infinity pools that are like something from Kakadu National Park with a view resembling the Bahamas.

For more than half a day, this creek will be my walking companion, rising on gently to the crest of a headland that's as far from the coast – about 3km (1.9 miles) – as I've been since arriving on the island. This crest feels like the beginning of the end because, for the first time, I can see Hinchinbrook Island's southern edge. Offshore, Orpheus (Goolboodi) Island and the Palm Islands rise from the sea, while Australia's longest jetty – 5.76km (3.58 miles) in length – pokes out from the mainland at Lucinda. The descent dips steeply in and out of creek beds, bottoming out at Mulligan Falls, where I will spend my final night on the island. From the campsite, I barely even need to walk to reach the namesake falls – I will hear them from my tent through the night.

I will venture to the waterfall several times this afternoon, including a final time after sunset. I have a long march along Mulligan Beach to George Point to come tomorrow, and a ferry ride back to the mainland, but as I stand in the pool at the base of Mulligan Falls, I'm soon surrounded by turtles and dozens of fish, with a tree snake watching down from the rocks above the pool. It's as though I've stepped into an aquarium, and as I push away into the pool, floating on my back, I ponder the realisation that the Thorsborne Trail is more about the water than the walking. And for that, it will forever be one of my favourite trails in Australia. **SR**

RAT CUNNING

The one camp companion you'll likely encounter on the Thorsborne Trail is the native Hinchinbrook rat, a cute creature with an irrepressible thieving habit. These animals have been known to gnaw through tents and even through tins to get at food, so all of Hinchinbrook's campsites are now equipped with rat-proof boxes in which you should store your food. It's use it or lose it – store your food anywhere else and the rats will outsmart you.

Clockwise, from far left: saltwater crocodile; dawn rises over the Hinchinbrook Island coastline; hike from beach to beautiful beach on the Thorsborne Trail. Previous page: teeming mangroves in the Hinchinbrook Channel

ORIENTATION

Start // Ramsay Bay
Finish // George Point
Distance // 32km (19.9 miles)
Duration // 4 days
Getting there // Absolute North Charters (absolutenorthcharters.com.au) runs ferries between the trailheads and Cardwell/Lucinda, and transfers at hike's end.
When to go // The dry season – April to September – is also the coolest and most comfortable season.
Where to stay // Camping is the only option along the trail – there are campsites at Nina Bay, Little Ramsay Bay, Banksia Bay, Zoe Bay, Mulligan Falls and George Point.
Things to know // Camping permits are required before walking. The trail is popular, and a maximum of 40 people are allowed on it at a time, so book well ahead.
More info // parks.des.qld.gov.au/parks/hinchinbrook-thorsborne

Opposite, from top: Hill Inlet, Whitsunday Island; up and down on the Aotea Track, Great Barrier Island

MORE LIKE THIS
ISLAND ODYSSEYS

WHITSUNDAY NGARO SEA TRAIL, QUEENSLAND

One of Queensland's 10 Great Walks, the Ngaro Sea Trail is more a multisport event than a pure walk. The trail weaves through the Whitsunday Islands, connecting a series of walks on Whitsunday, South Molle and Hook islands. To access them, you'll need to come by yacht or kayak, sailing or paddling across the Whitsunday Passage and between the islands. Whitsunday Island has the best of the walks, climbing to island views at Whitsunday Peak and Whitsunday Cairn and traversing a narrow section of the island from Chance Bay to the famed Whitehaven Beach. South Molle has an island-wide network of trails – you could spend a full day wandering here – while on Hook Island, the Ngaro Sea Trail accesses a short track to ancient Aboriginal rock art at the Ngaro Cultural Site in Nara Inlet.
Start/Finish // Shute Harbour
Distance // Walks from 350m (1148ft) to 8km (5 miles)
Duration // 4-7 days
More info // parks.des.qld.gov.au/parks/whitsunday-ngaro-sea-trail

BISHOP AND CLERK, TASMANIA

Almost dangling off the northern tip of Maria Island, this dolerite peak forms a dramatic full stop to Tasmania's premier island national park. From the ferry pier, the walk passes through the World Heritage-listed convict penitentiary of Darlington and heads out to the edge of the Fossil Cliffs, composed of 300-million-year-old fossils. The track turns here onto the wooded slopes of Bishop and Clerk before scrambling through boulders to the summit. The view is wide for a peak that's just 620m (2034ft) high, peering down onto the Fossil Cliffs and Darlington, and across the sea to Schouten Island and Freycinet Peninsula. Catch the early ferry from Triabunna and you can make the climb in time for the final ferry back, or you can stay the night in bunkhouse-style accommodation inside the old penitentiary cells (or camp).
Start/Finish // Darlington jetty
Distance // 11km (6.8 miles)
Duration // 4-5hr
More info // parks.tas.gov.au/explore-our-parks/maria-island-national-park/bishop-and-clerk

AOTEA TRACK, GREAT BARRIER ISLAND, NEW ZEALAND

Great Barrier Island, New Zealand's fourth-largest island in the main chain, is a place of dense bush, hot springs, kauri logging history and a complete sense of isolation (in 2017 it was named the world's first island Dark Sky Sanctuary). The Aotea Track makes a loop through the island's rugged central mountains, with two huts along the route (book ahead) making it a perfect three-day outing. There are several possible starting points, but by beginning beside the Oreville stamping battery (a relic of the island's gold-mining days) you'll hike past the Kaitoke Hot Springs, and a chance for a soothing soak, on the first and last days.
Start/Finish // Whangaparapara Rd
Distance // 27km (16.8 miles)
Duration // 3 days
More info // doc.govt.nz/parks-and-recreation/places-to-go/auckland/places/great-barrier-island-aotea/things-to-do/tracks/aotea-track

HANCOCK GORGE

Grapple with some of the oldest rocks on the planet as you slip, slide, clamber and climb in exhilaration through the red-rock wilderness of Karijini National Park.

Dawn arrives in a golden blaze. As I emerge from my tent full of the expectant joy of a new day in the bush, I blink out across the savannah-like plains of Karijini National Park, trying to identify the hoots and warbles rising from straggly gums and bottle-shaped boab trees, still silhouetted in early morning shadow. I pick red dust from my fingernails and look up at an infinitely blue sky.

Ever since my first trip to Western Australia many moons ago, I've had Karijini ringed on my 'one day' map, so finally making it to one of the country's remotest national parks feels like no small triumph.

Karijini doesn't give up its charms easily. Getting here is a challenge; a proper adventure. The previous day I'd travelled on a bone-shaking, seven-hour drive in a 4WD from Exmouth, dodging potholes as we blazed our way along dirt roads through the relentless rust-red rock and spinifex scenery of the outback. When we eventually reached the ripple of the Hamersley Range, storm clouds menaced on the horizon.

The journey here seems ancient and mythical – and it is. According to Aboriginal lore, the Dreamtime Creation Serpent slithered its way from the coast through the Pilbara of Western Australia, carving out Karijini's dramatic waterways as it snaked along.

Now I'm psyching myself up to explore these waterways on one of the park's most feted walks: Hancock Gorge. Billed as a Grade 5, it's as much canyoning as hiking. Involving a mix of bouldering, scrambling, wading and swimming, the trail can be rough, steep and slippery. It's tough. And the fact that the out-and-back hike is just 1.5km (0.9 miles) yet takes half a day

verifies this. There are no crocs – it's too far inland – but there is the risk of loose rocks, hypothermia and flash floods that can come out of nowhere. I'm going with a guide.

Kitted out in a neoprene suit and helmet, I join a small group to enter the gorge by descending a metal ladder. As we venture deep into the belly of the canyon, a layer-cake of ochre-red rock that our guide describes as 'the centre of the earth', the world falls silent. The only noise is moving water. In such a thirsty-looking landscape, there's a surprising amount of this in Karijini. We wade through crystal-clear creeks that are gaspingly cold, slide down waterfalls on our bums with childish glee, tube

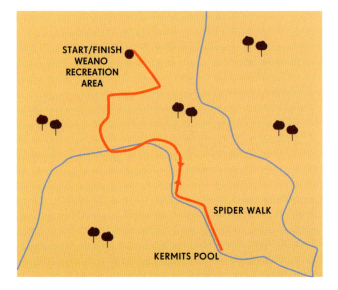

"As we venture deep into the belly of the canyon, the world falls silent. The only noise is moving water"

along ink-blue streams and swim in pools that glint emerald and turquoise when the sunlight catches them.

There are rocky ledges to negotiate, each one a test of agility, and sheer walls to clamber along, our fingers seeking handy crevices. Our break-time reward is a natural amphitheatre, where we rest in the calm and cool of a late spring morning, enjoying the view of rapids and watching a Wedge-tailed eagle circling overhead. There is no noise here, no phone signal – nothing to distract from the moment. Strip us of our modern gear and there would be no way of telling this was the 21st century. It's a scene from the dawn of creation.

This is no coincidence. Karijini is a geologist's dream, with rocks of banded iron ore spectacularly eroded over the course of 2.5 billion years. This primordial landscape gives an inkling as to how the world looked before humans, or even dinosaurs, set foot on it.

And it's vast on a scale that is hard to fathom. Karijini is Western Australia's second biggest national park, spreading over a whopping 6274 sq km/2422 sq miles (for perspective, that's more than twice the size of Luxembourg). The Aboriginal Banyjima, Kurrama and Innawonga people have called it home for at least 20,000 years. And its remoteness makes it a haven for wildlife like rock wallabies, echidnas and kangaroos, harmless Pilbara olive pythons, goannas, legless lizards and rare, rockery-building pebble-mound mice. Come winter (July to September), the landscape erupts with wildflowers like purple mulla mulla and yellow wattle, I'm told.

As we venture deeper, Hancock Gorge narrows and closes in. This is the 'Spider Walk', barely a metre wide, so named because the best way to tackle it is like a spider, scuttling along the rock walls with arms and legs outstretched, with the water rushing below. It's an act of amateur acrobatics, requiring balance and concentration. Some hikers turn back at this point as this is where things get trickier and more technical, but with a guide, harness and water shoes with decent grip it's possible to go that bit further.

We continue to Kermits Pool, cerulean blue and breathtakingly cold, where we briefly swim in the long shadows. On our return, we rope up to teeter along knife-edge ridges and abseil down near-vertical walls of red rock. I slip and lose my grip several times and, for a heartbeat, I panic, dangling off the precipice and sensing my own fragility. But then I'm down and we're on our way out, tracing the water back to where we began.

At the eco-camp that evening, we trade near-miss stories as day melts into dusk, the moon rises and the vaulted night sky glitters with stars. These are some of the darkest skies in the country and to gaze up at them is to feel like a speck on the face of the earth. I dig my heels into the ancient red dust and contemplate the past, the present, life, the universe and everything. The dust doesn't just coat your skin in Karijini, it creeps into your soul. **KC**

OXER LOOKOUT

The view from Oxer Lookout's elevated platform is quite simply unforgettable. Peering deep into four gorges – Joffre, Weano, Red and Hancock – it's as though the earth has been ripped open, with 100m-high (328ft) cliffs and pinnacles of ragged red rock sheering above glittering waterways and pools. Come at sunrise or sunset to see the rocks blush fiery red. The 800m (2624ft) trail to Oxer begins at Weano Recreation Area car park.

Clockwise from far left: dragon lizard, Karijini National Park; Pilbara dirt road; mesmerising Hancock Gorge colours. Previous page: turquoise waters in Hancock Gorge

ORIENTATION

Start/Finish // Weano Recreation Area car park
Distance // 1.5km (0.9 miles)
Duration // 3-4hr return
Getting there // The nearest airport is Paraburdoo, 80km (50 miles) from the park entrance and a two-hour flight from Perth with Qantas. A 4WD is recommended but not essential.
When to go // Best from June to August (winter) for warm, clear days and cold, starry nights. Summers are hot and rainy.
What to pack // Food supplies and water; a compass; hat; sunscreen; grippy water shoes; warm sleeping bag/tent.
Where to stay // Book ahead for Dales Campground; or camp/glamp at Karijini Eco Retreat (karijiniecoretreat.com.au).
Things to know // Note weather conditions and flash-flood warnings. Gorge pools can be very cold; hypothermia is a risk.
More info // parks.dpaw.wa.gov.au/park/karijini. Karijini Tours (karijinitours.com) arranges small group 4WD tours.

Opposite, from top: Hokitika Gorge swing bridge; a common crow drinks nectar along the Butterfly Gorge trail; spy flightless pukeko on the Ballroom Overhang Track

MORE LIKE THIS
GORGEOUS GORGE WALKS

HOKITIKA GORGE WALK, SOUTH ISLAND, NEW ZEALAND

The 'wow' never leaves your lips on this short, gentle but astonishingly scenic walk through the Hokitika Gorge. Frankly there are few better ways to spend an hour on New Zealand's West Coast. The Southern Alps hover on the horizon as you make your way over swing bridges and through ferny rimu and podocarp forest, which peels back to reveal tantalising views of the startlingly turquoise Hokitika River and its glacier-eroded granite rocks. It's tempting to swim, but take care of hidden rocks and currents. Come on a clear day to see the water at its dazzling best (it gets murky after rain) and be sure to bring insect repellent as the sandflies can be a real pest. The trail is easy to follow and suitable for families.
Start/Finish // Hokitika Gorge Scenic Reserve, 33km (20.5 miles) **south of Hokitika**
Distance // 2.1km (1.3 mile)
Duration // 1hr

BALLROOM OVERHANG TRACK, SOUTH ISLAND, NEW ZEALAND

Shadowing the Fox River, the Ballroom Overhang Track dives deep into a little-explored corner of the Paparoa National Park on New Zealand's West Coast. Brace yourself for a proper adventure on this wet, wild, deliciously remote track, which is reached via the Inland Pack Track. Negotiating climbs and drops, the trail threads through lush native bush and forest and along the riverbed to the Ballroom Overhang, an impressive limestone half-dome on a bend in the river. If you've brought your gear, camping for the night here is quite something. On quiet days, you might be alone on the trail but for the odd flightless weka or pukeko bird. Check weather conditions before setting out as the track involves numerous river crossings and can flood after heavy rain.
Start/Finish // Car park at the mouth of the Fox River
Distance // 11.6km (7.2 miles)

BUTTERFLY GORGE VIA YAMBI WALK, NITMILUK NP, NORTHERN TERRITORY

Out on a limb in Northern Territory, Nitmiluk National Park is a nature-run-riot spectacle of ochre-red sandstone canyons gouged out by the jade-green Katherine River and its waterfalls, rapids, torrents and swimming holes. The Katherine Gorge forms the park's backbone and is the focal point for a flurry of compelling day hikes, including the Butterfly Gorge via Yambi Walk. This half-day, moderately challenging hike slips through rainforest and the shadows of a gorge teeming with common crow butterflies. There are plenty of chances to dive off rock ledges into clear waters. It's best to avoid the roasting heat and rains of summer (November to April), which also attract crocs. Come instead in the dry season for hiking, swimming and canoeing. The park is home to the Aboriginal Jawoyn people: 'Nitmiluk' means 'Place of the Cicada Dreaming'.
Start/Finish // Nitmiluk Visitor Centre
Distance // 12km (7.5 miles)
Duration// Half-day

THE GOLD COAST HINTERLAND

Encounter fascinating wildlife, waterfalls and ancient rainforest on this three-day walk through two national parks in southern Queensland.

A glossy blue-black bird is assiduously arranging the scenery of its performance space. Blue petals and bottle tops are placed centre stage and anything that isn't blue is briskly flicked aside. This remarkable scene, starring a satin bowerbird, is happening metres from where I'm staying at O'Reilly's Rainforest Retreat in Lamington National Park, which is two hours' drive inland from Brisbane in the volcanic and forested region of the Gold Coast hinterland.

The park, a Unesco World Heritage site, sits on a plateau almost a mile above the coast and contains a portion of the world's largest stand of sub-tropical rainforest. More than 900 plant species, 200 bird species and 60 mammal species thrive up here, alongside 100 species of reptiles and amphibians. 'Many specialised plants and animals only live here,' says park ranger Kerri Brannon; 'It's all about the altitude.' Lamington National Park is also the starting point for the 54km (34-mile) Gold Coast Hinterland Great Walk, which descends through

LAMINGTON
NATIONAL PARK

BINNA BURRA

START/
O'REILLY'S

FINISH

PURLING
BROOK FALLS

SPRINGBROOK
NATIONAL PARK

dense rainforest, airy eucalyptus woodlands and even grasslands to Springbrook National Park on Queensland's border with New South Wales.

Lamington's altitude has another effect: no matter how steamy it is on the Gold Coast, it will be 50% cooler in the mountains, which makes for comfortable walking conditions in Australia's late summer. Pulling on my boots outside O'Reilly's Rainforest Retreat at the trailhead (you can walk from east to west instead, but you'd be going uphill for most of the way), the sun had yet to warm the chilly mountain air. Filaments of mist filter through the vines and around the buttressed tree roots; if it seems primeval, that's because it is. The forests date back hundreds of millions of years and were part of the ancient continent of Gondwana, before Australia broke apart from Antartica and South America, and ancient species such as cycads (which can be 500 years old), Antarctic beech and hoop pine were once dinosaur food.

On day one we follow the Border Track from the Green Mountains side of Lamington to Binna Burra, where another lodge has cabins and space for camping. This 21km (13-mile) section is the highest stage of the walk, with views to Mt Warning, the first place in Australia to get sunlight every morning.

My first wildlife encounter on leaving O'Reilly's is with a gaggle of unperturbed brush-turkeys. But unless you have sharp eyes or the patience to stand silently, your encounters with birdlife tend to be audio rather than visual. This makes the birds easier to identify. Does it sound like the crack of a whip? That's

"If you hear a car alarm or mobile phone, that'll be an Albert's lyrebird, an elusive but accomplished mimic"

a whipbird. Does it sound like a mewling cat? That's a catbird. A rifleshot? That's a Paradise riflebird. You get the idea. And if you hear a car alarm or mobile phone, that'll be an Albert's lyrebird, an elusive but accomplished mimic.

At the junction of the Border Track with the Coomera Falls Circuit I take the Coomera turning, where I meet Rusty and Nev, two park rangers attending to one of the regular rainy season landslips. 'Some parts of the trail date back to the Depression labour of the 1930s and the 1940s, when unemployed men, and war veterans who found it hard to adapt to civilian life, went into the woods to adjust to life,' explains Rusty. 'They'd fill backpacks with rocks from the creek and carry them along the trails. It was hard, dangerous work – there were no safety harnesses in those days.' Snakes were a hazard too, and it's a little later that I encounter Australia's third-most venomous reptile, a young male tiger snake warming himself on the trail.

The natural history lesson continues on the second section of the walk, which connects Lamington National Park with its eastern relative Springbrook. An intense fragrance in the air turns out to be patch of lemon-scented teatrees. A lattice of roots

Clockwise, from far left: deep in the woods of Lamington National Park; a strangler fig grips its victim; O'Reilly's Rainforest Retreat; an eastern whipbird. Previous page: the forested Gold Coast hinterland of Queensland

around a tree trunk is a strangler fig, imperceptibly killing its host over decades. And then my second Indiana Jones moment occurs: strung across the path, one after another, are spider webs 3m (10ft) wide at head height, each patrolled by a golden orb spider the breadth of my hand.

No sooner do we reach the valley floor than we start on the steep climb up to Springbrook National Park. Michael Hall, who has been a park ranger for 30 years and is the ranger in charge of Springbrook, explains that people have had as much influence on the landscapes of the Great Walk as volcanic power. 'Aboriginal people,' he says, 'burned the woods to create open spaces for hunting, leaving forest for shelter.' Controlled burning is a tool for defending the fragile eucalyptus forests from encroachment by voracious rainforest plants. Once fire has cleared a space, it's a starting gun for new life to race upwards to the light. 'Some forest likes a light burn every 10 years,' says Hall, 'other forest prefers a crowning fire up to the canopy of the trees every 100 years. A crowning fire can produce 100,000 kilowatts of heat per metre.'

Michael is pointing out more plants and trees on the final day's route past Purling Brook Falls, Springbrook's 100m (328ft) waterfall, when his eye is caught by a movement on a branch above us. After three days of prehistoric plants, ancient landscapes and deadly wildlife, he's spied one more little brown bird. 'It's a spotted pardalote,' he whispers. 'I haven't seen one of those for 20 years. Now that is special.' **RB**

ORIENTATION

Start // Lamington National Park
Finish // Springbrook National Park
Distance // 54km (34 miles)
Getting there // Several tour operators provide transfers from Brisbane airport to O'Reilly's lodge. From the end of the walk at Springbrook National Park there are also transfers to Gold Coast airport (closer than Brisbane).
When to go // Winter (June-August) is best.
What to pack // Sturdy boots; a first-aid kit (know what to do with a snake bite); water; hat; sunscreen; warm clothing; waterproof jacket; food and camping equipment if needed.
Where to stay // Accommodation is available along the walk, including at O'Reilly's Rainforest Retreat (oreillys.com. au) and Binna Burra Mountain Lodge (binnaburralodge. com.au). Camping permits are required for camping in Queensland's National Parks (www.qld.gov.au).
More info // npsr.qld.gov.au

Opposite: hike Girringun National Park's Djagany (Goanna) Walk to marvel at the mighty 268m (879ft) drop of Wallaman Falls

MORE LIKE THIS
EPIC NATIONAL PARK TRAILS

O'SHANNASSY AQUEDUCT TRAIL, YARRA RANGES NP, VICTORIA

If you don't fancy climbing Mt Donna Buang, the highest point in Victoria's Yarra Ranges National Park and all the more so thanks to a lookout tower at its top, then this trail is almost as epic an alternative. It runs for around 35km (22 miles) through much of this forested national park from East Warburton to Don Valley, a short drive northeast of Melbourne. The trail follows the route of the aqueduct that was built in 1914 to funnel fresh water to the city, an amazing feat of engineering. Being an aqueduct, it's a largely level route, with a few steep pitches. If you wish you could also run or ride it. Either way, it gives a flavour of the temperate rainforest of the Ranges, with ferns unfurling far above your head and above them the dense canopy of mountain ash trees. It's walk among giants.

Start // East Warburton
Finish // Don Valley
Distance // 35km (22 miles)
Duration // 2 days
More info // yarraranges.vic.gov.au

DJAGANY (GOANNA) WALK, GIRRINGUN NP, QUEENSLAND

Part of the Wet Tropics Great Walk, a 110km (68.4-mile) epic trail linking two of the Townsville region's most spectacular waterfalls (Wallaman Falls and Blencoe Falls), the Djagany (Goanna) Walk offers a great taste of the full tramp, which takes around 10 days. Admire Wallaman Falls – Australia's highest single-drop waterfall – before setting out on an old forestry track through a number of forest types that form part of the Unesco-listed Wet Tropics World Heritage Area. Look out for brilliant blue Ulysses butterflies fluttering through the rainforest, with tranquil creek crossings providing a welcome respite from the midday heat. The first two days on the trail end at remote walkers' camps, where you'll doze off to the sounds of the Aussie bush.

Start // Wallaman Falls camping area
Finish // Henrietta gate pick-up point
Distance // 56.8km (35.3 miles)
Duration // 3 days
More info // parks.des.qld.gov. au/parks/great-walks-wet-tropics- wallaman/walking

NEW ENGLAND WILDERNESS WALK, NEW ENGLAND NP, NEW SOUTH WALES

Descending over 1000m (3281ft) from the edge of New England Tableland, east of Armidale, to the headwaters of the Bellinger River, this multi-day hike invites experienced bushwalkers on a journey through one of NSW's most diverse wilderness areas. The first 1.7km (1 mile) of the trail takes you through lush, cool temperate forest to Wrights Lookout, where you can enjoy spectacular panoramic views over New England National Park, part of the Unesco-listed Gondwana Rainforests. From here the trail continues along Snowy Range, then down towards the valley floor – admire the changing environment as you descend. Once you reach the valley floor, you'll wander along an old farm trail over grassy river flats, passing historic farmhouses and stockyards on the way.

Start // Robinsons Knob Trail car park
Finish // Darkwood Rd
Distance // 33km (20.5 miles)
Duration // 2-3 days
More info // nationalparks.nsw.gov. au/things-to-do/walking-tracks/new- england-wilderness-walk

PICCANINNY GORGE

Walk on the wilderness side into this magnificent and rarely visited gorge system among the orange beehive domes of the Kimberley's enigmatic Bungle Bungle Range.

The woman at the visitors centre checked my emergency beacon, asked if I had enough water, charged a modest fee, and handed over the official Overnight Hike brochure. After a rough 53km (33 miles) of twisty, unsealed road from the highway, crossing five creeks and passing several stranded parties, I was now free to lose myself among the incredible sandstone karst formations known as the Bungle Bungles in Unesco-listed Purnululu National Park. But first I had another 27km (16.8 miles) of twisty, unsealed road to the trailhead at Piccaninny, an unforgettable place named in an (unfortunately) less enlightened time.

Water (five litres) made up the majority of my pack weight with the rest of my gear minimalist – tiny titanium stove, bivvy bag, lightweight down quilt, crackers, cheese, coffee. No need for warm clothing, this is the Kimberley, where it's only ever hot and dry or hot and wet. I was advised there was water in the gorge (not always a given), so the five litres gave me freedom to camp wherever I pleased tonight as it was already mid-afternoon.

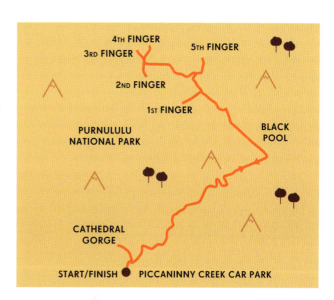

The route is well-defined and signposted from the car park to the junction with Cathedral Gorge – a cavernous, roofed amphitheatre and park highlight – well worth the short detour. However, I continue straight along the flat, dry creek, eager to make the most of the remaining light. Daytime temperatures can exceed 40°C (104°F), with the reflection off the brilliant white sand resembling a blowtorch, but today's breezy 21°C (70°F) makes the creek slog unnaturally pleasant.

The creek bed alternates between sand, gravel and rock (the latter most preferable) and walking is easy and spectacular, with massive orange conglomerate domes looming above. Winding to its own rhythm, the creek widens and narrows to the constraints of geology and wet season fury, splitting into channels and fossilised rivulets, sometimes completely choked by house-sized boulders. When the latter happens I search for an obvious detour up onto the riverbank, sometimes indicated by a small cairn or wind-scoured footprints in a sand-blow. Every so often I startle a white-quilled rock pigeon, diving out of the undergrowth heading for a cliff-face sanctuary.

Soon the creek enters the wilderness zone where there are no signposts, track markers, litter or seemingly people. I was aiming for The Elbow, a bend in the creek 8km (5 miles) from the car park where the gorge begins. Around 5pm, with the light fading, I call a halt, finding a sheltered spot on the bank, away from

> ## *"I am captivated by ever-changing palettes and patterns, of immense rock and sunbeams playing lightly on leaves and grass"*

the katabatic wind now blowing through the valley. I arrange my groundsheet, soak my dehydrated dinner and watch the rock faces glow crimson in the dying sun. There's no moon and the star show is infinite. I'd only been walking for 2.5 hours.

I wake with the dawn glow. Coffee, muesli, pack up then within 15 minutes I pass a couple camped in the sand. They're out for six days. I've opted for three, which seems like a good balance. Entering the gorge, the rock walls encroach and the views become even more amazing. A small cairn heralds the direction to Black Pool, a reliable water source under an enormous black streak on the cliff face – a wet season waterfall.

Most of the gorge is still in shadow, with only the cliff tops a brilliant orange. An hour and 15 minutes of easy walking from The Elbow, I arrive at the junction to the first side gorge, or 'Finger'. Cabbage palms and birdsong abound.

Most walkers establish base camp here and explore the rest of the gorge system with day packs. I opt for a small spot on the bank under a shady tree with a glorious view of 1st Finger's entrance cliffs. Leaving my main pack I head up the Finger with a water bladder, finding a lovely clear pool within two minutes. The resident fish don't begrudge me two litres, though I still nuke the bladder with chlorine tablets.

DID YOU KNOW?

Unesco regards the beehive-like Bungle Bungles of Purnululu as the finest examples of sandstone cone karst formation in the world. Their orange colouring derives from iron and manganese minerals while the black layers (more pronounced in the Wet) are evidence of cyanobacteria. Add sand, wind, water and a quadzillion years of erosion. 'Bungle' is possibly a local Gija corruption of the European 'bundle bundle' grass, readopted by later Europeans for a nearby pastoral lease.

Clockwise, from above: the Bungles' sandstone cones from above; looking into Piccaninny Gorge from The Elbow; striated rocks lining the Gorge. Previous page: Bungle Bungle 'beehives', Purnululu National Park

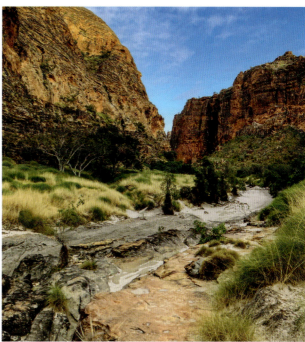

The deep and narrow creek forces me high onto the bank, revealing good views further up the gorge. A rough path descends steeply down a cliff face to the floor where further exploration seems possible.

Back up the main gorge I reach another pool minutes from camp and need to climb high to avoid it. This becomes the norm, follow the creek then climb to detour around obvious obstructions. The gorge must be fearsome in the wet season, if the height of flood debris is anything to go by – whole trees jammed between boulders high above the bottom, all split, riven and twisted.

A small side gorge, 5th Finger, curves off right which I note for later, the main gorge constricting dramatically after this junction, red walls towering 200m (656ft) above. The detours become more numerous and the scrambles more dodgy until the gorge widens again near the junction with the other fingers (2nd, 3rd and 4th), all promising adventures for another day. I retrace my route back to 5th Finger, a narrow, pretty gorge with beautiful trees and rocks – shapes, textures and patterns of light and shade all combining to make a beautiful elysian interlude.

Back at camp, I soak another dinner and daydream under the trees, captivated by ever-changing palettes and patterns, of immense rock and sunbeams playing lightly on leaves and grass.

I leg it out at first light, the rock burnt umber against a cerulean sky. With the sun at my back I catch a tail wind and make quick time back to the tourist lands, the occupants quite startled by this dishevelled character with flailing walking poles blowing out of the heat. **SW**

ORIENTATION

Start/Finish // Piccaninny Creek car park, Purnululu National Park

Distance // 40km (25 miles)

Duration // 3-5 days (water depending)

Getting there // Purnululu National Park Visitor Centre is 53km (33 miles) on a rough, unsealed road from the Great Northern Hwy. A high-clearance 4WD is essential.

When to go // The dry season (April to October) is the optimum time for the hike.

What to pack // Be totally self-sufficient and lightweight: groundsheet; bivvy bag; lightweight sleeping mat; good boots; hat; sunscreen; sunglasses; water containers; Personal Locator Beacon; GPS; fuel stove; water purifying tablets.

Things to know // Registering/deregistering at the visitor centre is mandatory; this is where park usage and camping fees are collected. An invaluable, free Avenza map is available for download from their website (avenzamaps.com).

More info // Piccaninny Gorge Overnight Walk (parks brochure); parks.dpaw.wa.gov.au

Opposite, clockwise from top: Mt Zeil,
highpoint of the Northern Territories;
big skies in the Gammon Ranges; take
a freshwater swim at Bell Gorge

MORE LIKE THIS
DESERT PEAKS AND GORGES

MT ZEIL, NORTHERN TERRITORY

At the far end of the West Macdonnell Ranges, the Northern Territory's highest peak is the tallest point on the Australian mainland west of the Great Dividing Range. A massive mountain (1531m/5023ft), Zeil can be climbed in one long day (10-12 hours) from the wilderness camp on its northern edge. Follow the marked trail 1.5km (1 mile) from the car park towards the obvious gorge where the trail abruptly vanishes. Climb steeply over the rocky, spinifex-studded slopes of the hill on your right, congratulating yourself for wearing long trousers, sturdy boots and gaiters. Descend to a saddle then start climbing again, keeping as far west as possible. There are many false summits and not an ounce of shade so carry water for the day and return the same way.
Start/Finish // Mt Zeil Wilderness Park, Narwietooma, Papunya Rd, Alice Springs
Distance // 17km (10.5 miles)
Duration // 1 day
More info // mtzeilwildernesspark. com.au

BELL GORGE, WESTERN AUSTRALIA

No road trip along the Kimberley's infamous Gibb River Rd is complete without a proper soaking in the soothing waters of Bell Gorge. After a bone-shattering 29km (18-mile) drive off the Gibb, descend steeply from the car park into a pandanus-lined creek frequented by honeyeaters and fairy wrens. In several hundred metres you'll arrive above the falls where the best views are on the left. White-quilled rock pigeons and agile wallabies frequent the sheer cliffs. Cross the creek and follow sporadic track markers up the scorched rock to a high point. The track now descends a steep gully to the majestic plunge pool where you might share the waters with a Mertens' water monitor. Save some time for exploration downstream.
Start/Finish // Bell Gorge/Dalmanyi car park, Wunaamin Conservation Park
Distance // 5km (3 miles) return
Duration // 2-3hr
More info // parks.dpaw.wa.gov.au

GAMMON RANGES CIRCUIT, SOUTH AUSTRALIA

Out in the South Australian desert Vulkathunha-Gammon Ranges offer unsurpassed off-track wilderness walking, where routes are limited only by water availability. From Loch Ness, head towards Bunyip Chasm, an interesting side-gorge. The main route climbs steeply over brittle rock and spinifex onto Steadman Ridge and Mt John Roberts (850m/2788ft) where sunsets are superb and the white salt crust of Lake Frome is visible in the distance. If time is limited turn left down North Italowie Creek, otherwise follow Wildflower Creek west to a saddle below Cleft Peak (835m/2739ft) where water might pool. The Terraces (a tiered creek bed) can be explored as a day-trip, alternatively drop into Streak Gorge and camp at Junction Waterhole. Follow the South Italowie back towards the car.
Start/Finish // Loch Ness Well, Vulkathunha-Gammon Ranges NP
Distance // 14-35km (8-28 miles)
Duration // 2-6 days

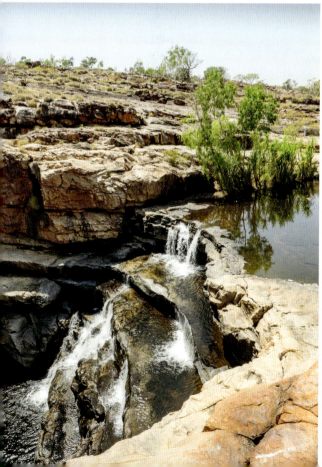

NEW ZEALAND

TONGARIRO
NORTHERN CIRCUIT

*Lap New Zealand's most striking volcano on this Great Walk, passing steaming craters,
neon-bright lakes and the raw beauty of the country's only 'desert'.*

Beside the Emerald Lakes, cradled between volcanoes in Unesco-listed Tongariro National Park, there's a track junction that's like the confluence of two streams. Along one track there flows an enormous volume of hikers as hundreds of people march across the famed Tongariro Alpine Crossing.

Branching off from this like a placid tributary is the Tongariro Northern Circuit, where I'm suddenly alone, about to descend into New Zealand's only so-called desert, with a mountain beside me that's so perfectly conical that it could be the blueprint for all volcanoes. The sound of the Alpine Crossing crowd falls behind me, and all is perfect.

It's my first day on the Tongariro Northern Circuit, one of New Zealand's 10 Great Walks and the country's greatest volcanic showcase. For three days I will weave among a trio of active volcanoes – Tongariro, Ngauruhoe and Ruapehu – witnessing their stamp on the landscape, from craters to vividly coloured lakes to New Zealand's lone desert studded with 'volcanic bombs'.

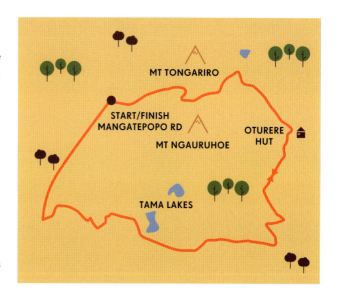

MT TONGARIRO

START/FINISH
MANGATEPOPO RD

MT NGAURUHOE

OTURERE
HUT

TAMA LAKES

For the first morning, my journey blurs into that of the Alpine Crossing as I set out among the hiking hordes from Mangatepopo Rd. Shuttle buses arrive at the trailhead before dawn, and first light is a faint scratch across the horizon as I set out walking. It's only as I begin the first significant climb towards South Crater that the sun finally reaches me, revealing a landscape stripped bare – a barren crust of earth and boulders, with Mt Ngauruhoe rising above. This portentous peak will be a constant presence for the next three days, with the Northern Circuit making a loop around it. It is the most active volcano on the New Zealand mainland and erupted 61 times between 1839 and 1975, though it hasn't blown its stack for nearly half a century. Little wonder it body-doubled as Mt Doom in *The Lord of the Rings* film trilogy.

The Alpine Crossing is almost universally described as the best one-day walk in New Zealand, and it's not hard to see why as I ascend to the angry-looking, wound-like Red Crater and then plunge down the slopes to the well-named Emerald Lakes, which in this desolate landscape are what passes for greenery. But there's still a sense of relief as I step off the Alpine Crossing and onto the more solitary path that is the continuation of the Northern Circuit. I descend into the Oturere Valley atop a thick spur of lava, entering a stretch of walking that quickly becomes my favourite, even with all those showy volcanic moments along the Alpine Crossing.

The Oturere Valley sits at the edge of the Rangipo Desert, which was once smothered in forest. In the world's largest volcanic

"Fire and water, desert and flood – the very combinations that make this harsh and startling landscape so compelling"

explosion of the last 5000 years – the 186 CE eruption that created nearby Lake Taupō – the forest was obliterated and no tree has ever grown back. It's not a true desert, with the area receiving more than 200cm (78.7in) of rainfall a year, but it so resembles a desert that the name has stuck.

I stay this night at Oturere Hut, which commands a grandstand view of Mt Ngauruhoe. When I wake in the morning, mist is rolling down its slopes like steam from a cauldron, recalling missionary and botanist William Colenso's description of this area as 'a fit place for Macbeth's witches'.

This short day I will be immersed in the Rangipo Desert as I walk a straight line south to Waihohonu Hut. The most curious feature of the landscape – the one that will lodge forever in my mind – is its boulders. These 'volcanic bombs' were spat from Mt Ngauruhoe during its many eruptions, plugging in the sandy earth like darts into a board. It's a reminder that a single eruption here can redraw the landscape like an architect. As recently as 2012, the Te Maari Crater, little more than 5km (3.1 miles) from Oturere Hut, erupted, spewing out molten rock. One of the rocks crashed through the

VOLCANIC LEGENDS

Māori lore tells of seven mountains at Lake Taupō's edge that were also gods and warriors. Each fell in love with Pihanga, the only female among them. A battle for her heart was won by Tongariro, who forced the others to move away from the loved-up couple. Some shifted a respectable distance, but Taranaki gouged an angry trail as he headed west – now the Whanganui River, with its headwaters in Tongariro NP.

Clockwise, from top left: 'kiwi crossing' near Mt Ruapehu; hiking the Northern Circuit toward Mt Ngauruhoe; crystal-clear waters at Ohinepango Springs. Previous page, from left: Mt Ngauruhoe under a cover of snow; Taranaki Falls, near the hike's end

roof of nearby Ketetahi Hut – which had often been used as an overnight hut by Northern Circuit hikers – crushing a bunk. The hut was empty (it was winter) but it immediately closed as an overnight shelter, and was removed altogether in 2019.

My day in the desert ends abruptly. Suddenly, where there were no trees, there are many trees, as I step into beech forest and, nestled among them, Waihohonu Hut. I dump my pack for the night and make the short stroll to Ohinepango Springs. Unlike many of New Zealand's thermal springs, these ones have no heat, pouring out cold from the earth, but it's an impressive volume of gin-clear water that suddenly pours through the desert.

As the name suggests, the full Northern Circuit loops back to Mangatepopo Rd and the start of the Alpine Crossing, but like many hikers I'm finishing in Whakapapa Village, cutting out the less-interesting final day. So, as I walk out from Waihohonu Hut, I'm beginning my final day of the (semi) circuit, funnelling between Mt Ngauruhoe and Mt Ruapehu, which is the North Island's highest mountain and scene of its only ski field. Midway, I detour up the lower slopes of Mt Ngauruhoe to the Tama Lakes, a pair of pools like blue eyes on the brown face of the national park. Ahead also, not long before I reach Whakapapa Village, is Taranaki Falls, pouring powerfully over a 20m-high (66ft) lava flow. It's another Tongariro moment of fire and water, desert and flood – the very combinations that make this harsh and startling landscape so compelling. **AB**

ORIENTATION

Start/Finish // Mangatepopo Rd, Tongariro National Park
Distance // 42km (26 miles)
Duration // 3 days
Getting there // Shuttle buses run to Mangatepopo Rd early each morning from Taupō, Tūrangi, National Park, Whakapapa and Ōhakune. There's a four-hour parking limit at the car park to discourage the use of private vehicles.
When to go // The Great Walk season is from mid-October to end-April; December to March is the warmest and best time.
Tours // Adrift Tongariro (adriftnz.co.nz) and Walking Legends (walkinglegends.co.nz) run three-day guided Northern Tongariro Circuit hikes, including transport, meals and camping equipment or hut bookings, respectively.
Things to know // Book ahead for Tongariro Northern Circuit's three huts and attached campsites at doc.govt.nz.
More info // doc.govt.nz

Opposite, clockwise from top:
Mt Taranaki, perfectly reflected;
Mt Tibrogargan from Mt Ngungun;
take a side-trip to Wai-o-tapu's
Champagne Pool after the Maunga
Kakaramea/Rainbow Mountain hike

MORE LIKE THIS
VOLCANO HIKES

MT TARANAKI, NORTH ISLAND

The westernmost of the volcanoes that run like a studded belt across the North Island, Mt Taranaki is ribbed with trails, but it's the summit (or very near to it – the summit area is sacred to Māori and hikers are asked not to stand right on its top) that is the 2518m (8261ft) mountain's true siren, with Taranaki said to be New Zealand's most climbed peak. This simple fact masks the challenge of this long day in the boots. From the park visitor centre, it's a climb of almost 1600m (5249ft) to the top of the volcano, which hasn't erupted since 1854. The going is steep – there's a section called 'The Puffer' for a reason – and there'll be snow (and possibly ice) in the crater, but the view out across the Tasman Sea and inland to the Tongariro volcanoes is exceptional.
Start/Finish // Taranaki/Egmont National Park Visitor Centre
Distance // 12.6km (8 miles)
Duration // 8-10hr
More info // doc.govt.nz

MAUNGA KAKARAMEA/RAINBOW MOUNTAIN, NORTH ISLAND

Rotorua is no stranger to geothermal activity and, as the name attests, Maunga Kakaramea/Rainbow Mountain is one of the most colourful displays of its volcanic underbelly. The 743m-high (2437ft) mountain sits beside State Hwy 5, 26km (16 miles) south of Rotorua, and the straightforward trail ascends past the Crater Lakes, a pair of bright-blue lakes pooled at the foot of colourful cliffs. The walk climbs on past the cliffs to the summit, which looks over some of Rotorua's other great moments in geothermal history: Mt Tarawera, which erupted violently in 1886; the deep incision of Waimangu Volcanic Valley; and the furiously steaming Wai-o-tapu Thermal Wonderland. Need to soak away some muscle soreness at walk's end? The Waikite Valley Thermal Pools are just 9km (5.5 miles) down the road.
Start/Finish // Rainbow Mountain Scenic Reserve car park
Distance // 7km (4 miles)
Duration // 3hr
More info // doc.govt.nz

MT TIBROGARGAN, QUEENSLAND, AUSTRALIA

One hour's drive north of Brisbane, 11 craggy peaks rise out of the macadamia and pineapple crops to form one of Queensland's most surreal landscapes: the Glass House Mountains. These peaks are remnants of volcanic plugs – solidified magma from inside the necks of volcanoes – and a number of the summits can be reached on foot. Perhaps the most imposing of the accessible peaks is Mt Tibrogargan, aka the Gorilla, which is also one of the most difficult but spectacular to climb. The 364m (1194ft) ball of rock can be lapped on a gentle 4km (2.5 mile) circuit trail, or there's a more intrepid route to the top. This involves plenty of steep scrambling – a gorilla grip truly needed – but leads to a vast view out to the Sunshine Coast and Pacific Ocean. Mt Beerburrum and Mt Ngungun – fellow Glass House Mountains – provide easier summit moments.
Start/Finish // Tibrogargan trailhead, Barrs Rd
Distance // 3km (2 miles)
Duration // 2-3hr
More info // parks.des.qld.gov.au/ parks/glass-house-mountains

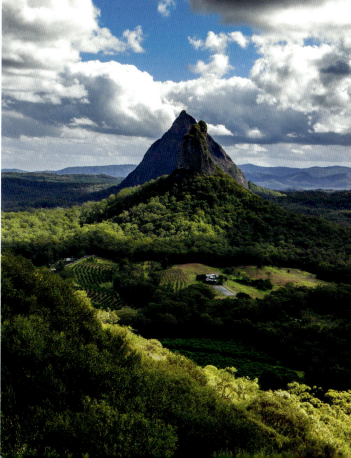

BEN LOMOND SUMMIT HIKE

This extremely enjoyable hike high above Queenstown delivers ever-widening views. Bribe your kids to come along by riding the Skyline Gondola, which shaves around 500m/1640ft from the total climb.

Queenstown has long been labelled the 'adventure capital of the world', and climbing Ben Lomond – the 1748m/5735ft peak that dominates the mountains behind town – generates some genuine excitement.

'Can we ride the luge at the top of the gondola? Before we do the walk?' pleaded son Ben, getting in some early negotiations before agreeing to hike to the peak.

'We'll ride the gondola up,' I said, 'and if you get to the top of the mountain we can go luging before coming down into town on the gondola,' I countered.

The boys looked at each other. 'Okay, deal!' said older brother Riki. 'Let's go!'

As a Queenstown family, we'd put off climbing Ben Lomond with the boys until we felt they were old enough. It's a few years ago now, but with Riki and Ben both having hit 10, wife Yuriko and I felt they'd both make it to the top fairly easily. I had been running hiking tours for a decade and knew the trail well. The boys were both energetic young sparks, and keeping them under control was going to be more problematic than actually getting them going.

Following the ride up the gondola we admired the vista from Skyline's viewing deck, long used by Tourism New Zealand in images to entice visitors to this southern wonderland: Queenstown far below, sparkling Lake Wakatipu and a plethora of captivating mountains.

'Can we ride the luge?' asked Ben. 'Now?' He was studying the luge tracks running just below the lookout, totally ignoring the view. The brightly coloured luges were whizzing by, ridden by excited youngsters.

'Not now – on the way down!' I replied. Heading out from the back of the Skyline building, we had to cross bridges over the luge tracks to get to the start of the hiking trail. I threw out a big carrot.

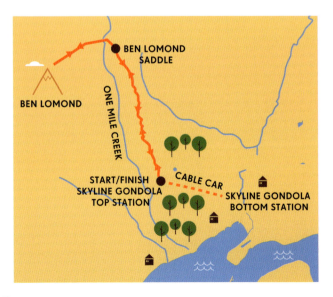

'If you get to the top of Ben Lomond, we'll get you both a three-ride luge package,' I said. The boys took off so fast that we could barely keep up.

There's not a lot to worry about when you take kids hiking in Aotearoa. No poisonous snakes – in fact, no snakes at all – and no dangerous animals such as bears for them to upset. But still, as responsible parents, you want to keep your kids in sight – which wasn't going to be easy. We'd picked a perfect blue-sky, midsummer day. Weather wasn't an issue; Mum and Dad keeping up might be.

Once we hit the trail, the boys hurtled ahead on the wide, easy-to-follow track through dark forest until, some 10 minutes in, Ben Lomond appeared, dead ahead, looking huge. We were soon above the tree line and climbing steadily towards Ben Lomond Saddle, our first target. There was only low-growing scrub and tussock lining the trail as it climbed, so it was relatively easy to see the boys as they raced ahead.

"As responsible parents, you want to keep your kids in sight – which wasn't going to be easy. We'd picked a perfect blue-sky, midsummer day. Weather wasn't an issue; Mum and Dad keeping up might be"

An hour or so into the climb, the views started to open up, revealing more and more of Lake Wakatipu and the Remarkables mountain range away to the east. Some early starters were already on their descent. 'Those two belong to you?' a young guy asked. 'Good luck keeping up with them!' I grunted a reply. We finally approached Ben Lomond Saddle, sitting at 1326m/4350ft between Ben Lomond (1748m/5735ft) and Bowen Peak (1631m/5351ft). An alpine extravaganza away to the north rolled into view as we reached the saddle. Endless valleys, mountains and snow-covered peaks. The boys were waiting for us.

While we'd been climbing more or less due north, Ben Lomond still towered away to the southwest. The well-marked track curled around to steepen and follow a ridge-line up towards the summit. Looking east, Queenstown Airport popped into view far in the distance and way below us. 'Look Dad! We're above that plane!' exclaimed Ben. An aircraft was approaching to land from the west, above Lake Wakatipu, but well below us in terms of altitude. There was absolutely no wind, despite the fact that we were on an exposed mountain ridge at over 1500m (4921ft). It was a perfect day.

Near the top, the track swung around to the western side of the peak and we were looking down on horseshoe-shaped Moke Lake, far below. There was no-one else at the summit when we eventually climbed to the high point, marked by a cairn. 'Named after Ben Lomond in Scotland,' I told the boys. 'Lots of the explorers and pioneers around here were Scottish.'

BEN LOMOND ADVENTURES

Extremely keen hikers can add 500m (1640ft) of climbing and descent to their day by not riding the gondola; walk up the Tiki Trail from the lower gondola station in town and add a couple of hours each way to your day. There are also a couple of gravity-fuelled opportunities for the final descent into Queenstown: tandem paragliding (nzgforce.com) down to land on Queenstown School's sports ground, or flying through the forest on one of the world's steepest ziplines (ziptrek.co.nz).

Clockwise, from left: Skyline Gondola cars; supplying a little extra height for tip-top trail views; Queenstown sunset from the Ben Lomond summit track. Previous page: Queenstown from the Skyline Gondola top station

My attempts to educate my sons were rudely interrupted by the arrival of three kea, intelligent alpine parrots who have seen it all before and know how to separate gullible hikers from their picnic lunches. 'Don't feed them,' I told the boys. 'Just enjoy them.'

The big green parrots had gone into standard formation: two entertaining us from the front while one tried to sneak up on unsupervised backpacks and lunches from the rear. Fortunately, I'd seen it all before too. But it was incredibly entertaining.

After a 20-minute break at the peak, playing with the kea and admiring the unparalleled alpine outlook, we started back down. It didn't take long. Once again, well behind our sons, Yuriko and I could pick up the occasional word in their conversation. 'Luge' seemed to pop up with great regularity. The descent on the same track seemed to take nowhere as long as the climb. The boys almost seemed to be running!

'Dad,' said Riki, when we arrived back at Skyline, 'climbing Ben Lomond was the most fun I've had in a long time. Now let's ride the luge!' **CM**

ORIENTATION

Start/Finish // Skyline Queenstown
Distance // 8km (5 miles) return
Duration // 5-6hr return
Getting there // The walk up to Skyline's bottom gondola station takes about ten minutes from downtown Queenstown.
When to go // November to April; weather can be extremely changeable – drop into the DoC's Queenstown Visitor Centre before you go to check forecasts and track conditions.
What to take // Refreshments; rain gear; warm clothing.
More info // DoC (doc.govt.nz)

Opposite, from top: Insta-worthy
views on the Roys Peak hike;
Diamond Lake from Rocky Mountain

MORE LIKE THIS
SOUTHERN LAKE-VIEW CLIMBS

ROYS PEAK

A long climb to a long view, this hike shimmies up to the 1578m/5177ft summit of Roys Peak along the rim of Lake Wānaka, passing one of Aotearoa's most popular mountain photo stops along the way. The climb to the peak can be a grind, ascending 1220m (4003ft) from near the lakeshore on a series of what may seem to be unending switchbacks, but the views make this a truly spectacular walk. Those very views have made this an extremely popular track, though many hikers aspire to only reach the ridge, about three-quarters of the way up, from where that famous selfie-with-Lake-Wānaka moment bombards Instagram. Take plenty of refreshments, and don't forget that the endless climb is followed by a knee-knocking descent on the same track.

Start/Finish // Roys Peak car park, Wānaka-Mt Aspiring Rd (6km/4 miles from Wānaka)
Distance // 16km/10 miles
Duration // 6hr
More info // DoC (doc.govt.nz)

LAKE ALTA & THE REMARKABLES

Drive up to the Remarkables Ski Area base (1600m/5249ft), then climb on a rough road to the top of the Alta Chairlift. From there, cairns and flagstones mark the way through alpine wetlands up to gorgeous Lake Alta, sitting at 1800m/5905ft above sea level and framed by jagged peaks. Cross the creek that exits the lake, climb directly north to the high point at the end of the ridge, then head across the rock scree to the top of the Shadow Basin chairlift. It's a short scramble from there up to the Remarkables Ultimate Viewpoint (1960m/6430ft). Vistas west over Lake Wakatipu, Queenstown and endless peaks are absolutely breathtaking. Follow the ski trails back down through Shadow Basin to the ski area base. This hike is a real winner, but keep it for a fair-weather day.

Start/Finish // Remarkables Ski Area car park
Distance // 6km/3.7 miles
Duration // 3–4hr
More info // DoC (doc.govt.nz)

DIAMOND LAKE & ROCKY MOUNTAIN

West of Wānaka, this low-level hill climb follows an excellent set of trails, with a 450m (1476ft) climb and descent, and lovely views over Lake Wānaka, the mouth of the Mātukituki River and a distant Mt Aspiring. From the car park, it's a gentle climb up to the willow-fringed shores of Diamond Lake, before the climb starts in earnest to the Lake Wānaka viewpoint, with bench seating and views east to Glendhu Bay and Roys Peak. Take the eastern track up to the 775m (2543ft) summit of Rocky Mountain before descending by the western track. The walk effectively takes in three conjoined circuit tracks so there are plenty of options, but don't forget to loop around the far side of Diamond Lake before heading back to the car park.

Start/Finish // Diamond Lake car park (18km/11 miles west of Wānaka)
Distance // 7km/4.3 miles
Duration // 3hr
More info // DoC (doc.govt.nz)

GILLESPIE
PASS CIRCUIT

Ferocious mountains, relentless climbs, river crossings and a celestial-blue glacier lake make this never-to-be-forgotten hike in Mt Aspiring National Park both a beauty and a beast.

Mt Awful. Mt Dreadful. Siberia Valley. Crucible Lake. One brief, daunting look at a map of the Gillespie Pass Circuit in New Zealand's Mt Aspiring National Park tells me what I am up against.

But I'm ready for a serious challenge. After several weeks tramping Great Walks like the Milford, Abel Tasman and Routeburn tracks, the rains have swept in and I'm hibernating in a log cabin, with tea and my next adventure on the boil. Something wilder. Something remoter. Something away from the crowds on *The Lord of the Rings* circuit. Somewhere to give the world the slip on dizzyingly high trails, with dark, gnarly mountains that are more than a little Mordor.

The Gillespie Pass fits the bill perfectly. Never heard of it? Neither had I. This is the secret star of New Zealand's backcountry hikes – a brutal-but-beautiful multi-day trek diving deep into the Southern Alps, where raging rivers, falls, glaciers, whopping great mountains and mossy silver beech forests that are pure Tolkien fantasy stuff await. I pack my tent and gear for a four-day expedition into the wilds, dismissing website warnings that you should only embark on the hike if you are experienced at crossing rivers.

More fool me.

It's a fine March day and the sun is beaming down on the river valley that sweeps past the trailhead in Makarora, which meanders south to Lake Wānaka. A ripple of wooded hills lifts my gaze to the jagged, blunt-faced mountains where I'll be heading, many topping the 2000m (6562ft) mark. There's a whisper of autumn in the air and the first brush of gold on the landscape. There isn't another soul to be seen.

The glassy turquoise Makarora River has swollen with recent rain and is broad and lively. But my map confusingly shows the river running a different course, so I waver as I decipher the safest place to cross. When I do, the water is gaspingly cold, knee-deep and faster than it looks. I struggle to keep my footing, but I manage to keep my momentum and reach the other side, where the Young Valley unfurls in all its Alpine glory.

Mountains. Forest. The river and its many lovely bends. These views are my constant companion as I push on. The first day is long and tough but I am conscious of making steady progress. I pass a swing bridge and enter ferny, lichen-draped forest, before

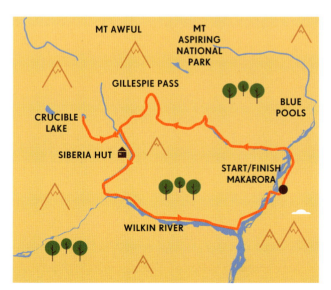

climbing steeply to the Young Hut at 550m (1804ft), where a simple bunk for the night has never seemed more welcome.

I'm awake with the first light. The tramp to the Siberia Hut is fierce, I'm told, so an early start is vital. The Young River feels forgotten in the peace of early morning. I hear the chorus of unknown birds reverberating through the forest, the rush of the river. Otherwise it's quiet enough to hear my own heartbeat. After a short, easy stride along the valley floor, I reach the start of the Gillespie Pass proper and pause to fill my bottle – this is the last water I'll see until the other side of the Alpine pass.

And water is essential. The pass is merciless: a relentless, zigzagging, thigh-burning, backbreaking, slippery, seemingly never-ending climb up a near-vertical rocky slope. At times the trail is little more than a thread vein – so narrow that I feel I will topple off with so much as a breath of wind. My pack becomes a lead-weight. The clouds hover low and threatening, but the weather thankfully holds out as I crest the ridge to reach the 1600m (5249ft) pass, with the black, ragged, snow-streaked face of Mt Awful (2192m/7192ft) looming menacingly above.

The summit is cold and exposed. A single edelweiss flower quivers in the wind, its furry white petals unmistakable. Just as unmistakable is the bird circling above: a startling flash of bright green and orange, a high-pitched cry. It's a kea, a species of parrot that inhabits the Alpine regions of New Zealand's South Island.

The descent is almost as gruelling as the climb: every fresh blister keenly felt as I sidle down through snow grass to a forest track leading to Gillespie Stream, then continue my zigzagging downward march to Siberia Stream. The name, I'm sure, is apt: the snowbound winters here must be bitter. The Siberia Hut is an hour away but I'm tired so decide to refresh with a wild swim instead, then I pitch my tent on the banks of the stream as day fades into starlit dusk.

A fellow hiker tips me off about the detour to Crucible Lake on day three. The walk from Siberia Hut picks its way gently through meadows initially, with views of Mt Awful at the valley head. But with a name like 'Crucible', you might expect a trial, and you'd be right. The trail steepens to enter native beech forest, where roots require scrambling and sidestepping, easing as I reach the stepping stone-forded Crucible Stream. A final stiff climb up leads to a moraine wall hiding the glacial cirque lake. It's the perfect magic trick – you don't see it until the last point, and when you do you can't believe your eyes. Crucible Lake is a wondrous, unforgettable place: dark, glaciated peaks thrusting above a ring of azure water. Icebergs chinking softly. Waterfalls streaming down sheer rock flanks. Worth every step and bead of sweat.

And the same can be said of the Gillespie Pass, I muse, as I begin the long hike out of the valley on day four, shadowing the Wilkin River. This trek doesn't give up its charms easily: you have to tease them out, face the torment of trail and weather, push limits. But it's all the sweeter for it. **KW**

RABBIT PASS

Craving more of a challenge? Hook up with a guide (aspiringguides.com; hikingnewzealand. com) to tramp the nearby Rabbit Pass in Mt Aspiring National Park. This four-day, off-the-radar hike is as astonishing as Gillespie, but tougher: much of it is unmarked and there are no huts (be prepared to wild camp). Waterfalls, glaciers, steep ascents, stream crossings and long descents will leave you exhausted and exhilarated.

Clockwise, from top left: Mt Awful from the Gillespie Pass; mountain daisy in flower. Previous page: Haast Pass Blue Pools, near the start of the Gillespie Pass hike

ORIENTATION

Start/Finish // Makarora
Distance // 58km (36 miles)
Duration // 3-4 days
Getting there // Young Valley is signed 2.5km (1.6 miles) north of Makarora. Queenstown is the nearest sizeable airport.
When to go // Mid-December to late March. The remote valleys and mountains are often snowbound in winter/spring and avalanches can present a risk.
What to pack // Warm layers; waterproofs; a tent; food and water; a compass and decent topo map (try linz.govt.nz).
Where to stay // Camp or hut-to-hut hike at at Young, Siberia and Kerin Forks huts. Bookings are required for Siberia Hut (doc.govt.nz); others are first come, first served.
Things to know // River-crossing experience is advisable. The circuit can be walked clockwise or anti-clockwise.
More info // Department of Conservation (doc.govt.nz)

*Opposite: take in eye-popping
Mt Ruapehu views on the
Round the Mountain Track*

MORE LIKE THIS
MULTI-DAY NEW ZEALAND HIKES

ROUND THE MOUNTAIN TRACK, NORTH ISLAND

The dramatic volcanoes of the Unesco dual-World-Heritage Tongariro National Park, bubbling up in the heart of the North Island, top every NZ hiker's wish list. The Tongariro Northern Circuit Great Walk is a limelight-stealer – and justifiably so. But for equally high-punching scenery, consider instead the comparably under-the-radar Round the Mountain Track, commanding sensational views of smouldering 2797m (9176ft) Mt Ruapehu, an active strato-volcano, with strong spiritual meaning for the local Māori, who refer to it as *koro* (granddad). In many ways this four- to six-day, extraordinarily diverse loop trail presents NZ in microcosm, taking you from mountain beech forest to alpine herb fields, glacier river gorges, crater lakes (among them the brilliantly blue Tama Lakes), waterfalls and the barren Rangipo Desert, with its wind-sculpted sands and volcanic rock. Check recent rains before heading out as there are unbridged river crossings to negotiate. Waihohonu Hut must be pre-booked during the Great Walks season (September to April).
Start/Finish // Whakapapa
Distance // 66km (41 miles)
More info // doc.govt.nz

ST JAMES WALKWAY, SOUTH ISLAND

This backcountry beauty shines a light on a less-tramped corner of South Island: Lewis Pass Scenic Reserve. A terrific introduction to multi-day-hiking, the five-day, four-night expedition takes you properly off the beaten track into thrillingly remote alpine wilderness, revealing views of ragged, oft snow-capped mountains without the slog and sweat. You'll often walk for miles without encountering another soul – through beech forest, over swing bridges and open farmland and bog, along silent river valleys and through gorges (most spectacularly the Cannibal Gorge on the Maruia River, reached via a steep, zigzagging ascent). The track is well signposted and there are five serviced huts en route if you're not up for camping. While the hike is easy-going, the climate can be extreme, so it's best tackled from October to April.
Start // Lewis Pass entrance (Lewis Pass Rd)
Finish // Boyle (other end of Lewis Pass Rd)
Distance // 66km (41 miles)
More info // doc.govt.nz

POUAKAI CIRCUIT, NORTH ISLAND

On the overlooked, underappreciated west coast of North Island, this extraordinary, moderately challenging two- to three-day tramp gets close to the perfect cone of 2518m (8261ft) Mt Taranaki – at its most photogenic wearing its cap of snow. The volcano is sacred to the Māori, who see the mountain as an ancestor and part of their *whānau* (family). The hike is a beauty, weaving through montane forest, alpine tussock fields and the 3500-year-old Ahukawakawa Swamp, with its unique microclimate and botanical rarities (sedges, sphagnum moss and red tussock). You'll observe how volcanic activity has left its mark on the landscape: from the erosion scar of the Boomerang slip to the towering lava columns of the Dieffenbach cliffs and the Bell Falls (an 18km/11-mile out-and-back detour), plunging over an ancient lava flow. The circuit is best hiked from October to April. Camp or stay at the two serviced backcountry huts. A good level of fitness and some backcountry experience (map reading etc) are advisable.
Start/Finish // Taranaki/Egmont National Park Visitor Centre
Distance // 25km (15.5 miles)
More info // doc.govt.nz

THE HEAPHY TRACK

The longest of New Zealand's Great Walks, this ancient Māori route traverses diverse terrain, from dense native forest to the wild beaches of the West Coast.

I've been descending into Heaphy Valley from the James Mackay Hut Campsite for what feels like hours, when a break in the greenery gives me a glimpse of the mouth of the Heaphy River. It should lead me to South Island's West Coast – my goal for the day. Energised, I press on. At the bottom of the valley, temperate vegetation gives way to thickets of nikau palms and then dense rainforest, its canopy closing above my head like some enchanted tunnel. In a clearing on the bank of the Heaphy River, I come across a large gathering of hikers, resting on the ground next to Lewis Hut. I join them, but not for long, with sandflies consuming more of me than I do of my sandwich.

Crossing several swing bridges, I finally find myself on a level trail alongside the Heaphy River, the fresh, salty breeze in my face signalling the proximity of the Tasman Sea. The undergrowth opens up and I limp across a grassy clearing overlooking a beautiful lagoon, with the powerful surf battering the massive

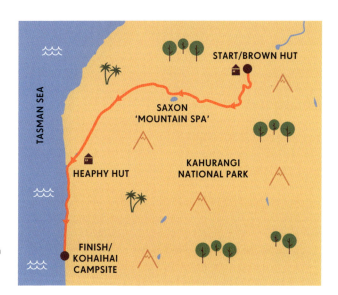

expanse of jetsam-strewn sand just beyond. My aches and blisters forgotten, I quickly put up my tiny tent, dump my gear and then spend ages padding barefoot along the damp sand, watching the waves roll in. A gaggle of freshly arrived hikers joins me on the strip of sand overlooking the river, and we swim in the cold water until we turn blue.

Later, sunburnt, salty-skinned and sweetly exhausted, I lie back in my tent in what must be the prettiest campsite in all of New Zealand, watching the clouds moving across the blue sky. 'This is the life,' I think contentedly, when my reverie is interrupted by someone shouting nearby: 'Hey! Come back with my socks!'

I poke my head out of my tent just in time to see a brown, speckled avian blur on legs disappear into the undergrowth, a pair of white socks clutched triumphantly in its beak.

I recognise the shouting woman as Linda, a fellow hiker I got chatting to the previous day at the Gouland Downs Hut – the snug 1930s construction where I stopped for lunch, to take advantage of the temporary shelter as the weather turned. Linda was making tea when I set up my little portable gas stove nearby, and told me that she was from Auckland, that this was her last Great Walk and that these brown flightless birds the size of a chicken, milling about outside the hut and seemingly not afraid of us, were wekas.

> ## "I lie back in my tent in what must be the prettiest campsite in all of New Zealand, watching clouds moving across the blue sky"

'You have to watch them like a hawk,' Linda explained. 'They are real characters – very curious and will steal anything that's not nailed down, particularly if it's shiny.' Sure enough, I turned around to see one of the wekas tugging at the foil packet containing my rehydrated lunch with its beak.

I told Linda about my first day on the trail when, worn out by the relentless switchback climb from Brown Hut – the starting point – through dense podocarp forest, I didn't make it to the campsite at Perry Saddle Hut, where hikers traditional stay on the first night, and instead pitched my tent at Aorere Shelter en route. There's something about camping alone: you're hyper-aware of every sound in the undergrowth. As the twilight thickened and the forest seemed to close in around me, I heard persistent rustling outside my tent and then watched in disbelief as one of my hiking poles slowly disappeared from view. I managed to apprehend the thief just in time.

'I thought it was a kiwi at first,' I said, since my ornithological knowledge of flightless birds is very limited.

'No, kiwis are very shy,' she explained. 'And they have a long beak. Also, they're nocturnal. You'd be really lucky to see one.'

'What brings you to New Zealand?' Linda continued. So I told her how getting off the grid for five days and hiking and

HEAPHY TRACK HISTORY

The Heaphy Track started out as part of a network of centuries-old Māori trails crisscrossing South Island. Māori pathfinders made tracks through dense forest and across mountains in order to reach the west coast – the only region rich in *pounamu* (greenstone), highly prized as an adornment, and also used to make tools and weapons. In the 19th century, European explorers used traditional Māori trails to explore the hinterland in search of pastoral land and gold mining.

Clockwise, from above: Heaphy River lagoon; nikau palms lining the route; Kohaihai River bridge. Previous page, from left: the Heaphy River meets the sea; hiking the Heaphy Track

camping among pristine, unique ecosystems really appealed, and how I've been wanting to do this particular Great Walk for a long time.

'How do you find hiking alone?'

'Great, actually.'

After weeks of frenetic work, being alone with my thoughts while walking at my own pace through groves of ancient lichen-covered trees and across tussock downs, then pitching my tent and savouring my dinner of boil-in-a-bag chilli con carne and energy balls while the sky became a tumultuous mess of reds and golds, had been wonderfully soul-restoring.

'The only time I wished I had someone with me was when I popped down for the dip in the Saxon "mountain spa",' I said. The water in the swimming hole was so frigid that the Saxon Hut staff posted the following warning by the trailhead: 'Please take a friend with you to administer CPR when your heart stops.' I wasn't entirely sure whether they were kidding.

Linda never recovers her stolen socks.

The last day of the trek dawns foggy and cool. I spot an eerie sentinel in the mist on the shore of the Tasman Sea – the tiny figure of a fellow hiker. Wary of the high tide cutting off the coastal track, I take off, through thickets of nikau palms, past headlands disappearing into the mist, past pristine white-sand beaches, until the bridge across Kohaihai River deposits me at the namesake campsite – my final destination.

Later, as the six-seater Cessna judders above the greenery-clad mountains and the meandering ribbon of Heaphy River, reversing the journey that took me five days in just 20 minutes, a part of me wonders if I'd dreamt it all. **AK**

ORIENTATION

Start // Brown Hut

Finish // Kohaihai Campsite

Distance // 78.5km (48.8 miles)

Duration // 4-5 days

Getting there // Golden Bay Coachlines (goldenbaycoachlines.co.nz) run daily shuttles from Takaka to Brown Hut (December-March). From Karamea, the best way to get back to Takaka is by air with Adventure Flights Golden Bay (adventureflightsgoldenbay.co.nz).

When to go // December to April is best for hikers; the rest of the year the trail is shared with mountain bikers.

What to pack // Insect repellent is essential.

Where to stay // The trail has seven huts and nine campsites; all must be booked year-round (via greatwalks.co.nz).

Where to eat // Bring all food supplies with you; there are potable water sources en route.

Tours // Bush & Beyond (heaphytrackguidedwalks.co.nz).

Things to know // Hiking east to west gets the biggest climb out of the way on the first day.

More info // doc.govt.nz

Opposite, from top: hiking the dunes at Farewell Spit; the wild and wonderful Kaikoura Coast

MORE LIKE THIS
MORE NZ COASTAL WALKS

FAREWELL SPIT & PUPONGA FARM PARK TRACKS, SOUTH ISLAND

Resembling the long beak of New Zealand's national bird, the kiwi, Farewell Spit is a 34km-long (21-mile), dune-backed sliver of sand that juts out into the Tasman Sea at the northernmost tip of South Island. You can explore this bird sanctuary, home to over 90 bird species, via a network of walking tracks that begin at Puponga Farm Park. They vary in length and difficulty, but highlights include the family friendly 1km-long (0.6-mile) Wharariki Beach track, with the most spectacular coastline in the region and views of Archway Islands; and the 6km (3.7-mile) Spit Track Circuit that cuts across rolling farmland, stretches of pristine sand and cliffs. To challenge yourself, try the 8km (5-mile) Puponga Hilltop Track – a winding loop trail passing the clifftop Pillar Point Lighthouse, with the option of combining the hike with the Spit Track Circuit.

Start/Finish // Puponga Farm Park
More info // doc.govt.nz

KAIKOURA COAST TRACK, SOUTH ISLAND

Hike between farms along a private track skirting Kaikoura coast, combining wild beaches with alpine views, and enjoy rural hospitality at night. Starting from The Beach House, Ngaroma, set off along the gravelly Big Bush Beach, overlooked by tall bluffs and battered by Pacific surf. En route, you'll see the stumps of ancient trees at the Buried Forest site, and pass the characterful Circle Shelter before reaching The Lookout, with its all-encompassing vistas of the Kaikoura peninsula. Beyond, you turn inland and pass through the Medina Conservation Area, with its ancient podocarps, including a formidable 800-year-old kahikatea tree. Staying overnight at the Medina Farm, you're dropped off at the second trailhead the following day, and make your way back to Ngaroma via Buntings Bush Gully, full of enormous podocarps, a scenic ridge walk in the Hawkswood Range, and a climb up Skull Peak (489m/1604ft), with wonderful coast and mountain views.

Start/Finish // Ngaroma
Distance // 26km (16 miles)
Duration // 2 days
More info // kaikouratrack.co.nz

TE PAKI COASTAL TRACK, NORTH ISLAND

Passing the sacred Māori site of Cape Reinga, this straightforward, scenic tramp encompasses New Zealand's northernmost tip, taking you along seven spectacular beaches and through ancient coastal forest. From the end of Te Paki Stream, cross the wide, flat Ninety Mile beach, pounded by the Tasman Sea, spotting oyster catchers and NZ dotterels on the way, then climb steeply up to Scott Point, before descending through scrub to Twilight Beach, home to one of the trail's four basic campsites. Go around a swamp and climb a ridge, passing the turnoff to the Cape Maria van Diemen lighthouse, then skirt Herangi Hill to reach the wild white-sand Te Werahi Beach. A stiff climb at Tarawamaomao Point brings you to Cape Reinga, where the Pacific meets the Tasman Sea; continue along the clifftops before going down to Tapotupotu Bay, flanked by thickets of giant kauri and pohutukawa trees. On the last day, traverse Darkies Ridge, with a side track up Te Paki (310m/1017ft), snorkel at Pandora Bay, then follow the long sweep of Te Horo Beach to Kapowairua via the Waitahora wetland.

Start // Te Paki Stream (Kauaparoa)
Finish // Kapowairua
Distance // 48km (30 miles)
Duration // 3 days
More info // doc.govt.nz

THE PAPAROA TRACK

A glorious trail created from a tragic tale – the latest addition to New Zealand's Great Walks, the purpose-built Paparoa Track, winds through rugged West Coast mountains.

Greymouth in Grey District on the banks of the Grey River is a gritty place with few pretensions – a West Coast town built on fishing, logging and mining accessed via winding mountain roads. West Coasters are renowned for their self-sufficiency and stubborn spirit, attributes hewn from the mountains shadowing them and distilled from the wild Tasman Sea forming the horizon.

The Paparoa is the first new Great Walk to be added in two decades in New Zealand, the only one to be purpose built, and the tenth in total. Built for both hikers and bikers, it weaves 55km (34 miles) through the ranges staring down onto the West Coast near Greymouth.

Gold drew miners to these ranges, then later coal. It was a tragedy of coalmining that led to the creation of the Paparoa. In 2010 an underground explosion at the Pike River Mine trapped and killed 29 miners. It was one of the darkest days in modern West Coast history. The devastated families resolved to create something in memory of their loved ones. The Paparoa Track is that memorial.

At Monteith's Brewery, the local speciality – a West Coast IPA washing down whitebait fritters – sets us up for the hike. The shuttle to the trailhead the next morning is hair-raising. En route we stop at Blackball village with its eclectic mix of businesses and buildings including Formerly The Blackball Hilton, a grand building offering accommodation, food and a bar. On the wall, proudly displayed, is a letter from the global hotel chain's lawyers with instructions to cease using the Hilton name. The owners just added 'Formerly' and carried on regardless.

It is raining steadily as Wendy, my hiking companion, and I don waterproofs beneath the marginal shelter of the trailhead

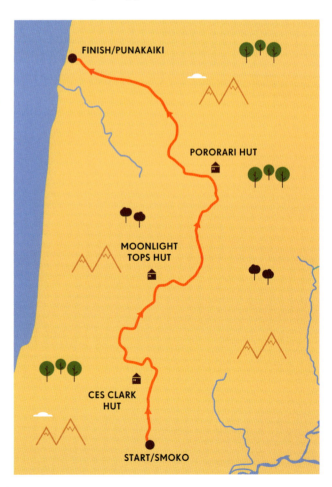

sign at Smoko. The first part of the Paparoa follows the Croesus Track, an old miners' route that has stood the onslaught of time remarkably well.

After climbing steadily through glistening beech and podocarp forest, we pop above the treeline and arrive at Ces Clark Hut. Our timing is impeccable for not only lunch, but also for the wind and heavier rain now starting to buffet the building. We are booked that night at Moonlight Tops Hut, 10km (6 miles) further and, with a forecast for worsening weather, know the most exposed part of the trail lies between our current safe haven and the next.

Conditions are certainly challenging – I hold onto Wendy a couple of times to stop her taking flight deeper into the Southern Alps. Jokingly I suggest we drop packs for the half-hour detour to 1200m-high (3937ft) Croesus Knob. But Wendy doesn't smile. Apparently, on a good day, you can see Aoraki/Mt Cook, New Zealand's highest mountain. Utterly drenched, we are very glad to reach Moonlight Tops before moonlight.

The spacious hut sleeps twenty. Twenty trampers moving wet gloves, thermals and waterproofs around the fire like a damp boardgame. A gap appears as a beanie is moved from hearth to head, a pungent sock soon taking its place.

Tramping is in the Kiwi DNA: respect for the land, an enjoyment of it, even when being out in all weathers is your day job. At the hut, stories are told. Indeed Roger, a North Island sheep farmer, allows his pasta to boil over three times in his quest to tell all, true or tall.

At dawn a mist hangs in the valleys, but we cheer when a watery sun warms the cloud and picks out the main escarpment in a glorious, tangerine light. To the north, the remote peaks of the Paparoa Range remain black in silhouette. With smiles on our faces and boots on our feet, we set off down a trail that drops into the most enchanted of mossy forest before emerging onto the

PANCAKE ROCKS

Be sure to visit Pancake Rocks at Punakaiki, ideally when the sea is surging at high tide. The short, cliff-top hike winds among pancake-stack-like formations and blowholes formed around 30 million years ago from dead marine life and plants that landed on the seabed and solidified into limestone as a result of incredible water pressure. The pancake-like stack was created over time by gradual seismic activity that pushed the limestone out of the seabed.

Clockwise, from above: the fern-forested banks of the Pororari River; a wild West Coast beach at Punakaiki trailhead; crashing seas at Pancake Rocks. Previous page: Punakaiki's stacked-up Pancake Rocks

escarpment. An airy few hours follow, the track clinging to a cliff edge dropping away to the west.

Far below, to the east, we pick out the final piece of the Paparoa jigsaw. The 11km (7-mile) Pike 29 Memorial Track, scheduled to open in 2022, leads steeply down 800m (2624ft) to the mine site. Here a memorial and interpretive centre unfolds the story of the disaster.

After lunch, overlooking distant Tasman surf, we plunge over the scarp, threading a route through the cliffs and across to the ridge holding Pororari Hut. Below the steepest section we meet Martin, one of the trail builders. With a family history steeped in mining – his mother from a mining family in Australia's Broken Hill, his father a miner on the West Coast – Martin, too, had worked the mines in both places. Now he puts his skills to work above ground, not below.

The drying games of the previous night are replaced, at Pororari Hut, with outside dining and a sunset over the ocean. Occasional sand flies do little to spoil the moment.

Our last day on the Paparoa leads us down through fabulous fern forest, to the Pororari River. Once across, via a swing bridge, the trail rolls on down the river. Now, deep in limestone country, the final few kilometres head below huge cliffs that step down into verdant vegetation along the banks. The sun is warm, a dip is tempting, the water cold.

When we pop out at Punakaiki trailhead, it feels right to continue the short distance to finish on a wild West Coast beach. The Paparoa, by boot or by bike, is a west side glory indeed. **HK**

ORIENTATION

Start // Smoko
Finish // Punakaiki
Distance // 55km (34 miles)
Duration // 3 days
Getting there // Drive from Christchurch to Greymouth (3.5 hours) or take the TranzAlpine Railway. Shuttle operators offer transport to/from either end of the track.
When to go // Year-round, but November-April is best.
What to pack // The huts have mattresses and stoves, but you need to carry sleeping bag, billies and utensils. The Paparoa is in the mountains of the West Coast of the South Island which is code for 'pack suitable clothing for all weather'.
Things to know // You can hike or mountain bike the Paparoa. Most hikers/cyclists travel south to north. No camping is allowed and the huts must be booked, often months ahead.
More info // greatwalks.co.nz/paparoa

Opposite, from top: Green Cape Lighthouse, at the end of the Light to Light Walk; hike or ride the Wangetti Trail through Wet Tropics World Heritage Area, amid beautiul blooms like the cocky apple flower

MORE LIKE THIS
LONG-DISTANCE TREKS

OLD GHOST ROAD, SOUTH ISLAND

Further up the West Coast from the Paparoa Track, near Westport, is the winding, weaving Old Ghost Road. The name would indicate this that trail would be a long-established route but it only opened in 2015, after a process that can only be described as persistent. The creation story is told in a thin book called *Spirit to the Stone*, copies of which are scattered in the five spectacularly located huts along the route. Required reading for anyone interested in trails and trailbuilding, it covers the story of landslides, proposed hydro dams potentially flooding its route, funding challenges, and mountains and gorges that would have sent lesser men and women away with their hands in the air, surrendering to the steeps and deeps of the New Zealand wilderness. The graded trail flows over mountaintops and clings to sheer gorge walls. It was built very much with mountain bikers in mind, but it is a work of art to be much enjoyed by hikers too.

Start // Lyell Campground
Finish // Rough & Tumble Lodge
Distance // 85km (53 miles)
Duration // 5 days
More info // oldghostroad.org.nz

LIGHT TO LIGHT WALK, NEW SOUTH WALES, AUSTRALIA

A beauty of a coastal walk that will impress anyone who loves to exercise with a side of clifftops and sparkling beach. The trail is bookended with celebrations of the maritime history of this far South Coast gem of New South Wales. Sea kayakers, too, often enjoy this section of coast but, with Bass Strait just around the corner, it can be a fearsome place. Paddlers often take refuge in the sheltered bays of Mowarry or Bittangabee. Like so much of the South Coast, the walk was impacted by the Black Summer bushfires of 2019/20. But, despite the torching, life is returning to blackened limbs, showing the resilience of the Australian bush. And, as part of the recovery, the Light to Light Walk is being redeveloped to offer both camping and hut experiences.

Start // Boyds Tower
Finish // Green Cape Lighthouse
Distance // 30km (18 miles)
Duration // 2-3 days
More info // nationalparks.nsw.gov.au/ things-to-do/walking-tracks/light-to-light-walk

WANGETTI TRAIL, QUEENSLAND, AUSTRALIA

Epic, purpose-built trails are appearing in all points of the Australian landscape, and the far northern reaches of Queensland are no exception. The Wangetti Trail takes a route exploring the coast and hinterland of the tropical landscape between Palm Cove and Port Douglas. Hikers and riders can explore the Wet Tropics World Heritage Area and Macalister Range National Park, among others, and should be on the lookout for everything from crocodiles to cassowaries. Being built in stages, the 33km (20-mile) section from Palm Cove to Wangetti was first to open, and the full trail with camping areas is due for completion in 2023.

Start // Palm Cove
Finish // Port Douglas
Distance // 94km (58 miles)
Duration // 5-6 days
More info // dtis.qld.gov.au/tourism/ qld-ecotourism-trails/wangetti-trail

THE GREENSTONE & CAPLES TRACK

At times you'll feel like the only soul on earth on this at-one-with-nature track through the beech forest-draped, mountain-backed, river-woven wilderness of New Zealand's Otago region.

Long ago, the indigenous Waitaha, Kāti Māmoe and Kāi Tahu Māori tribes made a journey beyond the realms of imagination. Pebble by pebble, they took greenstones from the Greenstone and Caples rivers and carried them over the mountains, through Fiordland and out to the West Coast, where they traded them for oil, seal furs and the like. As strong as steel, greenstone – or New Zealand jade or *pounamu* as the Māori call it – was prized for making tools, weapons and jewellery.

In the misty drizzle of an autumn morning, as I squeeze into damp boots, grab my backpack and gear up for a four-day tramp into the wilds, the Caples River is a stream of glassy, brilliant turquoise, rushing on to who knows where. I can well believe it has precious stones at its depths.

After the buzz of the nearby Routeburn Track, one of New Zealand's most raved-about Great Walks, the silence and solitude of the Caples Track is refreshing. I relish the hush in the glacier-carved valley, where moss-draped native beech forest sweeps up

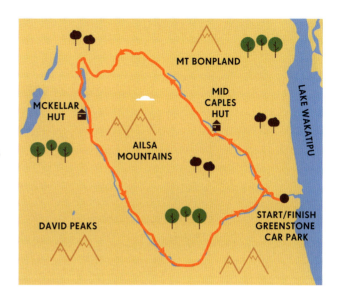

to the rugged backdrop of the snow-frosted Humboldt Mountains. River. Forest. Falls. Peaks. The view is New Zealand in a nutshell, yet there isn't a soul in sight at this early hour – just a falcon soaring in a lonely grey sky.

If you've ever wanted to unplug, give civilisation the slip and forget the century we live in, this is the place. Nature rules and there's little sign of human intervention, let alone a phone signal. Free from distractions, I resort to the slow-travel days of paper maps, pause often to dangle my feet in ice cold brooks, and use a pocket guide to identify birds, among them the kea, a vibrant green mountain parrot native to New Zealand that is now endangered.

The first day is a breeze on the tramp north; the Caples River is my constant companion: at times it is a broad green ribbon braiding the valley floor, at others it slips secretively through boulder-riven gorges. The gentle terrain means I have time to daydream and appreciate the detail: the mosses, ferns and fungi running riot across the forest floor, the silvery, cobwebby curtains of old man's beard lichen. There are creeks to cross and wispy falls spilling down lush-green cliff faces. The landscape has drunk deep of recent rains. The valley tightens and mountains appear dark and foreboding in the distance as I approach my base and simple bunk for the night: Mid Caples Hut.

With a seven-hour, 22km (13.7-mile) hike ahead of me to the McKellar Hut, I crawl out of my sleeping bag for a crack-of-dawn start on day two. Clouds hover low in the pleats and folds of the

> *"The view is New Zealand in a nutshell, yet there isn't a soul in sight at this early hour – just a falcon soaring in a lonely grey sky"*

mountains, tucking in the landscape like a blanket. The roar of water provides a soothing backbeat as I pick my way through beech woods, over grassy clearings and streamlets, trying to visualise the jagged, 2000m (6562ft) peaks above, whose summits are largely obscured by fog. And then the heavens open and it rains as though it has never rained before, in great fat droplets that soak me to the bone. A hunter spies me and ushers me into the Upper Caples Hut, where a small group of deerstalkers gathers in a steamy, wet-socked huddle around a wood fire. Before I know it, I'm trading stories over the best venison I've ever tried.

When I emerge from the glow of the hut an hour later, the Ailsa Mountains are fighting their way through the gloom. I push on.

The pace picks up as I begin the increasingly steep ascent to the exposed, 945m-high (3100ft) McKellar Saddle, the trail highlight in every possible sense of the word. Peeking over the edge, I gasp out loud as the view unfolds, with the inky expanse of Lake McKellar far below, the pyramid of Mt Christina on the horizon and the Humboldt, Ailsa and Darran ranges all around. A boardwalk unfurls across the boggy wetland at the summit, where the wind is picking

CONNECTING TO THE ROUTEBURN

Fancy extending your hike? From the Greenstone and Caples Track via The Divide, you can easily hook onto one of New Zealand's feted Great Walks: the Routeburn Track in Fiordland NP. The trail is well marked, but some sections can be steep and rough – your reward is out-of-this-world alpine scenery. The trail is accessible November-April (late spring or autumn are quietest); book huts and campsites ahead.

From far left: riverside terrain along the Greenstone and Caples route; Māori greenstone pendant; aerial of Lake McKellar.
Previous page: Southern Alps views from the Greenstone and Caples Track

up – a reminder that I shouldn't delay my zigzagging descent to the valley. The trail skirts the mountain-rimmed lake to bring me to the McKellar Hut on the edge of Fiordland National Park.

The third day dawns as bright as if the world has been made anew, and I cross a bridge and follow the river into the broad Greenstone Valley on the second leg of the circular hike.

Sunshine streams through the beech forest canopy, lights up golden tussocks and glints playfully on the green-blue Greenstone River as I head on through a boulder-strewn gorge and over a swing bridge that leaps across Steele Creek. Waterfalls plunge with new vigour down cliff faces spongy with moss and ferns. I shadow the river as the trail meanders through the open valley, dipping in and out of bush, before bringing me to another bridge over a gorge to the Greenstone Hut.

It's back over the bridge spanning the gorge the next morning for the easy onward march to the end. The views are quietly beautiful, with the valley narrowing to become a gorge saturated in every shade of green and the ragged Tooth Peaks puckering up to the south.

As I follow the Greenstone River to its confluence with the Caples River, the natural pools at the side of the trail are tempting for a swim. It's cold but what the hell. I wade up to my waist in the freezing water and roll my hand across the riverbed, my fingers sifting through pebbles in the hope of finding the greenstone that was so sacred to the Māori. I leave with no treasure but the memory. **KC**

ORIENTATION

Start/Finish // Greenstone Station Rd car park.
Distance // 61km (38 miles)
Duration // 4 days
Getting there // The car park/trailhead are 86km (53 miles) south of Queenstown via Glenorchy. Easyhike (easyhike.co.nz) provide car relocation, shuttle and gear-hire services.
When to go // Late October to mid-April when the huts are serviced. All have running water in summer.
What to pack // Warm layers; waterproofs; insect repellent; camping stove; utensils; sufficient food. NZ Topo50 map sheet: CB09 Hollyford covers the route.
Where to stay // Booking isn't required for the route's three DoC huts; get tickets from the visitor centre or buy a backcountry hut pass for unlimited stays (doc.govt.nz).
Things to know // Check weather conditions; McKellar Saddle is exposed, with no shelter. Boil or sterilise water from streams.

Opposite, clockwise from top:
Whakapapaiti Valley, overlooked by
Mt Ruapehu; taking in the Kepler
Track views; waterfall along the
Cameron Flat to Glacier Burn Track

MORE LIKE THIS
NEW ZEALAND ALPINE VALLEY WALKS

WHAKAPAPAITI VALLEY TRACK, TONGARIRO NP, NORTH ISLAND

With ravishing views of the perfectly pyramidal volcanoes in Tongariro National Park, you would expect this trail to be busy – you would be wrong. The Whakapapaiti Valley Track is a terrific circular day hike for enjoying the explosive scenery of New Zealand's oldest national park in relative solitude. Beginning at Whakapapaiti village, it passes through stunted beech forest and open tussocks as it wriggles up to the Whakapapaiti Hut, which sits at the foot of Mt Ruapehu, a glaciated, 2797m-high (9176ft), still-active stratovolcano that last blew its top in 2007. Stay the night, if you like, before returning to the trailhead. Billed as demanding, you'll need to be fit to tackle the rocky alpine terrain, 900m (2953ft) of elevation gain and unbridged river crossings on this hike, but it's worth the slog. It's best hiked counter-clockwise.
Start/Finish // Whakapapaiti village, 250m (820ft) north of Tongariro National Park Visitor Centre
Distance // 16km (10 miles)
More info // doc.govt.nz

CAMERON FLAT TO GLACIER BURN TRACK, MT ASPIRING NP, SOUTH ISLAND

Where...? If you've never heard of the Matukituki Valley in South Island's sublimely alpine Mt Aspiring National Park, you are not alone – but you are missing a trick. The half-day Cameron Flat to Glacier Burn track takes you properly off piste, with an easy-to-navigate trail that initially heads over farmland, building up the scenic pace as it dips into beech forest, climbs a saddle and descends to Glacier Burn, with the Humboldt Mountains looming on the horizon. Up-close views of tremendous bluffs, waterfalls and pearl-white Mt Avalanche await at the head of the valley. It's best tramped from November to April and is nearly always peaceful. This is just a taster of what the remote Matukituki Valley has to offer and can easily be combined with other more challenging routes.
Start/Finish // Cameron Flat
Distance // 10km (6.2 miles)
Duration // Half-day
More info //doc.govt.nz

KEPLER TRACK, FIORDLAND, SOUTH ISLAND

Ask a New Zealander to rattle off their all-time favourite tramps and the Kepler will invariably make the grade. This staggeringly beautiful circular hike is a baby in Great Walk terms, designed in 1988 to show off Fiordland from its most flattering angles, with alpine lakes, glacier-carved valleys, crash-bang waterfalls, lush native forest, limestone bluffs, deep gorges, sky-high mountains – the lot. The terrain is properly wild, but the route only moderately challenging as it's brilliantly organised, with bridges fording streams, boardwalks traversing boggy areas and steps negotiating the steepest sections. Keep an eye out for kea parrots as you clamber up to tussocky ridges, which afford dress-circle views of the Te Anau Basin, Takitimu and Earl Mountains. There are Department of Conservation-run huts and campsites en route; bookings are required from late October to April.
Start/Finish // Kepler Track car park
Distance // 60km (37 miles)
More info // doc.govt.nz

HOOKER VALLEY TRACK

This enjoyable day-walk takes hikers into a visual extravaganza of mountain peaks, glaciers, lakes, icebergs, suspension bridges and a close-up view of Aoraki/Mt Cook.

Excitement builds when you get your first views of Aotearoa's tallest mountain from Mt Cook Village. We'd been staring at the mesmerising peak for most of the 45-minute drive up the only-way-in road from State Hwy 8, but it had disappeared behind the closer peaks for the last few kilometres, before popping back into view from the village. It was a stunning early summer, blue-sky day, no clouds, and enough heat to cause the occasional audible crack of an avalanche breaking off the hanging glaciers clinging to the sides of the spectacular peaks on the western side of the Hooker Valley.

'Perfect day!' I said to wife, Yuriko, as we pulled into the car park at the end of the Hooker Valley Rd. While hiking is not at the top of her list of interests, Yuriko was also keen to make the most of the gorgeous day to walk what is known as one of the finest day-hikes in the country.

Crack!

'Look! Look!' I cried, pointing high up at the glacier hanging to the flanks of 3151m (10,338ft) Mt Sefton. 'An avalanche! See that snow and ice? Looks like a white waterfall!' The ice was still clearly visible tumbling down the steep sides of the mountain a good 10 seconds after we'd spotted it. It was far in the distance and of no danger.

'We're not going to get killed in an avalanche, are we?' Yuriko asked suspiciously, courtesy of decades of marriage and participating in various adventures, all the while being reassured that there was absolutely no danger.

'Don't worry, this track is in the middle of the valley, well away from where avalanches come down,' I said. 'No worries!' 'No worries' is a commonly used Kiwi term that, for some reason,

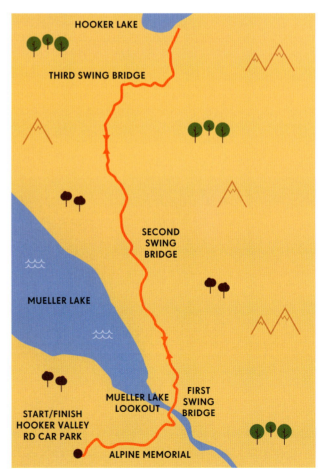

always seems to convince Yuriko that she should be worried. She definitely didn't look convinced not to worry.

Even less so, when only five minutes into the walk, we took a short side-track to the Alpine Memorial, a large pyramid of stone memorialising climbers who have been killed in the national park since the late 1800s.

'They were all climbers. Trying to summit Mt Cook, Mt Tasman, Mt Sefton and all these other peaks. We're just going for a walk up the valley. They won't need a plaque for us', I said encouragingly. Again, she didn't look convinced. Another crack. Another avalanche spotted up on high.

Ten minutes' down the track, we came to Mueller Lake Lookout, a magnificent spot overlooking the lake that sits at the foot of the Mueller Glacier, under the high peaks of Mt Sefton, the Footstool and their buddies. I gazed at the imposing peaks, the hanging glaciers and tried to spot avalanches before we heard them.

Yuriko wasn't looking up. She was looking down. 'We're not going to cross *that*, are we?' she asked, pointing below the lookout at the first of three swing bridges that I knew we'd be crossing, but hadn't mentioned. The river was swollen, muddy-brown and turbulent. Unfortunately, a strong breeze had suddenly built up and the suspension swing bridge appeared to be doing what swing bridges do – swinging.

'No worries!' I enthused again. 'Totally safe!'

Down at the bridge, I tried glossing over the swing factor. 'Do you know why the water is that murky colour? It's because it's laden with glacial flour, sediment produced when the moving glaciers grind up rock. It's what causes that beautiful aquamarine colour down in Lake Pukaki.' I may as well have been talking to myself.

THE SHRINKING MOUNTAIN

All mountains shrink or grow incrementally, but spectacular change happened in one hit on Aoraki/Mt Cook on 14 December 1991, when the summit of the mountain collapsed with 12 million cubic metres of rock tumbling 7.5km (4.7 miles) down the eastern face and into the Tasman Valley. Measurements later showed that 30m (100ft) had been sheared off the height of Aotearoa's tallest peak and the once 3754m (12,316ft) mountain's official height is now 3724m (12,218ft).

"It was a stunning early summer, blue-sky day, no clouds, and enough heat to cause the occasional audible crack of an avalanche"

'Hang onto the handrail,' I encouraged as we set forth onto the bridge, which seemed strong and sturdy to me, but if you've been brought up in Osaka in a risk-averse society, was obviously a bit of an ordeal. And, of course, in an act of utter stupidity, I suggested we stop in the middle of the bridge and take a photo. My suggestion was instantly rebuffed. I knew my wife as a classic Japanese photo-taker, but a deluge of murky water was roaring by a few metres below and she wasn't keen.

'That wasn't so bad, was it?' I asked, after we hit solid ground on the far side. No answer.

Mt Cook had disappeared behind the closer peaks, but after we crossed the second swing bridge, it reappeared, looking totally majestic. We stopped for photos and even better, at a long flat section of track featuring a wide boardwalk, Aotearoa's

From far left: crossing a Hooker Valley suspension bridge; Aoraki/Mt Cook, lording it over the Southern Alps; hiking the Hooker Valley Track. Previous page: the view to Aoraki/Mt Cook from Hooker Lake

most famous alpine flower, the Mt Cook Lily, was flowering in abundance. It was early December, and my flower-loving wife was ecstatic to see the gorgeous blooms, with their white petals, yellow stamens and large lily-pad-looking leaves.

'Misnamed by the early settlers,' I commented. 'Isn't even a type of lily. Actually, the world's largest buttercup.' She didn't seem impressed with my flower knowledge, but her normal good-humour had returned, just in time for us to cross the third and last swing bridge. The earlier breeze had dissipated, and the last bridge was barely creaking at all.

Twenty minutes later, we were at the end of the track, looking out on Hooker Lake and the Hooker Glacier. There were around 30 hikers enjoying the view. High ice cliffs marked the end of the glacier itself, and hundreds of icebergs, both big and small, sparkled on the lake between us and the glacier. Massive moraine walls lined the valley, and towering above it all in the far distance, Aoraki/Mt Cook glistened in all its glory in the bright sunshine. It was breathtaking. Without doubt, one of those moments in life well worth treasuring.

The walk back to the car park, including the swing bridges, was a breeze. **CM**

ORIENTATION

Start/Finish // Hooker Valley Rd car park
(or Mt Cook Village)
Distance // 10km (6.2 miles)
Duration // 4hr return
Getting there // Park in the large car park at the end of
Hooker Valley Rd; hikers without vehicles can walk to the car
park from Mt Cook Village (add one hour return).
When to go // Walkable year-round, but the weather can
be extremely changeable; check the forecast at the DoC's
Mt Cook Village Visitor Centre before you go.
More info // DoC (doc.govt.nz/hooker-valley-track);
DoC Visitor Centre at Mt Cook Village

Opposite, from top: mirror-calm and picture-perfect at Lake Matheson; glacial waters at Tasman Lake; hiking the trail to Mueller Hut

MORE LIKE THIS
SPECTACULAR AORAKI/ MT COOK VIEWS

LAKE MATHESON WALK

One of the classic views of Aoraki/ Mt Cook and the Southern Alps is the reflected panorama in Lake Matheson/ Te Ara Kairaumati on the West Coast, 6km (3.7 miles) west of Fox Glacier township. If you've been checking out the country's tourism websites and promotional pamphlets, you'll recognise the truly stunning mirror views instantly. This is a famous photo and if the weather is good, with little wind to ripple the lake, you'll likely be on the track with plenty of keen photographers. The trail itself starts at the road-end car park and cafe and is a loop track around the small glacial-carved lake, which is surrounded by ancient forest. It's an easy walk, with dawn and dusk the best times to enjoy reflections in the water. The first section, to the Jetty Viewpoint, is suitable for assisted wheelchairs.
Start/Finish // Lake Matheson Cafe
Distance // 4.4km (2.7 miles)
Duration // 1.5hr
More info // doc.govt.nz

MUELLER HUT HIKE

This is a tough hike with an ascent of more than 1000m (3281ft) to the barren tops of the mountains on the Sealy Range to the west of the Hooker Valley. Views of Aoraki/Mt Cook, its surrounding peaks and national park are unparalleled, but you'll have to put in some work for the rewards. Even better is the opportunity to overnight in the little red shed that is the Mueller Hut and enjoy its 'loo with a view'. Bookings for the 28-bed hut, originally built in 1914, are essential and can be made online on Department of Conservation's website. If you're out on a return day-hike, be well prepared and visit DoC's Visitor Centre in Mt Cook Village for advice and weather forecasts. It's easy to walk out to the start of the climb from just opposite the Hermitage Hotel.
Start/Finish // Mt Cook Village
Distance // 10km (6.2 miles)
Duration // 6-8hr
More info // doc.govt.nz

TASMAN GLACIER VIEW

For views of Aoraki/Mt Cook from the Tasman Valley, drive to the end of the Tasman Valley Rd, park in the large car park, then hike for around 30 minutes up to the impressive viewpoint on the top of the moraine wall. It's a relatively easy walk up past the Blue Lakes on a stepped track to absolutely stunning views. As well as glimpses of Aoraki/Mt Cook from its southeast, there are panoramic views of the surrounding peaks, the Tasman Glacier/ Haupapa, the country's longest glacier (23km/14 miles) and of Tasman Lake, the massive lake at the foot of the glacier, often speckled with icebergs. This is incredible alpine scenery and well worth the effort to get to, even if it is only a short walk. On the descent you'll be looking south, marvelling at the braided river system of glacial meltwater flowing out to Lake Pukaki.
Start/Finish // Tasman Valley road-end car park
Distance // 2.6km (1.6 miles) return
Duration // 1hr return
More info // doc.govt.nz

THE RAKIURA TRACK

At the southern frontier of New Zealand, the Rakiura Track is a stunning Great Walk offering the chance to see a kiwi in the wild – maybe.

Stewart Island is a dream destination for trampers – over 85% of it is national park, with 280km (174 miles) of walking tracks and only 28km (17.4 miles) of road. Named Rakiura in Māori, it's New Zealand's third-largest island, located 30km (18.6 miles) south of the South Island across the Foveaux Strait.

I arrived with a particular goal in mind. I was dying to see a kiwi in the wild. And Rakiura offers the country's best chance of spotting these elusive birds in their natural environment. In fact, the estimated 15,000 Stewart Island kiwis, or Rakiura tokoeka, far outnumber the human inhabitants (400). Plus, Rakiura tokoeka is the only kiwi active during the day.

So on my whistle-stop trip to Stewart Island, I reserved a precious day in my packed itinerary for the Rakiura Track. I had only one day, so I tackled the first day of the circuit. It involves an 8km (5-mile) walk from the start of the track, plus 5km (3.1 miles) to the trailhead from Oban, the island's only town. For me, that meant a 26km (16.1-mile) there-and-back day walk, easily doable with nothing to carry but my camera, a water bottle and a fresh-cut sandwich from the supermarket in town.

Stewart Island is 47 degrees south, in the notorious Roaring Forties. The climate is highly unpredictable, but it was T-shirt weather as I walked out through Oban's suburbs and along

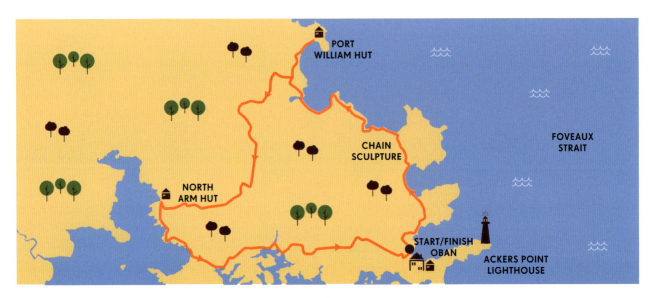

*"On the dirt road across the headland,
I passed a couple of tantalising
'watch-for-kiwi' road signs"*

pretty Horseshoe Bay. On the dirt road across the headland, I passed a couple of tantalising 'watch-for-kiwi' road signs.

At the Lee Bay trailhead, an enormous chain sculpture marks the start of the track. It recognises the story of Māui, who fished up the North Island of New Zealand using the South Island as his *waka* (canoe). Rakiura was the anchor stone that steadied his *waka* for this enormous task, and the sculpture represents Māui's anchor chain. There's a matching chain sculpture on the mainland at Bluff, where you catch the ferry to Stewart Island.

The trail hugged the coastline, providing moody vistas of the grey-blue water and rocky shores, before winding into shady rainforest thick with tree ferns, ground ferns, rimu and kamahi trees. It dipped and rose to cross a series of small streams and passed in and out of filtered sunlight, emerging at breathtaking Māori Beach. There's a basic campsite and historic relics of the sawmilling community that was here from 1913 to 1931.

I crossed the long arc of sand to the swing bridge, which took me over the creek and followed the path deep into the rainforest. Around me, the bush seemed alive with birds. I could hear bellbirds (korimako) and small parrots, fantails (pīwakawaka) and wood pigeons (kererū) and I knew others, including tūī, kākāriki, and little and yellow-eyed penguins were all around. Would a kiwi be among them? I investigated every scrape and rustle in the undergrowth, camera at the ready, but no luck.

I pushed on, past the turnoff to North Arm Hut and on to Port William Hut. Although this takes you off the Rakiura loop (following the trail of the 11-day North West Circuit Track), most walkers make the detour to spend the night in the hut. Previously the location of the Māori settlement of Pā Whakataka and later a European settlement, now the only human trace is a beautiful campsite and a hut with 24 bunks, a wood stove, pit toilets and rainwater. I had the place to myself as I ate my sandwich overlooking the lapping waves. Walkers overnighting here often report kiwi sightings, but for me, still no luck.

Next morning walkers on the circuit backtrack 40 minutes to the turnoff to follow the walk inland for 13km (8 miles) to North Arm Hut. Hard work by the Department of Conservation in recent years

RAKIURA TOKOEKA

The charismatic kiwi is a symbol of the nation, but most New Zealanders have never seen one in the wild. On Stewart Island, kiwi sightings are common, often in grassed areas and sometimes on beaches, where they mine sandhoppers under washed-up kelp. Get kiwi-spotting tips at Rakiura Track huts, and listen out at night en route for their signature song: a high-pitched kee-wee for males and a throaty kurr-kurr for females.

Clockwise, from far left: trailside kiwi crossing; ocean overlook along the Rakiura Track; passing through the chain sculpture at Lee Bay; into the Rakiura rainforest.
Previous page, from top: rimu trees droop over ground ferns along the trail; yellow-eyed penguins, Stewart Island

has reduced the amount of mud on this notoriously boggy stretch. The trail passes historic equipment, left in situ from the logging era, and undulates across valleys and ridges. North Arm has the same facilities as Port William and is in a stunning spot overlooking sheltered North Arm Bay.

On the final day, walkers are on flatter terrain close to the shore, with beautiful views of the water and the chance to swim in secluded bays. The 11km (6.8-mile) track ends at the Fern Gully car park, from where it's another 2km (1.2 miles) back to Oban.

My trip, however, was to backtrack the way I'd come through the rainforest and beaches of the island's eastern shore. By the time I reached the Lee Bay car park, the sun was low and when I made it back to Oban it was dark and I was hungry. I headed for the pub, disappointed that I had not caught a glimpse of New Zealand's most famous bird.

But there outside the South Sea Hotel, was a small group gathered for the start of a kiwi-spotting night tour, run by Ange of Beaks and Feathers – a passionate local guide with a knack for sniffing out kiwis in the wild. The next night I joined Ange's tour to Stewart Island's grassy airstrip, where I finally encountered half a dozen of the cute little critters. They walked purposefully about, and even between our legs, poking their beaks into the soil in a very businesslike manner. Rakiura tokoeka may sometimes be spotted in the day, but the ones I met on the airstrip seemed very happy to be foraging in the dark. **MP**

ORIENTATION

Start/Finish // Oban
Distance // 39km (24 miles)
Duration // 3 days
Getting there // Take a one-hour ferry from Bluff on the South Island to Oban on Stewart Island. To make a loop from Oban, walk 5km (3.1 miles) to the northern trailhead at Lee Bay or 2km (1.2 miles) to the southern trailhead at Fern Gully. Shuttles to the trailheads are also available. Water taxis can access huts.
Where to stay // There are basic campsites at Māori Beach, Port William and North Arm, and 24-bunk huts at Port William and North Arm. All must be booked in advance, which can be done on the Department of Conservation website.
More info // Search for 'Rakiura Track' on the Department of Conservation website (doc.govt.nz).

*Opposite: coastal views along
Stewart Island's North West Circuit*

MORE LIKE THIS
RAKIURA EXTENSIONS

NORTH WEST CIRCUIT,
STEWART ISLAND

Famous for its mud, this tough and epic hike has unbridged river crossings, knee-deep mud bogs, lots of up and down climbs – and it's prone to flooding. If that sounds like a fun time to you, you'll be rewarded with a stunning experience. You'll cross pristine beaches, clamber through forests, take in jaw-dropping views and climb into subalpine scrubland, spending over a week completely removed from civilisation. The trail follows the Rakiura Track as far as Port William Hut, then continues along the coast to loop around the north edge of Stewart Island. Ten basic huts are dotted along the way with 12 to 24 bunks – book them in advance on the Department of Conservation website. Be sure to call into the visitor centre when you arrive in Oban for up-to-date information and to purchase the essential topographical maps. Bush survival skills and a personal locator beacon are recommended for this one.
Start/Finish // **Oban**
Distance // **125km (78 miles)**
Duration // **9-11 days**
More info // **doc.govt.nz**

SOUTHERN CIRCUIT,
STEWART ISLAND

An optional add-on to the North West Circuit for truly hardcore hikers, the Southern Circuit can also be walked as a stand-alone loop. The big challenge here is negotiating the frequently flooded valleys of the Freshwater and Rakeahua rivers, which can inundate the track in waist-deep water. There are five basic huts on the circuit with six to 20 bunks – book them in advance. This hike is for experienced hikers with good fitness, way-finding skills and backcountry experience. Get the latest update on conditions from the Department of Conservation office in Oban before you set out. Many hikers take a water taxi to Freshwater Landing (or even Freds Camp or Rakeahua Hut to avoid the sections most prone to flooding), but you can also walk from Oban along the North West Circuit Track to Freshwater Hut (add 23km/14.3 miles, or two days each way, for this option).
Start/Finish // **Freshwater Landing**
Distance // **71.5km (44 miles)**
Duration // **4-6 days**
More info // **doc.govt.nz**

ULVA ISLAND/
TE WHARAWHARA

Established as a bird sanctuary in 1922, and pest-free since 1997, this tiny island paradise is a must-visit for anyone coming to Stewart Island/Rakiura. In the rainforest here, birds such as kiwi, saddleback and yellowhead, which are rare on the mainland, find a safe home in an environment mostly unchanged by human activity. Access is by a 10-minute boat trip (any water-taxi company will run you over, or there's a scheduled ferry). A network of trails wriggle through the island from the Post Office Bay ferry landing, such as a 20-minute hike to Flagstaff Lookout, or a three-hour loop taking in West End Beach and Boulder Beach. The shady, well-formed tracks are family-friendly and full of surprises. You'll definitely be pausing to birdwatch, whether or not you were a twitcher before landing on the island.
Start/Finish // **Post Office Bay**
Distance // **3.5km (2 miles)**
Duration // **3hr**
More info // **doc.govt.nz**

THE
ROUTEBURN TRACK

Follow ancient Māori paths through New Zealand's Southern Alps, where huge flightless birds once roamed and the rivers sparkled with sacred jade.

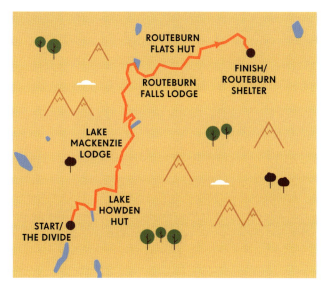

A late morning sun appears and disappears through a patchwork of high clouds, revealing a huge bushy expanse stretching hundreds of kilometres over hilltops and shaded valleys, surrounded by jutting peaks of grey rock.

This is the tail of New Zealand's mighty Southern Alps, a vast spine of sandstone and granite reaching nearly 483km (300 miles) along the South Island's western coast. It is remarkably isolated. No roads connect the mountains ahead to the rest of the world. Instead, to explore the peaks, lakes and river valleys that stretch from here in the Fiordland National Park to Mt Aspiring in the west, I must make my way on foot via a thin, winding hiking trail known as the Routeburn Track – a 32km (20-mile), three-day journey through some of New Zealand's most spectacular landscapes.

In a sloping green valley known as The Divide, the track begins. I set off with boots crunching into skittering gravel and packed earth. The path leads through thick stands of beech trees swathed in drooping moss, crowded in by the outstretched fingers of fern

fronds that grasp softly at my knees. The forest is quiet, save for the rhythm of footsteps, my blue waterproof jacket providing a bobbing spot of bright colour in a setting of endless green.

The track traces slowly around the northern lip of the Livingstone Mountains and climbs upwards, higher and higher, twisting with the curves of the terrain, to reach the crest of Key Summit. The wind, held at bay until now by the forested slopes, here whips around a broad grassy mountaintop, grabbing handfuls of my hair and buffeting against my eardrums.

It was along routes like this, climbing high mountain passes and detouring through the surrounding valleys, that the ancient people of this land walked hundreds of years ago. Hardy Māori hunters forged paths through the thick foliage in search of great boulders of *pounamu* – known as greenstone or New Zealand jade – lying like forgotten jewels at the bottom of the rivers and lakes stretching from here to the west coast.

Great ridges of snow-topped mountains fill the horizon before me, framing three of these great river valleys, stretching off in different directions – Hollyford to the north, Eglinton to the southwest and the bushy green slopes of the appropriately named Greenstone Valley to the southeast. All are shaped by shifting tectonic plates and the inexorable grinding of colossal glaciers.

I trace along the western flank of the Ailsa Mountains, the path growing steeper with every step. The Māori walked these paths in sandals made of woven cabbage leaves, making their way across

"A sheer drop of hundreds, then thousands of metres grows with each new switchback"

80km (50 miles) of treacherous terrain east to their settlements in Otago. Soon, spray from the thundering deluge of Earland Falls, a great forked waterfall cascading down from nearly 180m (600ft) above, creates a fine mist across the path. It winds up alongside a wide grassy meadow with groves of slender-trunked ribbonwood trees and down into a steep valley, where the night's rest stop, Lake Mackenzie Lodge, is neatly tucked. Plumes from its chimney promise a warming fireside within.

The next morning I pick up the track with a steep climb up a narrow, zigzagging path. Alongside, a sheer drop of hundreds, then thousands of metres grows with each new switchback, until I reach a rocky open area overlooking Hollyford Valley. The near-perpendicular granite slopes of the Darran Mountains line up before me. Sir Edmund Hillary cut his teeth here before making his attempt on Everest in 1953.

For early European settlers, these westernmost reaches were a dark, forbidding place, unmapped and unknown. Today, as I walk up to the grassy hilltop of Harris Saddle, I look out into the rumpled green distance and it's clear that great areas of dense forest and scrubland remain as they were hundreds of years ago – still rarely, if ever, visited by humans.

POUNAMU

The moss-green *pounamu* found here was prized by Māori tribes up and down the country, crafted into jewellery or simply used as currency. Harder than steel, it was also handy for creating the deadliest of weapons, such as razor-sharp axes and broad-bladed clubs called meres, which hung from the wrist with plaited twine and could be used to wrench open an opponent's skull. It was more valuable than gold.

Clockwise, from top left: Lake Mackenzie; trailside waterfall along the Routeburn; New Zealand is home to some 550 species of moss; crossing a walk-bridge en route. Previous page: Routeburn Track views

It was in remote areas like this that the last of New Zealand's giant flightless birds, the legendary moa, most likely clung on before succumbing to extinction. With some species growing close to 3m (10ft) tall, like a Jurassic-sized ostrich without wings, moa were considered imaginary – a fanciful story of the Māoris – until discovery in the mid-19th century of their long-necked skeletons up and down the country proved their existence beyond doubt.

I round the ridge overlooking Lake Harris, surrounded by snow-dusted peaks, and past the thundering cascade of Routeburn Falls before coming to the evening's rest stop at Routeburn Falls Lodge.

Routeburn Falls marks the edge of the treeline at more than 750m (2400ft). When morning light spills over the mountainside and into the valley, it reveals the undefined border where the craggy grey outcroppings of the mountains descend into forest. From here, the track winds alongside shaggy alpine pastures, over springy suspension bridges and through thick green bush, the downward path encouraging a light step after two days of uphill endeavour.

Before long, a strange noise is heard on the breeze – the rumbling motor of a bus in a nearby car park, sounding rough and foreign to the ears after three days spent isolated in nature – and soon, the Routeburn Track has come to an end.

After a journey of 32km (20 miles), I arrive down on the valley floor, and the soaring highlands above, with all their legends, mysteries and fantastical creatures, are once again out of sight beyond the trees. **CL**

ORIENTATION

Start // The Divide
Finish // Routeburn Shelter
Distance // 32km (20 miles)
Duration // Three days
Getting there // The nearest airport is in Queenstown, which is just over an hour from the Routeburn Shelter. Note: most hikers use a drop-off service such as Kiwi Discovery.
When to go // Late October to April.
What to pack // Plan carefully. Basics include: sturdy boots; waterproofs; lots of layers; first-aid kit; food and water.
Where to stay // There are four huts on the track. Book all accommodation passes for huts and campsites in advance.
Where to eat // Take food with you. The huts have basic cooking equipment.
More info // doc.govt.nz

Opposite: the view down to Queen Charlotte Sound's Grove Arm from the Queen Charlotte Track

MORE LIKE THIS
SCENIC MULTI-DAY NZ TRAMPS

QUEEN CHARLOTTE TRACK, SOUTH ISLAND

Deep in the heart of the Marlborough Sounds, a series of ancient sunken river valleys at the northeastern tip of New Zealand's South Island, the Queen Charlotte Track is double the distance of the Routeburn, but this intermediate trail can be completed in a similar amount of time. The adventure begins with a boat transfer to Meretoto/Ship Cove, from where the well-signposted trail weaves along a series of forested ridgelines offering superb views of the Queen Charlotte/Tōtaranui and Kenepuru sounds. Stay in Department of Conservation-run campsites or at private accommodation along the way. You can also opt to mountain bike the trail and arrange for your gear to be transported between overnight stops by a local boat operator.

Start // Meretoto/Ship Cove
Finish // Anakiwa
Distance // 71km (44.1 miles)
Duration // 3-5 days
More info // doc.govt.nz

INLAND TRACK, SOUTH ISLAND

Most hikers know the South Island's Abel Tasman National Park for the Abel Tasman Coast Track, one of New Zealand's Great Walks. But it's not the only multi-day hike to enjoy in this wonderful wilderness area in the Nelson/Tasman region. Linking Mārahau to Wainui Bay via Pigeon Saddle on the Takaka-Totaranui road, this challenging tramp passes through a range of forest types between sea level and the roof of the park, Evans Ridge (around 1000m/3281ft), where snow sometimes falls. Occasional granite outcrops offer great views of the coast, while the Moa Park moorlands, a basin of sub-alpine scrub and tussock, provide an intriguing interlude. Camp or stay in huts (operated on a first-come, first-served basis), keeping an eye out for endemic tūī and bellbirds as you go.

Start // Mārahau
Finish // Wainui car park
Distance // 41km (25.5 miles)
Duration // 3 days
More info // doc.govt.nz

LAKE WAIKAREMOANA TRACK, NORTH ISLAND

Remote, immense and shrouded in mist, Te Urewara National Park encompasses the largest tract of virgin forest on the North Island. The park's highlight is Lake Waikaremoana ('Sea of Rippling Waters'), a deep, 55-sq-km (21-sq-mile) crucible of water encircled by the Lake Waikaremoana Track. Along the way it passes through ancient rainforest and reedy inlets, and traverses gnarly ridges, including the famous Panekire Bluffs, from where there are stupendous views of the lake and endless forested peaks and valleys. Due to increasing popularity, in 2001 the track was designated a Great Walk requiring advance bookings.

Start // Onepoto
Finish // Hopuruahine Landing
Distance // 46km (28.6 miles)
Duration // 4 days
More info // doc.govt.nz

THE CAPE BRETT TRACK

Trek along a rugged coastal ridge to a lighthouse-tipped cape peering out to one of the most famous sights of New Zealand's Bay of Islands.

I t looks like any other forested pass on any other trail. I've been walking for five hours, and rainforest wraps around me. The trail is climbing towards an obvious notch in the ridge, where I'm expecting to step on to the pass and find an ordinary scene – another slope of forest rolling away ahead of me.

But nothing is ordinary here. I'm hiking on the Cape Brett Track, which runs like an underline beneath New Zealand's famed Bay of Islands, following the high line of the cape's ridge to a lighthouse on its point. I will stay the night in the former lighthouse-keeper's cottage before returning the following day.

As I step on to the pass, the world suddenly plunges away beneath my feet. I'm stopped in my tracks, literally, because to take two steps ahead would mean being toppled into the ocean almost 200m (656ft) below. Ahead of me, across the sea, the cape snakes and contorts to its end, the track looking like a razor cut through its high cliffs.

Nothing has prepared me for the curtains to pull back on a scene quite like this. Until now the hike has been beautiful, but I've just stepped across the line into extraordinary.

I'd begun my hike five hours earlier, setting out from the strung-out settlement of Rawhiti, where steps ascend to a low ridge. Within moments I'm looking down into paradise – unruly bush tumbling down the slopes to empty, cream-coloured sands washed smooth by the tide. I drop my pack and descend to the beach. I've been walking for two minutes after all, so I'm due a break.

When I return to my pack, an elderly Māori man is standing beside it. He's come to Rawhiti looking for an ancestor's grave. 'A local guy said the cemetery is over there,' he says, pointing back along the low ridge on which we stand. 'Can you imagine

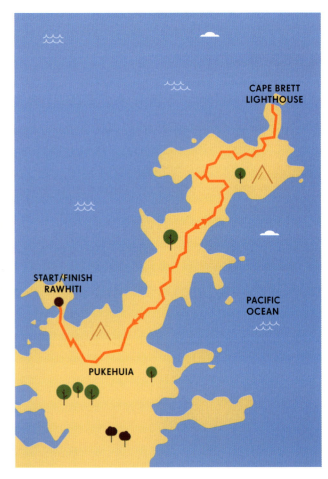

carrying a dead body up here?' I look up to the ridge where I'm heading, close to 300m (1000ft) above us, and the dead weight of the backpack beside me, and just nod.

From there my journey has been simple, if not always easy. The track ascends to the ridgetop that forms the spine of the cape. Like all spines, this one is full of vertebrae, most of which I have to climb, turning the next few hours into a sweaty grind broken by occasional peeps through the forest into the Bay of Islands, which from here look like the scattered pieces of a broken vase.

Atop the ridge, the sound of the ocean rolls up the slopes from both sides – the Pacific Ocean in stereo – and the climbs have the effect of hastening my fantasy of a swim ahead at Deep Water Cove. This narrow slot in the cape is reached on a short side trail just before the Cape Brett Track ascends to the pass that heralds the dramatic final couple of hours to the lighthouse.

At the junction I drop my backpack and, without it, it's as though somebody has given me wings. I plunge down the slopes to the cove, where the pebbly beach is covered in driftwood. The track is almost empty today, so I strip down and plunge into the chilly water, washing off more than four hours of effort.

Half an hour later I'm stepping through the pass that's like falling into Alice's Wonderland. The cape spools out ahead of me, attached to New Zealand only by a thin thread of land. Dead trees angle out from the slopes below me, adding yet more drama to an already dramatic scene. Whatever fatigue I've been feeling disappears in an instant as I look ahead to the line of the track etched along the cliff edges. A couple of exciting hours beckon.

"Nothing has prepared me for the curtains to pull back on a scene quite like this"

SHINING LIGHT

Cape Brett Lighthouse was first illuminated in 1910, and remained a working lighthouse until 1978, with the light from its 12m-high (40ft) station shining almost 50km (32 miles) out to sea. Three men originally staffed it, with a school for the lighthouse-keepers' children on the cape. Conditions were harsh, perhaps best evidenced by a storm in 1951, when a keeper reported waves crashing on to the roof of the cottage (now the hut for hikers), which stands a full 43m (141ft) above the sea.

Clockwise, from above: the cliffs of the Cape; the lighthouse at the end of the line.
Previous page: Cape Brett Lighthouse, standing tall in the Bay of Islands

At first the track buries itself in bush, but when the views return, they *really* return. The cape looms larger with every break in the bush, and the ocean swarms ashore in white fury around the black rock of the cliffs. By the time I return along the track the next morning, after heavy overnight rain, these dry cliffs will be pouring with waterfalls. Is it any wonder there are now helicopters buzzing about, gawking like me at this spectacular tentacle of land?

The trail climbs on and on, a protective handrail briefly testifying to the sudden sense of exposure as the land tumbles away 200m (656ft) either side into the sea. And then, suddenly below me, is the lighthouse and, just offshore, the island that forms the Bay of Islands' most famous attraction, the Hole in the Rock, its cave hidden from view by the angle.

Beside the lighthouse I indulge in a moment of self-congratulatory pride – I have made it. But it's at that moment that I spy a red roof far below – the old lighthouse-keeper's cottage, converted into a hikers' hut, where I will spend tonight, around 150m (492ft) lower down the slopes. I don't even want to think about the climb back out the next morning, and I'm certainly not the first to be intimidated by this hill.

Before a tramway was built linking the cottage to the lighthouse, a horse was used to haul goods between the two. It's said that the horse quickly learned the sound of the supplies boat arriving, and would run and hide. For me, however, there's nowhere to hide. I have to walk on. I'll worry about dragging my own dead weight back up the hill in the morning. **AB**

ORIENTATION

Start/Finish // Rawhiti

Distance // 32km (20-mile) round-trip

Getting there // The nearest major airport to the Cape Brett Track is Auckland, around four hours' drive from the trailhead. There's no public transport. A couple of homes in Rawhiti offer hiker parking for around NZ$5.

Tours // The walk to Cape Brett Lighthouse takes a full day, requiring an overnight stop at the lighthouse-keeper's cottage before returning along the same track. It's possible to walk just the most dramatic section, from Deep Water Cove to the lighthouse, with water-taxi company Bay of Islands (boiwatertaxi.co.nz) ferrying hikers to either point.

Where to stay // Stays in the lighthouse-keeper's cottage must be pre-booked, which can be done through the Department of Conservation website (doc.govt.nz).

Opposite, from top: Rarotonga views from the slopes of Te Rua Manga; Barwon Heads Bridge, at the start of the Rip to River trail

MORE LIKE THIS
OCEAN-VIEW ODYSSEYS

RAROTONGA CROSS-ISLAND HIKE, COOK ISLANDS

In the midst of the Pacific Ocean, the Cook Islands might be best known for their lovely lagoon-stroked beaches, but inland there are other adventures to be explored. On Rarotonga, an extreme hiking trail crosses the spine of the volcanic isle, taking walkers to Te Rua Manga (The Needle). Go north to south from Avatiu Rd, following orange markers along a jungle track to Ridge Junction, from where Needle Lookout is another 650m (2132ft). Fixed chains and ropes lead those brave enough to trust them to the base of the cloud-scraping Needle, which offers eye-popping views across the reef-fringed island. Don't attempt to touch the 413m (1355ft) point, though, unless you're an experienced climber with your own equipment. Descend via a path that follows Papua Stream.

Start // Avatiu Rd
Finish // Papua Rd
Distance // 4 miles (6.5km)
More info // cookislands.travel

NUKAN KUNGUN HIKE, COORONG NATIONAL PARK, SOUTH AUSTRALIA

All you have to do is take a quick look at the map to see why the Ngarrindjeri people named this place a word meaning 'long narrow neck' (*Kurangk*). Part of South Australia's rugged Limestone Coast, this is where the Murray River empties into the ocean to form Coorong's unique coastal lagoon that stretches down in a long skinny isthmus to separate a vast dune system from the mainland. There are plenty of walking trails in the park but the two-day Nukan Kungun is one of its best, taking you through the scenery where the original *Storm Boy* movie was filmed. Fringed by indigenous grasslands and forest, its brackish waters are rich with birdlife and you'll share the trail with kangaroos, emus and wombats, before spending a night camping under the stars. The walk concludes at 42 Mile Crossing, where you'll cross over the dunes to finish up with spectacular views of the Southern Ocean.

Start // Salt Creek
Finish // 42 Mile Crossing
Distance // 25km (15.5 miles) one-way
Duration // 2 days
More info // parks.sa.gov.au/parks/coorong-national-park

RIP TO RIVER HIKE, VICTORIA, AUSTRALIA

Mixing shipwrecks, rugged surf and rock pools, this sandy stroll from Barwon Heads to Point Lonsdale is one for those who enjoy the romantic cliche of 'long walks on the beach'. Starting off from the Bluff – a hulking rock headland overlooking Bass Strait – you'll make your way over Barwon Heads' famous bridge where the Barwon River meets the ocean. You'll then proceed along its blonde sands to pass Ocean Grove's surf club before continuing ahead along the blissfully long and isolated stretch of beach to reach Point Lonsdale Lighthouse. It makes for an atmospheric finishing point, where you can look out to the notorious stretch of water known as 'the Rip' that divides the Bellarine Peninsula from Mornington Peninsula. Just below is a cave where the escaped convict William Buckley spent some time during his 32 remarkable years living with the Wathaurong, the Aboriginal people who've resided in this region for many thousands of years.

Start // The Bluff, Barwon Heads
Finish // Point Lonsdale Lighthouse
Distance // 16km (10 miles) one-way
Duration 3-4 hours

THE ABEL TASMAN COAST TRACK

One of New Zealand's Great Walks, this world-class beachcombing caper tiptoes around tides and bounds between the bays and golden coves of the South Island.

If the huge piece of driftwood hadn't suddenly sprouted a head and let out an indignant snort, I'd have sat on it to eat lunch. Apparently, this log isn't wood at all. It's a heaving, breathing, belching lump of grumpy New Zealand fur seal, which had been enjoying a morning snooze under shimmering sun until I ruined its reverie by gatecrashing the secluded beach.

Evidently, my new friend isn't as excited about our encounter as I am – something he makes cacophonously clear when I begin bagging silly sealy selfies. I keep a respectful distance, not wanting to end up in a fist/flipper fight with a hefty, rudely awakened sea mammal, especially not quarterway through a 60km (37-mile) walk, beyond limping range of human habitation or help.

So I leave him to snore and seek an alternative snack spot. Fortunately, picnic places with epic ocean views are plentiful along the Abel Tasman Coast Track, and before long I stumble into another beautiful bay, gilded by golden sand and gently stroked by the waters of Tasman Bay, a glassy puddle becalmed between the protective arms of Farewell Spit and D'Urville Island.

Once lunch is munched, an internal debate begins: should I have a quick swim, or keep walking towards the hut? And therein lies the problem with this trail, a rambling route through rata forests fringing the coastline of Abel Tasman National Park, linking a series of idyllic coves at the top of New Zealand's South Island.

The hike isn't physically tough – not compared with most multi-day Kiwi capers – and covering 15km (9 miles) a day allows walkers to enjoy the experience at a comfortable clip. No, here the challenge is different. For round every corner is a beach so fine it would be unforgivable not to stop, strip and plunge into the blue. And then you continue, only to find another sublime bay. And so it goes on.

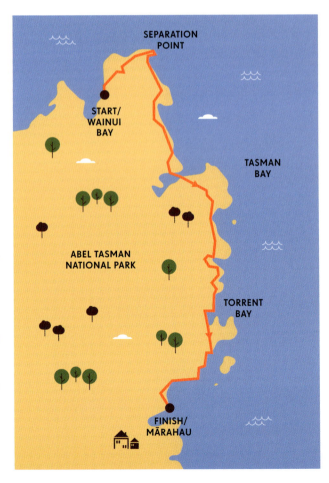

Small wonder the Coast Track is an original member of New Zealand's much-feted group of Great Walks, a list that features the nation's top trails. In a country well-endowed with epic hiking routes, it takes something special to feature in this premier league of paths. Tongariro has dramatic volcanoes and multi-coloured mineral-stained lakes; the Routeburn, Kepler and Milford Tracks make the grade through the magnificence of Fiordland; and the Abel Tasman Coast Track gets the nod because it's one of the world's best beachcombing adventures.

The walk can be done in either direction, but most people start at Mārahau and spend several days strolling north, returning via water taxi from Tōtaranui. A decade earlier I'd walked the route this way. Then, tramping around New Zealand on a backpacker's budget and unable to afford the boat transfers, I had continued to Whariwharangi Hut and spent three days trekking back to Mārahau via the Abel Tasman Inland Track (a 41km/25.5-mile path along Evans Ridge and through the beech forests of Moa Park), a more challenging and less trafficked trail than its coastal cousin.

This experience taught me that the top part of the Coast Track offers quieter paths, better vistas and more wildlife encounters than the rest of the route. Armed with this insight and angling for new views, I've returned to walk north-to-south, after being dropped off at Wainui Bay. Trekking in this direction involves an extra layer of logistics, but it launches you straight into the wildest sections of the trail, and soon after rounding scenic Separation Point, the decision pays off, as I meet the seal in Mutton Cove.

"Round every corner is a beach so fine it would be unforgivable not to stop, strip and plunge into the blue"

KAYAKING THE COAST TRACK

The Coast Track is a cracking walk, but Abel Tasman National Park's shores can also be explored from the cockpit of a sea kayak. Several operators offer combined hiking and paddling adventures, where it's possible to kayak across translucent lagoons and between bays, before swapping blade for boots and walking back. Mārahau to Anchorage Bay is a popular paddling section, with walkers wandering onward usually to Bark Bay or Onetahuti before catching a water taxi back.

Clockwise, from above: kayaks at Watering Cove; walking the beaches of Abel Tasman; another glorious bay. Previous page: footsteps in the golden sands of Mārahau

My dilemma – to take a dip or dawdle on – begins just around the corner, in Anapai Bay, one of the most beautiful bitemarks found along this whole sensationally serrated shoreline. I don't hesitate long. Once past Tōtaranui, I'll be sharing the huts and the trail with trampers and paddlers aplenty, and the water will be busy with boats, so I embrace the empty beach and dive into the translucent brine that's all mine for a few magical moments.

Sometimes you simply have to get wet. The Coast Track isn't a technical trail, but the tidal range here is large, and there are several estuary crossings to negotiate. At Bark Bay and Torrent Bay, high-tide inland walk-around options exist, but Awaroa Inlet can only be crossed two hours either side of low tide. Campsites and huts have tide tables, and sometimes it's necessary to set off before dawn to avoid delays, but even when you nail the timing, socks and shoes must be removed while you wade across.

The delightful distractions continue as the track tramps over the 260m (853ft) Tonga Saddle and drops to a sensational stretch of sand at Onetahuti Beach, before ambling past Arch Point – an extraordinary exhibition of rock art sculpted by the elements.

I enviously eye kayakers departing from the beach at Bark Bay, and make a mental note to return and paddle the park for a new view of this epic coastline. Now, though, I have a bigger boat to catch, to the North Island. I wobble over the famous Falls River swing bridge to Torrent Bay, where another tidal crossing lies in wait en route to Anchorage and the trailhead at Mārahau. **PK**

ORIENTATION

Start // Wainui car park
Finish // Mārahau
Distance // 60km (37 miles)
Getting there // Mārahau is easily accessed from Picton, where the Interislander ferry arrives from Wellington.
When to go // The Abel Tasman can be done any time of year, but the trails and campsites heave with hikers (and kayakers) during summer (December-February). October to November and March to April offer better conditions.
Where to stay // The Department of Conservation (DoC) operates huts and campsites along the route; book ahead.
What to pack // A relatively gentle multi-day hike, the Abel Tasman can easily be done in running shoes. The route rarely rears above 200m (656ft) and the weather is temperate, but take waterproofs and warm layers for evenings. Pack swimming gear, and a mask and snorkel.

Opposite from top: hike Rainbow Beach on the Cooloola Great Walk; Cape Arid views from the Tagon Coastal Trail

MORE LIKE THIS
CRACKING COASTAL HIKES

COOLOOLA GREAT WALK, QUEENSLAND, AUSTRALIA

One of Queensland's 10 'Great Walks', this 102km (63-mile) hike weaves through the Great Sandy National Park's vast and varied coastal hinterland. Count on five days to complete this overland adventure, one that'll take you through the diverse landscapes of Cooloola Recreation Area. You'll pass through rainforest, eucalypt woodland and coastal heath, studded with freshwater lakes, before you land on Cooloola's giant dunes and untamed surf coast. For this Grade 4 hike you'll need to be self-sufficient and carry your own camping equipment and cooking supplies, as you'll be pitching a tent at the designated hiker camps. The walk starts just north off Noosa and extends through to Rainbow Beach, just below the Unesco-listed K'gari (Fraser Island).

Start // Noosa Heads
Finish // Rainbow Beach
Distance // 102km (63 miles) one-way
Duration // 5 days
More info // parks.des.qld.gov.au/ parks/great-walks-cooloola

KANGARUTHA WALKING TRACK, NEW SOUTH WALES, AUSTRALIA

Tucked away on NSW's South Coast, this magnificent day-walk zigzags through Bournda National Park's dramatic coastline of rocky inlets and pristine beaches. Starting from the south of Tathra, it follows an undulating route (best suited to seasoned hikers) through a varied terrain of melaleuca woodland, cliff-top trails and beach walks with stunning bay views. There are plenty of secluded coves along the way for exploring rock pools and opportunities for leisurely dips in the ocean, in between picnicking on the sands. It's a popular walk for nature lovers, with some great birdwatching, including sea eagles and glossy black cockatoos, as well as other wildlife including kangaroos, wallabies and echidna. From October to November, keep an eye out for whales that pass along this 'humpback highway'. Finishing up at scenic Turingal, you can enjoy some time on the beach at Wallagoot Gap, before plunging into the glassy waters of nearby Wallagoot Lake, then drying yourself off to retrace your steps for the return walk.

Start // Tathra (Kianinny Bay)
Finish // Turingal Head
Distance // 9km (5.6 miles) one-way
Duration // 3.5-4hr
More info //nationalparks.nsw.gov. au/things-to-do/walking-tracks/ kangarutha-walking-track

TAGON COASTAL TRAIL, WESTERN AUSTRALIA

Set along the remote coastline of southern WA's Golden Outback region, this spectacular half-day's walk takes you across the white sandy beaches of Cape Arid National Park. Starting from the Thomas River Campground, the trail leads through the land of the Wudjari people, taking you up along coastal heathland filled with blooming banksia and, from August to October, spring wildflowers. It's nice and remote out here so other than emus, kangaroos and sunning lizards you'll likely have this trail to yourself; though come July to October you'll have the company of frolicking whales, too, along with bottlenose dolphins and seals year-round. The trail winds down to the soft powdery sands of several secluded beaches to finish at the eastern end of the coastal wilderness of Kennedy Beach. Take some time to relax before making your way back on the return trek.

Start // Thomas River Campground, Yokinup Bay
Finish // Kennedy Beach
Distance // 15km (9.3 miles) return
Duration 4-5hr
More info // parks.dpaw.wa.gov.au/ site/tagon-coastal-trail

THE MILFORD TRACK

Touted as 'the finest walk in the world', the Milford Track boasts dripping rainforest, deep glaciated valleys, towering peaks, thunderous waterfalls and a glorious alpine pass.

A keen hiker and enthusiastic cartophile (a lover of maps), it didn't take me long to get my head around the route of Fiordland's legendary Milford Track. Take the boat up to the head of Lake Te Anau, walk up the Clinton Valley, climb up and over the Mackinnon Pass, descend into the Arthur Valley, walk out of that valley to Sandfly Point, then board another boat to Milford Sound.

It all looked fairly straightforward, but I knew there was a major wildcard – the weather. Fiordland is one of the rainiest places on earth. While Te Anau, on the eastern side of the mountains, averages a little over 100cm (39in) of rainfall each year, Milford Sound, on the west coast, averages around eight times that.

Weather comes in from the west, from the Tasman Sea, with the air picking up moisture along the way. That air is forced up as it hits the Fiordland mountains, cools, the moisture condenses as water vapour, and the western side of the mountains are pounded with regular heavy rainfall. The air carries on over to the eastern side of the mountains, but is relatively dry by this stage, producing little rain. This process is known as 'orographic rainfall' and Fiordland is a classic example.

My problem was that the Milford Track is popular and requires booking far in advance. I wouldn't have the luxury of checking weather forecasts before choosing my departure date. There are three Department of Conservation (DoC) huts along the way at which 'independent walkers' overnight and DoC rules are strict. The Milford Track can only be walked in one direction, from the Te Anau end, and independent walkers must book and stay at each of the three DoC huts in order. Walkers get onto

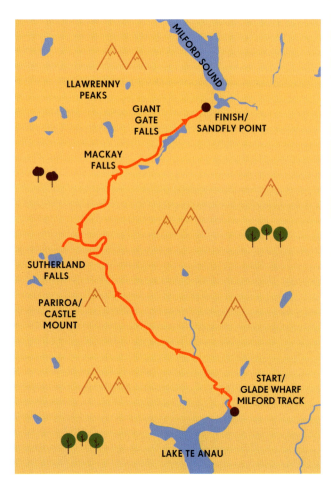

the track at the head of Lake Te Anau by boat, and get off it by boat from Sandfly Point at the end of the track, so the rules are easy to police. I opted for a date in late February, the least rainy month on the track. Being late summer, it would still be warm.

As I hopped off the boat at Glade Wharf at the head of Lake Te Anau, 202m (663ft) above sea level, I congratulated myself on the decision. It was a sunny, blue-sky day and weather forecasts I'd checked at Fiordland NP Visitor Centre in Te Anau were showing a massive anti-cyclone arriving from the west, bringing four to five days of good weather.

I only had a leisurely 5km (3-mile) walk through beautiful beech forest along the banks of the Clinton River to contend with on the first day. I spotted three trout and an eel in the pristine waters while crossing the Clinton on the first swing bridge, and even dawdling and taking a swim in the refreshing river, it only took a couple of hours to get to Clinton Hut, where all independent walkers spend the first night.

Guided walkers, on the Ultimate Hikes package, have their own luxurious lodges along the track, with the accompanying price tag. I'd already passed the first, Glade House, and while the thought of hot showers, flush toilets, cooked meals, cold beer and a sheeted bed appealed somewhat, I was more after the

> *"Hot showers, flush toilets, cooked meals, cold beer and a sheeted bed appealed, but I was more after dinner out of my pot, a sleeping bag and a shared bunk at a DoC hut"*

'rough and tumble' of dinner out of my pot, a sleeping bag and a massive, shared bunkroom at the DoC hut.

Day two was a six-hour, 16.5km (10-mile) gradual climb following the Clinton River to its source, Lake Mintaro, at the base of the Mackinnon Pass. Nothing steep, but a climb nonetheless, up this iconic U-shaped glacial valley, dwarfed by towering rock walls on both sides. While I'd spent most of the day enjoying my own company, Mintaro Hut (615m/2018ft) was full of the same faces from the evening before.

Day three started with a solid climb on a zigzagging track up to Mackinnon Pass, and the memorial to Quintin MacKinnon, the first European to discover the pass in 1888. The highest point on the track, at 1154m (3786ft), sits between the memorial and Pass Shelter. The high point revealed a stunning 360-degree alpine panorama on that perfect day, while the shelter and its 'loo with a view' looked back down the Clinton canyon, the direction from which I'd come.

QUINTIN McKINNON

On the Te Anau waterfront, near the Fiordland NP Visitor Centre, look for the bronze statue of Quintin McPherson McKinnon (1851–1892), erected in 1988, 100 years after he and Ernest Mitchell were credited for crossing the Mackinnon Pass and establishing the Milford Track. An adventuring Scotsman, McKinnon went on to become the track's first guide, taking parties over the pass to Sutherland Falls.

Clockwise, from far left: Fiordland forest along the route; Quintin MacKinnon memorial at Mackinnon Pass; cool aching feet in track-side pools; marvellous Milford Sound. Previous page: Milford Track waterfall

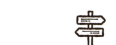

ORIENTATION

Start // Glade Wharf/Lake Te Anau
Finish // Sandfly Point/Milford Sound
Distance // 54km (33.5 miles)
Getting there // Independent walkers need to find their way to Te Anau; Ultimate Hikes guided walks depart by bus from Queenstown.
When to go // November to April
Things to know // Book Milford Track hut tickets online with DoC first. You'll also need to book: transport from Te Anau to Te Anau Downs; the boat from Te Anau Downs to Glade Wharf; the boat from Sandfly Point to Milford Sound; overnight accommodation at Milford Sound (if you want to stay); and transport from Milford Sound back to Te Anau. There are links to transport operators on the DoC website.
More info // DoC (doc.govt.nz/milfordtrack); Ultimate Hikes (ultimatehikes.co.nz)

The track then dropped steadily down to the west, down the other side of the pass, through an attractive alpine garden, then thick rainforest and past gushing falls, to the valley floor a full 900m (2953ft) below. Along the way, it teased with views of the Sutherland Falls, NZ's highest at 580m (1903ft). I couldn't resist taking the sidetrack to visit the falls close up. It took an extra 1.5 hours to return, but was well worth it for the thrill of standing at the base of the thunderous three-leap waterfalls.

It had been a strenuous 15km (9-mile), six-hour, up-and-over-the-pass day, plus extra for the falls side trip. I had no problems dropping off to sleep in Dumpling Hut that night.

Day four was an 18km (11-mile), six-hour valley walk following the Arthur River out to Sandfly Point. There were plenty of highlights, though. Dramatic Mackay Falls, a clamber inside intriguing Bell Rock, and impressive rock cuttings for the track alongside Lake Ada. Sandfly Point is appropriately named (lots of pesky sandflies), but I'd timed things well and only had a short wait for the boat to Milford Sound/Piopiotahi Visitor Centre.

While the Milford Track had lived up to its reputation – the *London Spectator* labelled it 'the finest walk in the world' way back in 1908 – the cruise on magnificent Milford Sound the next morning was just as unforgettable. **CM**

*Opposite, from top: Lake Hauroko,
at the start of the challenging
Dusky Track; Hump Ridge
Track marker, Te Waewae Bay*

MORE LIKE THIS
FIORDLAND MULTI-DAY HIKES

HOLLYFORD TRACK

This is a moderate hike through the Hollyford Valley – the longest in Fiordland National Park – that is low-level and can be walked year-round. The track starts at the end of the Hollyford Rd, stemming north off the Te Anau-Milford Sound Hwy, and ends at magnificent Martins Bay on the West Coast. There are splendid mountain and lake vistas, beautiful beech forest, extensive birdlife and a magical coastline. With an extra day at the bay, you can view a seal colony and possibly get a peek at a penguin. Many hikers fly out from Martins Bay airstrip back to Te Anau. The Department of Conservation has six huts along the track. Hollyford Track Experience (hollyfordtrack.com) offers guided walks that include private lodges, a jetboat trip the length of Lake McKerrow, and end with a flight out to Milford Sound.

Start // Hollyford Rd end
Finish // Martins Bay
Distance // 56km (35 miles)
Duration // 4-5 days
More info // doc.govt.nz

HUMP RIDGE TRACK

Access for this three-day loop hike, best from late October to late April, is from Tuatapere in western Southland. A partnership between the Tuatapere community and the Department of Conservation, run as a private walk through a Charitable Trust (humpridgetrack.co.nz), hikers can 'Freedom Walk' or take a full-on 'Guided Walk'. Hiking days are long, and some sections of the track are steep and rugged, especially on the climb up to Okaka Lodge on the first day. Up high, there are panoramic views of southwest Fiordland, the Southern Ocean and Stewart Island. The track later descends to the south coast, passing over historic viaducts (bridges) in the heart of native forest. Port Craig Lodge, at sea level, offers trampers the chance to soak weary limbs in the ocean, while the track winds around the coast on its final day before depositing you back where you started.

Start/Finish // Rarakau car park
Distance // 61km (38 miles)
Duration // 3 days
More info // doc.govt.nz

DUSKY TRACK

This is one for super-fit, experienced adventurous sorts, happy to do plenty of homework and preparation before they go. The challenging track traverses three valley systems, crosses two mountain ranges and has 21 three-wire bridges to cross. Although the track is reasonably well marked, expect to encounter tree falls, deep mud, river crossings and rough terrain. The Dusky Track can be walked in either direction. From the south, hikers take a boat to the start of the track at the head of Lake Hauroko. From the north, access is across Lake Manapouri by boat. Along the way there is a two-day optional detour off the main track to Supper Cove in Dusky Sound. Contact the Fiordland NP Visitor Centre in Te Anau or Department of Conservation Invercargill Office for current track and weather information, and to purchase hut tickets.

Start // Lake Hauroko
Finish // Lake Manapouri
Distance // 84km (52 miles)
Duration // 8-10 days
More info // doc.govt.nz

INDEX

Epic Hikes of Australia & New Zealand
August 2022
Published by Lonely Planet Global Limited
CRN 554153
www.lonelyplanet.com
10 9 8 7 6 5 4 3 2 1

Printed in China
ISBN 978 183869 508 8
© Lonely Planet 2022
© photographers as indicated 2022

General Manager, Publishing Piers Pickard
Associate Publisher Robin Barton
Commissioning Editor Kate Morgan
Designer Jo Dovey
Cartography Kristina Juodenas
Picture Research Heike Bohnstengel
Editors Clifton Wilkinson, Polly Thomas
Index Polly Thomas
Print Production Nigel Longuet

Lonely Planet Global Limited
Digital Depot, Roe Lane (off Thomas St),
Digital Hub, Dublin 8,
D08 TCV4
Ireland

STAY IN TOUCH lonelyplanet.com/contact

Authors Andrew Bain (**AB**); Anna Kaminski (**AK**); Anthony Ham (**AH**); Bob Brown (**BB**); Christa Larwood (**CL**); Charles Rawlings-Way (**CRW**); Craig McLachlan (**CM**); Emily Matchar (**EM**); Glenn van der Knijff (**GV**); Huw Kingston (**HK**); Kerry Walker (**JR**); Kate Armstrong (**KA**); Kerry Walker (**KW**); Monique Perrin (**MP**); Patrick Kinsella (**PK**); Paul Bloomfield (**PB**) Sally Nowlan (**SN**); Sarah Reid (**SR**); Sophie Davies (**SD**); Steve Waters (**SW**); Trent Holden (**TH**).

Cover illustration by Ross Murray (www.rossmurray.com).